AF539768

THE SINGULAR SELF
ESSAYS ON INDIAN AUTOBIOGRAPHIES

THE SINGULAR SELF

ESSAYS ON INDIAN AUTOBIOGRAPHIES

By

Dr. Meena Sodhi

Professor
Deptt. of English
Banaras Hindu University
Varanasi

DISCOVERY PUBLISHING HOUSE PVT. LTD.
NEW DELHI-110 002

Published by:
Tilak Wasan
DISCOVERY PUBLISHING HOUSE PVT. LTD.
4831/24, Ansari Road, Prahlad Street
Darya Ganj, New Delhi-110002 (India)
Phone: +91-11-23279245, 43764432
Fax: +91-11-23253475
E-mail: parul.wasan@gmail.com
info@discoverypublishinggroup.com
web: www.discoverypublishinggroup.com

***First Edition:* 2011**
ISBN: 978-81-8356-725-1

The Singular Self: ***Essays on Indian Autobiographies***

Printed at:
Shree Balaji Art Press
Delhi

Preface

"All artistic creation is absolutely subjective." This remark of Oscar Wilde made as early as in nineteenth century, is as efficacious and potent today as it was then. In coming days it also became the corner stone for all biographical writings.

Confessions (AD 398-400) by Saint Augustine, was the initiator for all modern western autobiographies. It marked not only a historical beginning of life-stories, but also became an archetype for other such forms of writing. Scargill's book titled *The Autobiography of a Dissenting Minister*, published in 1809 introduced the term 'autobiography' for the first time. Then the form was understood to be only a factual account of the life of the writer. The location of the author to the life, he narrated was not at the core of discussion. With the passage of time, autobiography, as a literary form, came to mean a definitive exhibition of the individual self, culminating in the achievement of a state of self consciousness. It was also perceived that the creative process necessitated the initiation into self actualisation which is determined through the act of writing, which in turn becomes subjective and personal reconstruction of the author's life. The period following World War II focussed the attention on man and his subjectivity; the post-industrial Western society seemed to threaten and annihilate the very existence of an individual. As such he felt the need to establish his identity and supremacy; autobiographical writing thus got a fillip and became one of the popular modes of self-expression.

Philippe Lejeune defined autobiography as "retrospective prose narrative produced by a real person concerning his own existence, focusing on his individual life, in particular on the development of its personality." W. B. Yeats very tersely summed up the act in a single sentence: "It is myself that I remake."

Mid twentieth century witnessed the waning of interest in biography, thus giving an impetus to the writers of autobiographies. The genre could easily be paired with the theories of structuralism and post-structuralism; it was not only a fertile ground for considering the division between fact and fiction but could also be challenged in the objective representation of life. Its very identity as a form of literary writing was questioned when Paul de Man expressed his doubts about the authenticity of autobiographical texts, which he felt were more fictional than truthful. The implied pun in Paul de Man's "de-facement" encouraged the deconstructionists to use the metaphor of murder for biography and suicide for autobiography. The challenge thrown up by a deconstructionist is that the human language is a language of deprivation and is therefore "not the thing itself but the representation, the picture of the thing and, as such, it is silent, mute as pictures are mute". The critic argued that autobiography was not a life but a text.

Notwithstanding the above criticism autobiography has still flourished remarkably well. It is appropriate to remember that writing is an embodiment of the writer's imagination in language and can clearly be distinguished from the other forms. Thus the writing of an autobiography is an act like any other act performed by the humans. It is defined as "a biography of a person written by himself". Like the worm inside a cocoon, the writer spins a yarn, creating a life, weaving a story. The work has to be narrative, which covers a temporal sequence to allow the emergence of the contour of life. Even if we grant that the representation of one's life is impossible, we have to realise that autobiography as a genre has its own formal features and is worthy of study by literary critics.

The present century is an age of enquiry and the spirit encourages the probing into the self on a "voyage of inner discovery". It is an act of revealing the "inner recesses" in "outer spaces"; hence the articulation of consciousness is the author's entry into the public arena. The urgency to have two-pronged approach, the juxtaposition of the world within and the world without, accentuates the complex dimensions of the autobiographical mode, the necessity of appropriating two opposite elements: the indigenous self-consciousness and the socio-cultural conditions of the writer's era. Thus this form of writing becomes a fascinating and compelling subject for literary deliberations.

The urge to reveal the self is a universal manifestation; Indians, who perhaps had felt inhibited in sharing their life experiences with others, are not so reticent in the post-modern Indian society. Autobiography as a literary form is thus captivating not only the writers but the readers as well. Such writings in regional languages have always been copious and rich. Today we find more and more well known people and public figures turning to autobiographical writing in English. The Indian writer has a distinct advantage over his western counterpart due to the breadth of his experiences particularly in the family. This is the "fulcrum of his creativity".

A critic had observed that "genres rise and genres fall." The dawn of the new millennium can initiate a boom in life writings, which have become universal and emerged as a distinct field of study. Thus the genre, which in the last century was at the periphery of the world literary studies, is slowly moving towards the centre and is all set to capture the imagination of the present generation. Social networking sites like Facebook or Twitter encourage the Gen Next to be more forthcoming in self revelation. Blogs written by litterateurs, public figures and icons have aided and abetted urge for personal display of feelings and emotions, and are read curiously by all.

The book is a comprehensive assessment of autobiography in its myriad forms. It lays out a sophisticated, theoretical approach to life narratives and the components of the autobiographical acts including memory, experience, identity, space ad agency. An attempt has been made to discuss and critically analyse some of the autobiographical texts which have helped to form the predominant tradition of autobiographical writings in English in India. These life stories not only help to formulate a history of selfhood, but interpret a "paradigmatic narrative through which the subject has learned to know who she is." The focus has been specifically on the Indian literary writers in English because it is expected that a creative writer approaches the task of writing his own life with an artistic intent and the autobiography of a literary writer is bound to contain aesthetic composition. However, the chapter on the historical reviews of Indian autobiographies in English also considers all those life narratives by non-literary figures, which competent critics have found to be of literary merit. Two translated life-stories, originally written in Bangla by non-literary writers, have also been incorporated as they are important milestones in the survey of the form. Therefore, I have not tried to make an unbridgeable divide between the two groups or categories because from the point of view of literary theory they are both worth consideration. It is hoped that like my earlier work, *Indian English Writing: The Autobiographical Mode*, this volume, with the addition of seven more essays, will facilitate the readers to form new perspectives about the autobiographical genre.

My husband, Prof. Ajit Sodhi, has always reassured and supported my academic pursuits. He has helped in typing and formatting of the chapters. However, any errors or lapses in the book are solely due to laxity on my part.

My daughters Pooja and Anooja are constant in their enthusiastic approval of their mother's critical and creative activities. Their young minds generate new ideas which give an impetus in initiating new points of view in our discussions.

May 2010 **Meena Sodhi**
Banaras Hindu University

Contents

CHAPTER 1

Autobiography : A Re-creation of the Self

The multitude of voices raised by the structuralists, the deconstructionists over the complete extinction of the author's personality from his created work, found its culmination in Roland Barthes' *"The death of the author"*. The discussions, debates and arguments by the supporters of this theory tried to annihilate the author's biography from the text. It was an anti-thesis of the Romantic cult of Narcissism, the fascination with one's own image. The Romantics did not consider man's reflection or his encounter with himself to be a taboo or a mythical death sign. The development of the Venetian Mirror in the Middle Ages had made even a child, conscious of his own personality and identity. And so, for the Romantics, the image in the mirror became a part of man's everyday life.

Eliot's *"Tradition And The Individual Talent"* (1917) was written mainly to combat the idea that a poet should be praised in proportion to his originality. No poet or artist, Eliot asserted, could be understood solely in terms of himself. It was a reaction against the excessive expression of personality, the exaggerated display of `I', the uninhibited revealation of the self by the Romantic writers. Therefore, as a zealous and self-proclaimed classicist, Eliot declared:

> "... the poet has not a personality to express, but a particular medium, which is only a medium and not a personality, in which impressions and experiences

combine in peculiar and unexpected ways. Impressions and experiences which are important for the man may take no place in the poetry, and those which become important in the poetry may play quite a negligible part in the man, the personality".[1]

Eliot's theory of "impersonality" is in conformity with a scientific analogy, which he gives in the essay, to demonstrate the production of sulphurous acid:

"I shall, therefore, invite you to consider, as a suggestive analogy, the action which takes place when a bit of finely filiated platinum is introduced into a chamber containing oxygen and sulphur dioxide".[2]

Here Eliot compares the mind of the poet to a platinum shred, which remains unchanged and neutral during the process of a poetic creation. He very cogently and authoritatively concludes that "the more perfect the artist, the more completely separated in him will be the man who suffers and the mind which creates ..." [3]

Northrop Frye's *Anatomy of Criticism* (1957) recommends the stance taken by Eliot in treating any kind of writing, which includes literary criticism, as objectively as a scientific endeavour.

Similarly Eliot's emphasis on depersonalisation, in the scientific context, finds an echo in Wayne C. Booth's *The Rhetoric of Fiction* (1961). Booth shoots out a number of synonyms for the Eliotian act of "depersonalisation": "impersonality, detachment, disinterestedness, neutrality etc."[4] Giving examples from Flaubert and Chekov, he says:

"Like many literary enthusiasts, the passion for neutrality was imported into fiction from the other arts relatively late."[5]

For Flaubert the model novelist should have the attitude of a scientist or a chemist and the human soul should be treated with a kind of impartiality which is shown by the physical scientist in his study of matter. Once the writer has perfected this dispassionate technique, he would have taken a giant leap in the right direction. Art, Flaubert says, must achieve "by a pitiless method, the precision of the physical sciences".[6]

Another critic voicing the same thoughts is Foucault, who, in *"What is an Author?"* (1969) concludes that the author's name does not have a legal status and is not located in the fiction of the work:

> "A private letter may have a signifier - it does not have an author; a contract may well have a guarantor - it does not have an author. An anonymous text posted on a wall probably has a writer - but not an author. The author - function is therefore characteristic of the mode of existence, circulation, and functioning of certain discourses within a society".[7]

Foucault, no doubt has the scientific discourses in his mind, which do not have an authorising subject as such; the subject is replaced by a discussion based on the results of an experiment, a theory which the subject has been able to arrive at. But, he says, the authorising subject may be absent even from non-scientific discussions like those on literature, philosophy, psychology and history. Various forms of discourses in modern intellectual life, like novel, poems, plays, philosophical and psychological experiments they are quite independent of the personality as well as the authority of the writer. Plagiarism and photoreproduction are the two most evident examples. The authority of the author is reduced merely to the signature, which is attached to his work in the form of his name on the title page. For the past several years critics like Roland Barthes and Jacques Derrida have tried to establish the supremacy of the "textual non-subjective I" as the creator of a discourse.

Booth says that for a writer to forget his "individual being" and his "peculiar circumstances", would be to underestimate the relevance of his individuality.

"As he writes, he creates not simply an ideal, impersonal 'man in general' but an implied version of `himself' that is different from the implied authors we meet in other men's works".[8]

Booth goes on to say that in many cases it has seemed that the novelist while writing is discovering or creating himself through the narrative. So the process of writing could be what Prof. Rajnath states the "death of the empirical author which Eliot announced in his *'Tradition And The Individual Talent'",*[9] and the birth of Booth's "implied author" which aptly conveys Eliot's point of view of the personality. With the extinction of the empirical self of the author is born an "official scribe" or as Booth adopts the recently revived term by Kathleen Tillotson, "author's 'second self'"[10]. Booth maintains that "The 'implied' author chooses, consciously or unconsciously, what we read; we infer him as an ideal literary, created version of the real man; he is the sum of his own choices".[11]

Augustine's *Confessions*, written between the years 397 and 400 AD, was a landmark in establishing the conversion of experience into narrative, that is, in an autobiography. It is conversion of life into textual self-representation. The life of the writer is made to conform to certain narrative forms and thus appears unique. However, Paul de Man[12] was prompted to take an extreme stand:

> "... he argued that the whole referential foundation of autobiography was based upon an illusion, that autobiography was not a life but a text. Such an argument, tendentious as it may be, is quite unsettling to most Americanist's and all readers who would like to believe, with Whitman, that when they touch a book they are touching a living person - or coming as close to one as they can."[13]

The stand of the deconstructionists and the implied pun in Paul de Man's "de-facement" often uses the metaphor of murder for biography and suicide for autobiography. But, as Robert F. Sayre summarises that it is necessary to remember that while reading an autobiography we only metaphorically read "a life." We read a book. The writing of an autobiography is an act like any other act performed by the humans.

What this paper seeks to exemplify is the supremacy of the "implied" author and his importance in the literary sub-genre, the autobiography, where the self of the writer is remade through the process of writing and therefore the text does not exhibit "The death of the Author". The autobiographical process is not the mere depiction of the author's personality, but rather a recreation of his personality, which is seen in retrospection in his autobiography. The *autos,* the "I" of the autobiography determines the "bios" or the life. But it is the third element, the *graphe* or the act of writing, which is of real importance. It combines the self and the life and gives them a certain form, and enables them to reflect the image back and forth as between two mirrors. The artistic activity helps the autobiographer in establishing his true identity and enables him to present an accurate picture of himself.

This self-referentiality of autobiography is in the language, the narrative and the structure of the work and is also self-interrogative. It establishes tension and drama within the work and also asserts the life of the writer. It is to be noted that the autobiographical writing is undoubtedly a process of self-alteration. The man writing about his life, becomes almost a stranger to himself. The life which he has lived belongs to the past, whereas the life about which he is writing, or shall we say creating, belongs to the present. It does remind us of the importance of the Eliotian concept which demands the writer to be conscious not only of the "pastness of the past, but of its presence".[14] Although when

Eliot coined the phrase, he had the notion of Tradition in his mind.

Yeats in his autobiography says "It is myself that I remake"; this is exactly my contention: that the art of autobiography involves a process of reconstruction of the writers life; it is the self-picturing in which he indulges. It is a contradiction of the theory of the "New Critics" and later of Eliot and Barthes. The urge to portray oneself is obvious: "Self-portraiture.... is a synonym of self-knowledge".[15] And it should not be doubted because, as Coleridge had observed: "when a man is attempting to describe another's character, he may be right or he may wrong - but in one thing he will always succeed, in describing himself".[16]

The autobiographical genre was transformed during the Romantic period, from an objective memoir to a personal subjective remembrance, "the attempt to connect, by retrospective reflection, disparate and discontinuous experiences and states of mind into a self conceived almost solely in terms of a maturing consciousness, rather than embodiment".[17] The embodied self or the real self is replaced by a new, self-made object, an artistic artefact - the "implied self" of the autobiographical text. Emphasizing the death of the author, Roland Barthes's point of view more or less expresses the same idea:

> "The Author, when believed in, is always conceived of as the past of his own book: book and author stand automatically on a single line divided into a before and an after".[18]

What I am trying to stress is that even if we accept the death of the author in a text, the writing process results in the birth of a new person in an autobiography; it is a creation of a new self. The autobiographical act collects the scattered material of an individual's life to convey a comprehensive vision of the writer. Georges Gusdorf compares the autobiographer to a historian, who narrates his own history.

He is the hero of his own tale and wants to unfold his past "in order to draw out the structure of his being in time". It is a reconstruction of life in its entirety; the path, which he traverses in tracing his history of life, is undoubtedly a very long one; but it always leads him to himself. Unlike the historian he is not engaged in an objective endeavour but in a personal exoneration, in a search for himself through the history of his life. It is most often the work of an aging man who thinks like the historian of his life, he can overcome all the difficulties which he encounters enroute quite impartially. He struggles against the loss of memory in portraying the course of events and there is always the temptation to reject the obsession with truth. But a sense of moral alertness checks him from deviating from the path of factual truth and he succeeds in giving a mirror image of his life.

It is a difficult process and Georges Gusdorf thinks that "integral resurrection of the past" can seem meaningless due to its complete relation to the present. The autobiographer, who is also a historian of himself, is faced with a complex situation in revisiting his past. Gone is the child, the young man and the mature man of yesterday; the man of today knows the end of his story. The tension faced by the writer in trying to overcome the time gap between the life lived in the past and its depiction in writing, should be evident in the narrative. Gusdorf says:

> "Thus the original sin of autobiography is first one of logical coherence and rationalisation. The narrative is conscious, and since the narrator's consciousness directs the narrative, it seems to him incontestable that it has also directed his life. In other words, the act of reflecting that is essential to conscious awareness is transferred, by a kind of unavoidable optical illusion, back to the stage of the event itself".[20]

The chief criticism directed against this seemingly meaningless historical method is that it tries to substitute the completely formed for something, which is in the process of being formed. The narrator finds himself being caught in the motif of the narrative, which joins his past to the future. The past events, which were probably meaningless or had multiple meanings at the time of occurrence, acquire a new meaning. This demand for a meaning makes him choose the details of his past life in a presupposed intelligible manner. We can say that an autobiography is a "revised and corrected version" of the writer's life. Therefore, an autobiography "cannot be a pure and simple record of existence, an account book or a log book; on such and such a day at such and such an hour, I went to such and such a place .... A record of this kind, no matter how minutely exact, would be no more than a caricature of life; in such a case, rigorous precision would add up to the same thing as the subtlest deception".[21]

For an autobiographer the factual truth is subordinated to the truth about himself; he presents to us a dialogue with himself; the narrative becomes an affirmation of the man who seeks the innermost fidelity. He does not try to repeat the scene but gives it a new perspective. It is an enactment of the drama of the life of a man who tries to reassemble himself at a certain time in history. Georges Gusdorf thinks it to be a "document about a life" and its historian has every right to check its accuracy. But more than being a mere historical record it is a work of art; the literary writer is well aware of its style, beauty and the harmonious image, which he desires to project. So it is primarily valuable for its artistic excellence; its being termed fiction or fraud becomes irrelevant. Consequently the literary value of an autobiography is of far greater signification than its historical or objective function.

"Every work of art is a projection from the interior realm into exterior space where in becoming incarnated it achieves consciousness of itself".[22]

Therefore as a work of art the autobiography is not only a focus on the author's life, but an artistic creation which employs all narrative devices and restrictions like accuracy, impartiality and inclusiveness; it is not merely a recapitulation of the past but also an attempt by the autobiographer to reconstruct himself in his own likeness.

"Confession of the past realises itself as a work in the present: it effects as true creation of self by the self".[23]

The autobiographical act is a reconstitution of the writer's self, and is viewed from a distance in life: the writer sees himself as a special entity, having a unique identity across the wide space of time. The external events are not responsible only for the restructuring of life; they certainly constitute a limitation but what plays an essential role in this structural design, on the themes of life, is the writer's personality. The reinterpretation of life helps the autobiographer to get a clear perspective of himself, of what he has been. The recomposition of life is termed as "a second reading" by Georges Gusdorf, which he claims to be truer than the first. It is like having an aerial view of a fortification or a city, revealing the important lines which the viewer had failed to notice earlier in himself; the clarity of values which he holds dear to himself without being aware of them and which ascertained the most crucial decisions of his life. It is a search of self through his own history.

It is an interesting fact that the autobiographer emphasizes the past "I" to be different from the present "I".

"The narrator describes not only what happened to him at a different time in his life but above all how he became - out of what he was - what he presently is".[24]

It is imperative for the writer of an autobiography to seek the genesis of the present condition. The dictionary defines "autobiography" as "the story of one's life written by himself". But there is a world of difference in that "himself". Stephen Spender[25] detects objectivity in the depiction of the autobiographer's subjective experiences and feels that unless he is able to achieve this transformation, his experiences are of no value to his art. It does not remain his own experience but it becomes that of everyone. He creates a life, which is new and revealing. He is himself the thesis of his book but views himself as he were another person writing about himself. Since the autobiographer is the "unique and unknown I", it is a case of depersonalised autobiography.

James Olney feels that the views expressed by phenomenologists have been conveyed metaphorically in a classic expression from Heraclitus, which more or less emphasizes the autobiographer's dilemma:

> "Heraclitus somewhere says that all things flow and nothing remains still, and comparing existing things to the flowing river, he says that you would not step twice into the same stream".[26]
> (Plato, Cratylus, 402)

Recollection or recapitulation is dependent upon a creative memory, "that apes and reshapes the historic past as in the image of the present, making the past as necessary to this present as this present is the inevitable outcome of that past".[27]

The factuality being an essential part of all those things which involve perception, consciousness; memories, which Heraclitus thought to be like a flowing of a river. Memory and the present reality bear a reciprocal relationship: the now, shaping the memory, just as the present moment, the now, is shaped by the memory. And the autobiographer, while trying to remember the past in the present imagines himself to be another person and lives in another world of existence. Roland Barthes also concedes the estrangement between the two personalities of the writer:

> "When a narrator (of a written text) recounts what has happened to him, the I who recounts is no longer the one that is recounted".[28]

The recomposition, reexamination or to use the word appropriated by John Sturrock, a "conversion", takes place only through the medium of language. The autobiographer shapes his past according to the restriction of the language and the language is shaped to suit the restraints of his past. He then concludes that the work is a "textualization of that pretextual life", and "that autobiography is not life itself but a certain artful representation of life".[29] Thus the means of language is absolutely essential for the communication of meaning.

A deconstructionist might argue that language is an abortive gesture, since it cannot mean anything beyond itself; and he will not hesitate in dissolving the text of an autobiography into thin air. But critics like Georges Gusdorf believe writing to be a second incarnation and language to be "an outpouring of the thought" and also "thought's externalised form, which once expressed, is able to return to its point of departure. Thus it becomes consciousness, an inner speech, man's discourse to himself, self debating with self, by virtue of which the individuals destiny is formed. Deprived of speech, the mind would fall back into confusion analogous to an animal's, with an unclear consciousness clinging to the present moment.... like the torpor of sunbathers on the beech who have made their minds a blank".[30]

Paul John Eakin[31] too is opposed to the viewpoint of the deconstructionists, which says that since an autobiography is supposed to refer to a past context, the act of reference distorts the image of the past as it really was. So, they argue, all the historical references are mere fictions by nature. Defending the autobiographical genre as a recreation and not merely as a creation of the past, Paul John Eakin contends that the deconstructionist unnecessarily bothers about the unbridgeable gulf between "the thing itself (the experiences of the past) and the "picture" (the representation in the language). His submission is that whereas on the one hand, the language cannot encompass anything beyond itself, the "picture" in language maybe taken for the human experience or "the thing itself". Since we experience in language, we cannot analyze pure experience outside its linguistic experience or the verbal text. He finds similar viewpoints expressed by Ricoeur, Fleishman, and Janet Varner Gunn who postulate a phenomenological correlation between the temporal structure of autobiography and what they take to be the essential narrativity of human experience. This point of view finds affirmation in **The words** by Sartre who demonstrates that the living of the life, which he records, was already firmly steeped in the teleology of nineteenth century biography; a teleology which gave him the basic structure for the design of a life and the creation of an identity.

The deconstructionists may talk about the genre or its linguistical import or about its deep lying structures. But what they have still not understood nor fathomed is the knowledge of self and consciousness even though, in a flamboyant attitude, they may deny rather than affirm its reality. The created self is resultant of the autobiographical process, where it is not only created, but discovered and asserted in the process of writing; and it "requires the reader or the student of autobiography to participate fully in the process, so that the created self becomes at one remove, almost as much the reader's as the author's".[32]

It is a work of enlightenment, which gives a glimpse of the individual's inner privacy, hitherto unknown, unseen not only to the readers but also to himself, so that he is able to view himself not as he is but as he wishes to have been. Or the autobiographer may ask and answer the question "How did I become what I am?" "Writing is liberation", wrote Sainte-Beuve and it is true of autobiography; having indulged in self-examination and having written about it, the writer is not the same person that he was before the artistic creation. The past has been successful in altering the present. The process continues as the human being is constantly being remade. It is a never-ending dialogue with the self, a remaking of self which goes on forever.

REFERENCES

1. *The Sacred Wood,* Methuen & Co. Ltd.,1967, p. 56.
2. *Ibid.,* p. 53.
3. *Ibid.,* p. 54.
4. *The Rhetoric of Fiction,* The University of Chicago Press, 1970, p. 67.
5. *Ibid.,* p. 68.
6. *Ibid.,* p. 68.
7. *Modern Criticism and Theory,* ed. by David Lodge, Longman, 1989, p. 202.
8. *The Rhetoric of Fiction,* p. 70.
9. "The Death of the Author": T.S. Eliot And Contemporary Criticism", *The Journal of Literary Criticism,* Vol. 5, no. 2, p. 3.
10. *The Rhetoric of Fiction,* p. 71.
11. *Ibid.,* p. 75.
12. *"Autobiography as De-facement",* Modern Language Notes, Vol. 94(1979), 919-30.
13. Robert F. Sayre, *The Examined Self,* The University of Wisconsin Press,1988.
14. *"Tradition and Individual Talent",* The Sacred Wood, p. 49.
15. "On Writing Autobiography", *Studies in Autobiography,* ed. James Olney, O U P, New York, 1988, p.166.
16. *The Notebooks of Samuel Taylor Coleridge,* ed. Kathleen Coburn, I (London: Routledge & Kegan Paul), 1957, p. 74.
17. "Romantic Autobiography As Cultural Artefact", *Studies in Autobiography,* ed. James Olney, p.143.
18. "The death of the author", *Modern Criticism and Theory,* ed. David Lodge, p. 170.
19. "Conditions And Limits of Autobiography", *Autobiography: Essays Theoretical and Critical,* ed. James Olney, Princeton University Press, 1980, p. 43.

20. "Conditions and Limits of Autobiography", *Autobiography: Essays Theoretical and Critical,* p. 41.
21. *Ibid.,* p. 42.
22. *Ibid.,* p. 44.
23. *Ibid.,* p. 44.
24. Jean Starobinski, "The Style of Autobiography", in *Autobiography: Essays Theoretical and Critical,* ed. James Olney, p. 79.
25. "Confessions And Autobiography", *Autovuigraogt Essays Theoretical and Critical,* p. 117.
26. "The Ontology of Autobiography", Autobiography: Essays *Theoretical And Critical,* pp. 237-238.
27. *Ibid.,* p. 243.
28. "The Death of the Author", *Modern Literary Theory,* p. 276.
29. *The Language of Autobiography,* Cambridge University Press, 1994, p. 24-25.
30. "Scripture of the Self; Prologue in Heaven", *Studies in Autobiography,* ed. James Olney, pp. 113-114.
31. "Narrative And Chronology As Structure of Reference And The New Model Autobiographer", *Studies in Autobiography* ed. James Olney.
32. Autobiography And The Cultural Moment", *Autobiography: Essays Theoretical and Critical,* ed. James Olney, p. 24.

CHAPTER 2

Autobiography : An Agency of Man and His Self

The desire to express oneself and the urge to reveal the world within has universal connotations and can be found from the beginning of the human civilisation. Man has always tried to express his inner feelings, his desires and his life through the medium of art. Being a multi-dimensional phenomenon, he has used various ways and means to depict his inner urges. And in this rootless, ever-changing modern life, he wanted to leave some testimony of his existence. Therefore, it is no great surprise that the form of writing which is moving from the periphery to the center is autobiography, which records the life-history of a man, helps him in establishing his identity, and also guarantees the agency of the self.

The most lucid definition, which can be given of an autobiography, is that it is an account of the writer's life written by himself, as he wishes others to view it. The act of writing an autobiography is a discovery, a creation and an imitation of the self. James Olney has emphasized a shift in the autobiographical writings in the modern times from *bios*, the life of the writer, to *autos*, the self. This shift has made the study of autobiography seek recourse to philosophical, psychological and literary methods for analytical purposes. The pre-eminence of *autos* allows the "I" to take a form of its own and has infact decided the nature of autobiography:

"It was this turning to *autos* - the `I' that coming awake to its own being shapes and determines the nature of the autobiography and in so doing half discovers, half creates itself - that opened up the subject of autobiography specifically for literary discussion, for behind every work of literature there is an `I' informing the whole and making its presence felt at every critical point, and without this `I', stated or implied, the work would collapse into mere insignificance".[1]

Therefore it can be implied that what appears to be autobiography to the person concerned, is likely to be viewed as history, philosophy, psychology or sociology by other people.

Philip Dodd thinks that the autobiographical form deserves special mention and that it should be "deployed by such writers to articulate their rejection of Stalinism, which denied the self any agency. What characterises each of these works is the representation of the self discovery that it is not simply an effect of history, but free.[2]"

The autobiography or "the narrative of self" or "the voyage of inner discovery", indulges in the glorification of man. George Gusdorf[3], the special critic on autobiography, says that this mode of writing "is limited almost entirely to the public sector of existence". It is a search of self through the annals of history; an act which embodies the self where the "real" or "actual" self is replaced "by a new, self-made object, a cultural artifact - the book at hand, the autobiographical text".[4]

The image of the self is an important concept: Narcissus viewing his own face in the depth of the fountain; a fascination with one's own image. The development of the Venetian Mirror in the Middle Ages made the image in the mirror a common occurrence in the everyday life of man. The human infant becomes aware of the mirror and his reflection in it from the age of six months. As he grows older he discerns the importance of his own identity; he learns to differentiate that which is outside from that which is within. The man of civilisation dwells in leisure in rediscovering himself and exults in the fascination of Narcissus. Similarly autobiography is the mirror in which the writer reflects his own image. And with the technical achievements of modern times, the appeal of the reflection in the mirror boosts the tradition of self-examination in man not only in the West, but mostly all over the globe. However, Man's appearance in the mirror is visible not only to himself but also to the people around him. The reflection is the sum total of his personality, his relationship and his achievements. And the world is aware of all these aspects; but what the world is not aware of, is the self inside man; this side of his personality is known only to himself.

The individual, therefore, writes the story of his experiences from within and provides us with a privileged insight, which is quite often guarded, into his past life. He alone is capable of recounting the events of his life and, what is more important, he alone is aware of its secrets:

> "..... there is also himself known only to himself, himself seen from the inside of his own existence. Thus inside self has a history that may have no significance in any objective 'history of his time'. It is the history of himself observing the observer, not the history of himself observed by others".[5]

The autobiography is also the story of a distinctive culture written in individual characters, which no other form of writing is capable of giving. The man who writes his autobiography thinks himself to be a special entity. Infact all the humans imagine themselves to be of great significance to the world, which, they feel, would be incomplete after their death. And therefore, by writing an account of their lives they want to leave some precious record of their existence on this planet. The emphasis on the uniqueness of the individual's life came into focus only after he had attained civilisation. Man is dependent on a community and is never isolated from it. But the life in a community demands that each man must play a role which had some time or other been played by his ancestors and will also be played by his offsprings, who would take on the names of their forefathers. Thus the community life helps in maintaining a continuity of the individual's self-identity. It, therefore, implies that the writing of an autobiography is not possible in a culture, which does not give prominence to man and to the self.

Keeping in view this line of argument, it is not possible to accept the dictum that the autobiographical genre is more appropriate and more well-suited to a western writer, who is less inhibited in revealing his past life, its secrets, its mysteries, than his Indian counterpart. The revealation of self in the West is particularly a product of the Christian doctrine. Augustine's *Confessions,* written between the years 397 and 400 A.D., is self-analytic and gives an insight into the complexity of the soul; it is also a record of a great and powerful mind undergoing religious conversion. It is the first example of great autobiography even though the form was not identified until the early nineteenth century:

> "Christianity brings a new anthropology to the fore: every destiny, however humble it be, assumes a kind of supernatural stake. Christian destiny unfolds as a dialogue of the Soul with God in which, right up to the end, every action, every initiative of thought or of conduct, can call everything back into question.... The rule requiring confession of sins gives to self-examination a character at once systematic and necessary".[6]

The Renaissance and the Reformation in Europe made Man discover himself in a new way. The individuality of man was established, which has been re-emphasized by the modern man today. Since the post-industrial Western Society imposes a threat on the self, the obsession with it can be seen as a reaction to a widely discursive feeling that the days of the individual are numbered:

> "..... people increasingly experience themselves to be powerless before anonymous and virtually omnipotent corporations and institutions, and, at the same time are rendered superfluous by the rapidly advancing automation of the sphere of work".[7]

World War II had demeaned the value of man and it did not make the great world thinkers very happy. They were not pleased at the state of affairs, whether it was in the field of science, religion or politics. Consequently once again the interest is on man, on his supremacy, on his subjectivity, the latter makes him probe inward, reconstruct himself and his life. Dr. S. Radhakrishnan had said:

> "We have to understand ourselves, understand man behind all his activities, scientific, ethical, spiritual. Science cannot dictate what man is to be; but man must understand what scientific activity is .... A true theory is that which works, and work is human activity".[8]

It has been a practice to differentiate the "eastern man" from his western counterpart. But what we forget in the process is the fact that they do not belong to two different species. However, the only difference we can concede between the two is that while the eastern man is intuitive, spiritual and an introvert, the western man is materialistic, ethical and an extrovert. Therefore, it is argued that the autobiography, which reveals the innermost secrets of the writer's life, is not an appropriate medium for the Indians to take up: they are being mostly introverts and not so forthcoming in sharing the secrets of their lives. But without going into a historical survey of Indian autobiographies, it is necessary to point out that the first evidence of autobiographical writing in India is found as early as 1500 B.C., in the *Rigveda* (10:2:34) in *The Lament of the Gambler,* where a gambler, who was once a Rishi, confesses how he ruined his life by gambling. Later the Moghuls felt importance of writing their life history or getting it written by someone else. Sultan Firoz Shah, who ascended the throne of Delhi in 1351 wrote his autobiography *Futuhat-i-Firoz Shahi. Babar-nama,* another autobiography bears testimony to this fact. This form got a fresh impetus after the Indian Renaissance in the nineteenth century, which had been initiated by Raja Rammohan Roy. And Lutfullah wrote the first work, which can be identified as the modern autobiography, in 1854. What is more important is that the concept of self has been prevalent in India since the Vedic and the Upanishadic times. The *Taitreya Upanishad* (600-500 B.C), the *Manduka Upanishad* (500-400 B.C) and the *Mahabharata* (1 A.D) have glorified man and the self. The last work extols man as the highest creature in the chain of living beings on the earth:

> "Guhyam brahma tadidam vobruimi
> na manusat bresthataran ki kincit".

Meaning thereby that "I tell you this, the secret of the Brahman: there is nothing higher than man". *The Upanishads* admonish man to know his true self, "know thy self" (atmanam vidhi) and the Socratic ideal "know thyself" also becomes the ideal of the Indian philosophy. However, there is a difference; Socrates would not have separated the "self" from "thy" and would not have said, "know thy self" which the Indian thinkers did. According to them the Self is not the body:

> "There is indeed a sense in which, according to Socrates, it is not the body. If the distinction between the rational soul and the irrational is Socratic and if

> the rational soul alone is eternal, then the true self will be the rational soul, not the lower; and in that case man's true self will not be the body, but reason. Even then, however, according to Indian thought the self (**atman**) is higher than reason".[9]

The "I", the inwardness of the physical body, is given a focal function in Indian philosophy. The great philosophers all over the world have given the same advice, "Man know thyself". The Indian philosophers do something more: they say that man is in direct communication with God. But since God is not an external figure, where is He? The only logical conclusion, which comes to the mind, is that he dwells in man. This concept is supported by all religions; the Divine Spirit pervades within each man who has a private experience and the existence of the material world outside. The Indian philosophers assert that the Indians have a tendency to see God in the external nature, who unifies the world under his control:

> "But then, how can He control man, who has an inward mind? Can He do it by controlling only man's external circumstances? Here the inward-looking religion supplied an answer: He does it by controlling from outside and from inside. The *Brhadaranyka Upanishad* (700 B.C.) says that the light of the *atman* is the same as the light of the sun; the self within is the same as the sun without".[10]

But the Gods were all subordinated to the *Atman*: the source of light both external and internal. It was the Supreme Spirit, which dwelt in man:

> "In the *Upanishads* the *Atman* is clearly conceived as dynamic and as full of bliss and consciousness. Indeed it is not merely dynamic, it is also static, because it is self-subsistent".[11]

The true self has also been called the *Brahman*, the *Atman* being the Supreme Self. It is not revealed to the ordinary mind, which is too engrossed in the unending, everyday activity of the world. But as soon as one is able to rise above the day to day mundane activity, one is able to discover the intuitive, non-mediated experience of the self. It is here that the autobiographical writing helps man to unravel the dark recesses of his being. The writing of his life history breaks a spell and the writer attains a deep sense of peace for the first time in his life:

> "..... self-observation becomes an instrument of self-change. Letting thoughts take their course, they are brought under the magnifying glass of critical examination, being looked upon as an other than the present individual, the energy frozen in them is broken and detachment reached".[12]

M. Hiriyanna[13] explains the two terms, "*Brahman*" and "*Atman*", the first is a "prayer" and the primary cause of the universe. While the "*Atman*", he says is "the inner self of man". It is the essence of man and it is primarily distinct from his physical body. The *Taittiriya Upanishad* (600-500 B.C.) emphasizes the *atman* to be the real man and also his ultimate self:

> "From the *atman*, which is the *Brahman*, aether (*akasa*) is born; from akasa air; from air fire; from fire water; and from water earth. From earth are born plants and from plants food is derived; and from food man is born. But this is only the physical body to which we refer as 'I'. The 'I' disappears at death, although the physical body may remain for some time. Hence, body is not the true 'I'. What disappears at death is life, the vital principle; then the vital principle *prana*, must be the *atman*, the 'I'."[14]

P.T. Raju in *The Concept of Man,* argues that modern philosophy has still not been able to solve the question of the relation of matter, life, mind and spirit. The *Upanishads* included two more levels of reality, but even then they were not able to provide an answer to this problem. However, what they did realise was that all levels were unified in man and they also observed the relation between them. But modern science does not find this kind of relationship very satisfactory; nevertheless it modifies the seriousness of the problem. No doubt the empirical scientific approach helps in the study of man:

> "If, for instance, we wish to study how men behave individually and collectively and are interested in its classification, prediction and control, the scientific empirical approach has a definite utility. But when our concern is not such a utility-oriented study but a true understanding of the self, this method is external, contrived, and superficial. Each man lives, feels and experiences as 'I'."[15]

The "depth-psychology" studies do not provide a direct inquiry into this question. However, the *Moksha* philosophy, offered by the Vedanta and re-emphasised in our times by Swami Rama Tirtha, Raman Maharishi and Sri Aurobindo, does discuss 'I', the knower. And we are concerned to know more about man, this wonderful creature, who has a mind of his own, and can look backwards into the past and forwards into the future.

What is more important is that he has an inwardness, which is his very own and is very private. He thus becomes a psychological being. The world is the right place for man's self-realisation, the process through which he realises his inward reality. The Upanishad also says that the realisation of one's self can never be lost. The ultimate aim of education in man's life is to help man in realising his true inwardness. The duties in his life have also to be performed with this aim in mind, the aim of self-realisation. Buddhism too supports this theory:

> "..... Buddhism overemphasized inwardness and said that man, if he is intent upon self-realisation, need not bother about pleasing Gods and ancestors. To a man of self-realisation, God themselves pay homage, as they did to Buddha.[16]

The uniqueness in man was emphasized by Tagore in *Sadhana:*

> "I am absolutely unique, I am I, I am incomparable. The whole weight of the universe cannot crush out this individuality of mine. I maintain it inspite of the tremendous gravitation of all things".[17]

The individuality, the self of man is absolutely important, and if this special quality is gone, Tagore feels, the humans will become "bankrupt". It will be not only the loss of an individual, but also a "loss to the whole world".

It was once pointed out to Tagore that the annihilation of the self was the ultimate goal of the Indians. Tagore thought otherwise; he did not think it correct to take every meaning in the literal sense. And sometimes a dictionary did not prove to be very helpful. Selflessness is preached not only by the Indian religions but also by Buddhism and Christianity. But what is more important is the deliverance of man from *avidya*, from ignorance:

> "It is our ignorance which makes us think that our self, as self is real, that it has its complete meaning in itself. When we take that wrong view of self then we try to live in such a manner as to make self the ultimate object of our life".[18]

Due to his ignorance man lets the self imprison him in fetters, thus restraining him from knowing his true soul.

Therein comes religion or 'dharma', which helps man in attaining this goal:

> "Dharma is the ultimate purpose that is working in our self.... When we know the highest ideal of freedom which a man has, we know his *dharma*, the essence of his nature, the real meaning of his self...."[19]

Tagore projects two ways of looking at self: one is to see the self as a display of itself, and the other to see the self transcend itself and thus disclose its own meaning. Self is like a lamp, when it illuminates and holds the light high, it reveals itself. And when it decides to keep itself dark it violates its true design. Thus the Indian concept of self also favours its revealation rather than its concealment.

According to Tagore the wish for self-gratification is strong in everyone, but the self can attain higher heights only if its fulfillment is accompanied by some desire for the good of the society too. This attitude helps in the attainment of *bodhi* or the true awakening, as also in the acquisition of infinite happiness. All the things in this world have two aspects, *maya* or appearance, and *satyam* or truth. The self is only *maya* where it strives to be only individual, finite and considers itself separate from all the other things. But once it recognises its quintessence in the universal and infinite, in the supreme self, in *param atman*, then it achieves the distinction of being termed as *satyam*.

"This is what Christ means when he says `Before Abraham was *I am*'. This is the eternal *I am* that speaks through the *I am* that is in me. The individual *I am* attains its perfect end when it realises its freedom of harmony in the infinite *I am*".[20]

The world never ends, it is always old and always new. And the self has to know that it is borning new every moment of its life. It has always to ask, "who am I?" Apparently it appears to be a very simple question to answer, because nothing could be closer, more personal than a person's "I".

And it does appear to be quite an absurd question, which one puts to oneself. But it does not seem so illogical when the autobiographer puts it to himself to establish his identity. He has to answer the question, "How did I become what I am today?"

The autobiographical writing, an inward adventure as well as an inward concentration, has the complete absorption with the self. Robert F. Sayre[21] defines the autobiography as a "loose self-history". Roy Pascal[22] thinks that "True autobiography can be written only by men and women pledged to their innermost selves" and therefore the form requires dedication to internal as well as external events. Robert F. Sayre supports this viewpoint and reiterates:

> "Autobiography is an examination of the self as both a sovereign integrity and a member of society. In fact, the self is at all times both these things, and autobiography is an endless stream of demonstrations of their inseparability".[23]

Patricia Meyer Spacks says that "To read an autobiography is to encounter a self as an imaginative being".[24]

Autobiographical writing is an inward concentration in which there is complete absorption with the self. This view has been expressed by V.S. Naipaul in *India: A Wounded Civilization.* It is a kind of inward adventure. Discussing the Indian concept of the self, while analysing Gandhi's *My Experiments with Truth,* Naipaul says, that to the Indians:

> "The outer world matters only in so far as it affects the inner. It is the Indian way of experiencing; what is true of Gandhi's autobiography is true of many other Indian autobiographers, though the self-absorption is usually more sterile".[25]

Naipaul gives long extracts of the conversation he had with a psychotherapist based at Jawaharlal Nehru University, Dr. Sudhir Kakar, who was of the opinion that the Indians use the outside reality only "to preserve the continuity of the self amidst an ever changing flux of outer events and things".[26] The western style of an individualistic and assertive personality is out of place in the Indian context. It explains the concept of ashram life in India and the concept of communal life in it. This gives coherence to the statement made earlier that the community life helps in the establishment of the individual's self-identity.

Self remains mysterious and subsequently increases the fascination for itself. The autobiographical writing, says James Olney[27], is indeed the result of "the lure of the self". With its special charm, its recondite nature, its enigmatic appeal, the magic of self has drawn not only the writers all over the world, but the students as well as the critics to the study of autobiography. Similarly the historiographers have also insisted that the *autos* of the historian are and always present in the historical writings. The phenomenologists and existentialists agree with the psychologists when they say that the self defines itself from minute to minute amid the confusion of the external reality and as a security against the hurly-burly which exists in the outside world:

> "The study of how autobiographers have done this - how they discovered, asserted, created a self in the process of writing it out - requires the reader or the student of autobiography to participate fully in the process, so that the created self becomes, at one remove, almost as much the reader's as the author's".[28]

A work of art is a representation from the inner realm into its embodiment as an external form; it then achieves consciousness of itself. So does autobiography constantly return to the elusive center of the self which lies buried in the unconscious, where it discovers that it was already there where it began. The self is forever in the process of making itself, it never takes a complete shape; hence the act of self-creation is everlasting. Man is a complex creature and in order to establish his identity in his own social sphere, it is absolutely necessary for him to first re-establish himself and to find out the denominator which helps him in understanding his life, his actions and his values.

REFERENCES

1. "Autobiography and the Cultural Moment", *Autobiography: Essays Theoretical and Critical*, ed. James Olney, Princeton University Press, 1980, p. 21.
2. "Criticism and the Autobiographical Tradition", *Modern Selves, Essays on Modern British And American Autobiography*, ed. Philip Dodd, Frank Cass & Co. Ltd, 1986, p. 8.
3. "Conditions and Limits of Autobiography", *Autobiography: Essays Theoretical and Critical*, ed. James Olney, p. 36.
4. Charles J. Rzepka, "Romantic Autobiography as Cultural Artifact", *Studies in Autobiography*, ed. James Olney, Oxford University Press, 1988, p. 143.
5. Stephen Spender, "Confessions and Autobiography", *Autobiography: Essays Theoretical and Critical*, ed. James Olney, p. 117.
6. Georges Gusdorf, "Conditions and Limits in Autobiography", *Autobiography: Essays Theoretical and Critical*, ed. James Olney, p. 33.
7. Michael Mundhenk, "Appropriating (Life-) History through Autobiographical writing: Andre Gorz's The Traitor, A Dialectical Inquiry into the self", *Modern Selves*, ed. Philip Dodd, p. 81.
8. "Introduction", *The Concept of Man*, ed. S. Radhakrishnan and P.T. Raju, Harper Collins, 1995, p. 17.
9. P.T. Raju, "The Indian Thought", *Concept of Man*, p. 225.
10. *Ibid.*, p. 216.
11. *Ibid.*, p. 218.
12. Hans Jacobs: *Western Psycho-therapy and Hindu Sadhana*, London, George and Unwin Ltd., 1961, p. 118.

13. *Outlines of Indian Philosophy*, London, George Allen & Unwin Ltd., 1951, p. 55.
14. "The Indian Thought", *Concept of Man*, p. 225.
15. S.N. Mahajan, " Freedom: An Indian Perspective", *Concept of Man in Philosophy*, ed. R.A. Sinari, B.R. Publishing Corporation, 1991, p. 116.
16. "The Indian Thought", *Concept of Man*, p. 256.
17. "The Problem of Self", *Sadhana*, Macmillan, 1988, p. 57.
18. *Ibid.,* p. 60.
19. *Ibid.,* p .62.
20. *Ibid.,* p. 70.
21. *The Examined Self*, The University of Wisconsin Press, 1988.
22. *Design and Truth in Autobiography*, Cambridge Mass.: Harvard University Press, 1960.
23. *The Examined Self*, p. 6.
24. *Imagining A Self*, Harvard University Press, London, 1976, p. 19.
25. *India: A Wounded Civilization*, Penguin, 1979, p. 101.
26. *Ibid.,* p. 103.
27. "Autobiography and the Cultural Moment", *Autobiography: Essays Theoretical and Critical*, p. 23.
28. *Ibid.,* p. 24.

CHAPTER 3

De-marginalising Autobiographical Writing

The mainstream literary culture tends to exclude and marginalise various forms of "life-writing" such as diaries, letters and autobiographies. Out of these autobiographies, which seek to represent the unique individual life, should normally be adopted as topic of central interest for literary and cultural theory rather than face exclusion and be neglected in the construction of literary canons. A number of critics in the United States have been adopting a stand in favour of this form and their efforts have contributed towards the formation of a distinctive genre of autobiographical criticism. However, the situation in India is very different and here we have to primarily not only defend autobiographical writing but also recognise it as an important form of literary creation before we can even think of forming principles of theory on it. Since the autobiographical narrative expresses the individuality, and the wisdom of India believes in depersonalisation, it has been claimed to be essentially a Western genre. This claim, seen as "culturally self-serving rules of the genre", has been challenged and refuted by non-western researchers in India as well as elsewhere too. It has been a practice to differentiate the "eastern" man from his "western" counterpart. But what we tend to forget is that man everywhere he is, is the same and the desire to know and to express one's self has universal connotation; and while we can concede a difference in the outlook of life between the two we cannot slot them into two different species.

> "We are entitled to suppose that there is something like an urge to autobiography within any individual, seeking expression at every level from the loosely and ephemerally conversational to the enduringly artistic".[1]

Autobiography is all about the stories of the lives of various people and we, as a nation of story-tellers, can use it to monumentalise the self by using art's shaping powers in order to transform the incoherences of a life into the regularities of an artistic story, thus preserving the tension between life and literature. It is through art that man discovers his infinite range.

The inner urge or a compulsion to reveal his private and hitherto unknown self helps the autobiographer not only in exploring his identity but also in affirming its singularity. The act of writing assists him in getting a better understanding of his own self, the development of his own personality, so that at the end of his writings he is able to answer the most valid question associated with this form of writing, "How did I become what I am?" In a way the method he adopts is similar to the Bildungsroman technique for the analysis of a personal life. Autobiography therefore, not only records the life history of man, it also facilitates in establishing man's identity. The sense of identity is a sustaining force, "a kind of spiritual odyssey" for the post-colonial man, who is ever keen to affirm himself as a 'free', independent individual; the loss of identity may lead to all kinds of problems. Writing about his life, he realises that "*This* is the real me". Kamala Das, who has frequently been accused of a "striptease" in her writings, observes in *My Story:*

"One's real world is not what is outside him. It is the immeasurable world inside him that is real. Only the one who has decided to travel inward, will realise his route has no end".[2]

The individual alone is capable of recounting the events of his life and reveal more and more the "inner recesses" of his life. The autobiography then becomes "a quest for self-discovery", "a parable of individualism", a "site upon which subjectivity will be saved, and saved for literature".[3]

The autobiographer takes an immense interest in life through himself and indulges in an analysis of memories and records. The writings have to be conceived as the potential meaning of a life as a dynamic process, a "constantly self-revising totalisation, involving a mobile network of relational meanings"[4] and not as a fixed structure involving a chain of causes and effects. If literature has to be made out of life, then it is better to be made by a person who is uniquely placed to defy the bounds of bookish convention. Such life-narratives have the 'I' as the subject and object, standing in for past and present selves. The act "serves both to confirm the prerogatives of the present 'I' which describes how it became what it is out of what it was, and shows up the 'ambiguous constancy' of the 'I'"[5]

Stephen Spender in *World Within World* tells us that he thought of putting his experiences into the form of a novel, however he restrained from doing so and decided on autobiography for a more honest relationship between him and his work and between the reader and the author. The hero of the novel is removed from the actual world and has no existence outside it.

The autobiography has the advantage over the novel where the author himself is the hero of his own story depicting the real world.

Autobiographical writing in India has been slow in evolving as a favourite form with the writers who have felt more comfortable in putting on the mask of a persona in an imaginative world of fiction rather than write a factual text. The critics may frequently have predicted the death of the novel, more so with the advent of the television age, yet it continues to be written and read and receive much attention, infact more than Indian English poetry. The media hype associated with the appearance of *The God of Small Things* or *An Equal Music* or even *Difficult Daughters* is much more than can ever be expected with the *Selective Memory* or *The Tunnel of Time* or *A Double Life* or *No Holds Barred.* These life stories may find a reference in the critics' columns of good journals and newspapers; but how many readers are genuinely interested in picking them up to know the inner life, the inside story of the writer's self and to browse through the life and times of bygone eras? How many students studying R.K. Narayan as a novelist are curious to read his *My Days* and get a deep insight into the man, Narayan? We tend to classify the poems of Kamala Das as autobiographical; but do we advice the scholars to, also?, read her *My Story*? Surely such texts also guarantee an enduring shelf life. Perhaps the only readers of these books have been people like us who have procured a copy to "study" and to analyse the genre for a research paper.

In the pre-independent India "A host of biographies and autobiographies by or about national figures appeared .... In such works it was taken as self-evident that the experience of the writer or subject – usually the leader of a mass nationalist movement – was in some way typical. His (almost invariably his) development captured in cameo form the emergence of the self-conscious nation".[6]

The world of the freedom movement is remembered for being documented by men and women; it was a period when fundamental changes occurred in the nation's cultural consciousness. Autobiographies like Lal Behari Day's *Recollections of My School* (1873-1876), Mahatama Gandhi's *The Story of My Experiments with Truth* (1927), Jawaharlal

Nehru's *An Autobiography* (1936), Mulk Raj Anand's *Apology for Heroism* (1946) to mention a few, were written which could be considered as important representations of the period. At this time the autobiography was limping for recognition and was tentative and apologetic; it was a document of the external world. As such the autobiographical act was ignored or relegated to the background and the book was only a testimony of the social period.

The post colonial writings saw the slow emergence of the self which felt liberated and free and the autobiographers chose "to focus on specific episodes in the greater narrative of journeying, the idyllic childhood and the dawn of self-consciousness; or the time following, of severance and departure, and the loss of roots, home or motherland .... And, indeed, the culminative event in the journey narrative is that of homecoming, a moment which appears under a range of moods, extending from celebration to disillusionment"[7]

Life-writings like *The Autobiography of an Unknown Indian* (1951) by Nirad C. Chaudhuri, *From Fear Set Free* (1962) by Nayantara Sahgal, *My Son's Father* (1968) and *Never At Home* (1992) by Dom Moraes, R.K. Narayan's *My Days* (1974), *My Story* (1976) by Kamala Das, *Chintaman and I* (1980) by Durgabai Deshmukh, *Inner Recesses Outer Spaces* (1986) by Kamala Devi Chattopadhya are not only individual versions of history but also offer a rich resource of redefinitions of the self, and have become a part of the literary history too. Sometimes even a sociologist or an historian may not be able to give a correct and detailed account of life inside an Indian home, which we may get in an autobiography of an Indian woman, with her penchant for a more detailed account of customs, traditions, festivals, life-patterns like births, deaths, marriages, socio-cultural set up. Best examples are books by Vijay Lakshmi Pandit *The Scope of Happiness* (1979), *Prison and Chocolate Cake* (1954) by Nayantara Sahgal, and more recently Shobha De's

Selective Memory (1998) to mention a few. Salman Rushdie in one of his essays in *Imaginary Home Lands* (1991) expresses similar views when he says that the post-colonial literature (he uses the term "Commonwealth Literature") becomes interesting because of its "expression of nationality" and

> "Books are almost always praised for using motifs and symbols out of the author's own national tradition, or when their form echoes some traditional form, obviously pre-English, and the influences at work upon the writer can be seen to be wholly internal to the culture from which he 'springs'".[9]

The Indian writer has a distinct advantage over his Western counterpart in the scope of his experience, which forms the "fulcrum of his creativity". The family as a unit is dying in the West, particularly in the U.K. and the U.S.A., but it still makes a wonderful subject in India. The Indian family life provides plenty of rich material for any kind of writing and the autobiography is a genre which thrives on personal life-accounts and benefits most from this kind of set-up. Ved Mehta's series of autobiographical writings like *Daddyji, Mamaji, Vedi* depict the importance of the familial relationships. Prof. U.R. Anantha Murthy has frequently talked about a traditional division in an Indian home which had two parts —the front yard and the backyard. It is an interesting example of classifying the Indian household where the front yard was always dominated by the male with their discussions on the affairs of the world. On the other hand the back yard, the world of women, was the hub of activity with its inexhaustible treasure of themes for any creative writer. "It is at moments of cultural crisis that the traditions in the back yard make a come-back and revitalise the language"[10]

In the present era of increasing globalisation traditional life and beliefs in an Indian's life, particularly the one living in cities, is rapidly declining. It is affecting our language, which is similarly facing a cultural crisis. While maintaining a 'universal' outlook it is equally important to pay heed to what is authentically local. This crisis can definitely be overcome, to some extent, by the literature that is getting produced, particularly in English, which is easily understood by almost all those youngsters belonging to the Pepsi generation. Autobiographical writings, especially those written by people who celebrated their golden birthday with that of the nation's Golden jubilee of independence, are a vital source of the traditional Indian customs and traditions, particularly those written by women. The practice of reading autobiographies has to be popularised among the present set of readers inorder to make them familiar with the Indian culture, the Indian festivals, the folk traditions and so on. The Indianness in the writings is important and autobiographies, we feel, are a good medium for expressing it since they have to recount the past events of the writer's life in the form of a story.

The present Indian home may not be having the two basic sections prescribed by Ananthmurthy, having been lost in the concrete jungles we inhabit, with homes being mostly the apartments in multi-storeyed buildings, but the Indian's love of story-telling based on their experiences of life continues and most of these autobiographies of the last fifty years do recount stories from such traditional homes. Story telling, down the ages has been both a pleasure and a basic human need. And it "seems that readers are fed up of half-baked fiction and political drivel. That is why they are going back to read about the life of people who grew up in another age." [10]

Thankfully human bonds, relationships, customs and traditions are still very much in the ambit of curiosity of not only the readers in India but also the readers in other Asian countries too. And it is a better proposition to write about one's own relationships than invent a medley of such associations in a fictional world. The basic raw material for any writer is provided by the past (we can call it memory too), which is then reconstituted with imagination. Besides for most writers, "the line between autobiography and the novel has never been as blurred as in the recent past". After all Arundhati Roy, in the *God of Small Things* (1997) or Amitav Ghosh in *The Shadow Lines* (1988), *The Antique Land* (1992), *The Calcutta Chromosomes* (1996); earlier it had been R.K. Narayan in *Swami and his Friends* (1935) and *The English Teacher* (1946) to take recourse to the autobiographical material for writing such novels and build on a particular personal experience for a fictional outcome; anecdotes from real life help in stimulating the novelist's imaginations'

> "The inventions of the autobiographical novelists indicate infact a general principle of the novel. All are based on experience of life, ofcourse, and many on particular and identifiable originals of character or incident".[11]

An article which appeared in *The Hindustan Times* (April 11,1999) critically evaluated the hype created by the novelists from Rushdie to Raj Kamal Jha. The critic's conclusive remarks decried not only the lack of novelty in the themes in most of these novels but also the absence of the "multi-layered complex experience of this country". The progeny of Rushdie had been churning out one novel after another causing a surfeit of more fictional works than can be read. With the monotony of the thematic material in novel after novel, we have to question the readability of most of these works after ten years from now. The lack of universal themes dealing mainly with the human relationships is perhaps not the only malady affecting the Indian fictional writing in English today. Social realism is unmodish and what needs to be focused is the person within and how this affects his personality. "This sense of interiority needs to be understood in terms of active agencies for self-possession and self transformation".[12]

The Indians are slowly and cautiously getting ready to write their life-stories and the nostalgia season has finally arrived. Life stories are suddenly hot material and are finally coming of age; writers are brushing up their memories to make literary debuts. Manifestation of ideas in persons and the tales of their happiness, pain, hope, strength, sacrifice, courage in autobiographies have more appeal to the readers. Our sympathies are aroused and we want to be a part of their lives in one way or another. It is therefore not surprising that the last twenty to twenty-five years have seen autobiographies being written by businessmen, celebrities, politicians and army personnel. These books satisfy the country's curiosity for inside news. Ashok Chopra of UBSPD, who has launched a Book Club in collaboration with *Living Media* and *India Today*, had the first inkling of the growing popularity and the suddenly emerging market of the autobiography, when a rather shoddily written biography of Kiran Bedi, *I Dare......*, sold 30,000 copies, matching the sales figure of a Shobha De sizzler.

The Book Club in itself is a commendable undertaking to encourage and to develop reading habits in the youth of today, where the latest editions of all categories of books are offered at subsidised rates. The club's main aim is "a continuous surveillance on what is being brought out by publishers, both in India and the West where Indian writing in English is enjoying a boom of sorts, is a must".[13] It is a boon to the publishers who get a chance to offer their products through the club to its members; the books vary from fiction to biography to current affairs, cookery and autobiography. Here it is important to mention that the July 1997 catalogue of the Book Club offered four autobiographies to its members. These were *No Holds Barred* by Amita Malik, *An Actor's Journey* by Saeed Jaffrey, *A Double Life* by Alyque Padamsee and *The Lamp is Lit* by Ruskin Bond. They are writers from totally diverse backgrounds, each with a different and unusual point of view. Moreover, the incidents or the events, which constitute their experience, are very different from what we normally find in non-autobiographical works. There are no inhibitions and they have written freely and expressively.

The advent of the television age predicted the demise of the printed word. We do not want to argue the validity of this forecast and we sincerely believe that the book will outlive the Kindle. The human being and the human mind are far more important and no computer can ever produce a *Gitanjali* or *The Suitable Boy*. However the closing decades of the last decade saw the changing scenario with the dominance of elerctronic media being utilised positively with visual autobiographies, like the ones made on Nirad C. Chaudhuri, Mulk Raj Anand or Kamala Das. Programmes like *Ek Din Ek Jivan* with Tavleen Singh, *Rendevous with Simi Garewal*, *Star Talk* with Vir Sanghvi all on Star Plus, give an impetus to the autobiographical and biographical urges in the person being interviewed. It is incredible to see how the speakers open up and reveal the "inner recesses" of their life in the full glare of the camera; it makes us believe that there is an intrinsic affinity between television and autobiography. Both provide a kind of "sentimental illusion of intimacy" to audiences.

The Indian sensibility has been vociferously expressed down the ages through various forms of writing. The end of a supposed millennium is the time to take a stock of a variety of happenings; it is a time of apocalyptic endings and new beginnings. The last fifty or sixty years in the history of any nation do not necessarily signify a distinct or self-evident period in its cultural life. But what is more significant is that the period may witness some fundamental changes in the country's cultural consciousness, which suggest and signify an undeniable break with the past. These changes have an obvious and distinct effect on its literature, in the writing and reading of autobiography as individual versions of history. The transformation is evident in the fellow countrymen who are seen shedding their inhibitions and being enthusiastic in talking about themselves on Facebook, Twitter and other social networking sites. The blogs written by Amitabh Bachchan are popular reading material with the actor sharing the events of his life, talking about his concerns, his family and his other activities directly to his readers. Gurcharan Das, Shobha De are other well-known writers to have popularised blogs, with an aim to reveal about themselves.

A recent technological development all set to overpower the Kindle, is Infibeam Pi. With it the creator, Vishal Mehta, hopes to revolutionise the reading habits of the Indians. He started his retail portal, Infibeam.com with over two lakh e-books, whose copyrights have expired. The Pi, which supports English as well as ten Indian languages, is an online programme for publishing houses and bookstores. It is a reader-friendly device and Mehta is confident that slowly and gradually the reader will download all the old books (one assumes they will include autobiographies too!), which are available in bookstores.[14]

The present era may change the concept of autobiography as a kind of "poor relation" to the other prose form, the novel. It is very much related to the role, which the media plays in popularising the latest novels, even by first-timer writers. If the same writer were to write an autobiography would it get relegated to the second category of writings? One hopes not. But another noteworthy inadequacy in the propagation of the form has been that "the study of the genre has not yet been institutionalised in our curricular"[15]; consequently any kind of "non-fiction prose" remains neglected. Infact this very term denotes the dominance of fiction in literary studies. The study of autobiography has slowly been included in the American and British literatures, but such studies have still to be established in our universities. The only autobiography, which finds its way into the class rooms, is the one by India's first Prime Minister, Pandit Jawaharlal Nehru, which offers "life as an emblem of the nation's coming into being"[16] in beautiful English language. Whatever may be the reason for this oversight or apathy the prevailing situation has to be altered if the life-narratives have to be established as a popular genre and given a new lease of life. Many of such books are by achievers who can become role models to the present generation of Indians by providing them with a good incentive to emulate and to learn about India, its people and its past. The great autobiographies should become college textbooks and the inclusion of autobiographies in the syllabus does not indicate an attempt to replace poetry, fiction or drama. And since they are not mere figments of imagination, are not reel-life stories but real-life narratives, they cannot and should not be slotted as works of fancy; they can even have profound social and cultural impact. These books are "literature of responsibility" and must be approved for study in all our departments of language and literature. After all Indian writing in English includes or should include "every written document that will respond to literary analysis" and autobiographies must be made a part of the academia.

REFERENCES

1. John Sturrock, *The Language of Autobiography*, Cambridge University Press, 1994, p. 286.
2. *My Story*, pp. 109, 159.
3. Laura Marcus, *Auto / biographical discourses, Criticism, Theory, Practice*, Manchester University Press, 1994, p. 183.
4. Michael Sheringham, *French Autobiography Devices And Desires*, Clarendon Press, Oxford, 1993, p. 3.
5. *Auto/biographical Discourses,* p. 195.
6. Elleke Boehmer, *Colonial & Postcolonial Literature*, Migrant Metaphors, OUP, 1995.
7. *Ibid.,* p. 201.
8. Salman Rushdie, *Imaginary Homelands*, *Essays And Criticism* 1981-91, Granta Books, London, 1992, p. 66.

9. *The Hindustan Times*, February 2, 1997.

10. *India Today*, June 1997.

11. Roy Pascal, *Design And Truth in Autobiography*, Harvard University Press, 1960, p. 176.

12. Book Club, July 1999.

13. *Ibid.*

14. India Today, April 26, 2010, p. 68.

15. Paul John Eakim, *American Autobiography Retrospect and Prospect*, The University of Wisconsin Press, 1991, p. 3.

16 *Colonial & Postcolonial Literature*, p. 192.

Indian Autobiographies in English

> "It is a difficult thing to tell the story of a life, and yet more difficult when that life is one's own".
>
> Annie Besant
>
> An Autobiography (1893)

The desire to express one's self and the urge to reveal the world within, has universal connotations and can be seen in man from the earliest times of civilisation. Man has always tried to express his inner feelings, cravings, desires and aspirations through the medium of art. No wonder then that Oscar Wilde was prompted to say "All artistic creation is absolutely subjective". Today this yearning for self-expression has acquired a formidable dimension and more and more people are trying to find various means of self-portraiture. The contemporary society is forever in a state of flux and man feels impelled to indulge in the act of self-creation as well as to leave behind some testimony of his existence.

People are writing autobiographies, says Roy Pascal[1], because more and more readers are fascinated to read about the private lives of various people. Their secrets, beliefs, convictions, intentions, interests engross the readers who feel privileged to be admitted into the autobiographer's intimate circle. Therefore, it is no surprise that during the last two decades or so, many writers have turned towards this hitherto neglected genre of writing. There have been success stories of businessmen, celebrities, confessions from politicians, servicemen; memories of sports persons highlighting their lifetime achievements; literary writers penning forth the secrets of their lives and so on.

Regarding the practice of writing one's life-story, James Olney says,

> ....although it is widely practised by self-proclaimed non-scriblers, autobiography exercises some thing very like a fatal attraction for nearly all men and women who call themselves 'writers'"[2]

We cannot but agree with Philip Dodd[3] when he comes to the conclusion that in recent times autobiography, as a genre, has moved from "the periphery towards the center of the canon".

The most lucid definition, which can be given of an autobiography, is that it is an account of the writer's life and his personal experiences written by himself. Roy Pascal calls it a "reconstruction of the movement of a life, or part of a life, in the actual circumstances in which it was lived"[4].

The autobiographical form concerns the self and not the external forces of the world; however, the outer world is taken into account as the selfhood is shaped and moulded by these external forces. The autobiographical process, which is a reconstruction of the past event, which have no doubt formed a significant part of the author's life, takes place with the aid of the *autobiographical memory*[5]. The recreation of the past events is termed as a life- narrative by Ulric Neisser, which, he says, is a "way of defining the self".

> "They [life narratives] are the basis of personal identity and self-understanding and they provide answers to the question 'who am I?'"[6].

Self-narrative does not only ask the question "who am I?;" it also asks and answers the query "How did I become what I am?"[7]. It is a case of the writer enlightening himself as well as his readers. The whole procedure of writing an autobiography, says A.O.J. Cockshut, is an exercise in "inner assimilation, which involves qualities like "articulateness, fidelity to experience, sensitiveness to small currents of feeling, and, above all curiosity"[8]. The practice provides self-knowledge to the writer, it being the primary motive of autobiography, says Roy Pascal[9]. "This self-knowledge depends on perception, conceptualisation and private experience as well as narrative"[10].

Man has since times immemorial loved to tell stories about himself on his environmental surroundings or the people he lives with. The image of people gathered around a fire on a winter's evening, narrating stories to each other, is alive in the mind of every individual. The autobiography is nothing but a story - the story of an individual's journey in this world which he narrates for the world to read; he takes the "advantage of art's shaping powers in the effort to transmute the incoherence of a life into the regularities of a story"[11]. It involves the process of selection, rejection, proper distribution of facts, emphasis on certain aspects of life. However, the story should not be taken only at its face value, as it cannot reveal the final and complete truth about a man. The mystery of the self has remained unresolved and comprehending it is beyond the scope of even the most modern critical method. Nevertheless, an autobiography is a work of enlightenment in this direction where a glimpse of the individual's most private thoughts is revealed not only to the readers but also to the writer himself.

An autobiography is a work of art and conforms to the prerequisites laid down by it. A work of art, says Susanne K. Langer

> ".... is intrinsically expressive; it is designed to abstract and present forms for perception - forms of life and feeling, activity, suffering, selfhood - whereby we conceive these realities which otherwise we can but blindly undergo"[12].

James Olney[13] breaks the word "autobiography" into three different parts: "autos", the self, the "I", stated or implied, without which the work would become meaningless. The "bios" or the "life", which is the entire life of the individual upto the time of writing. Lastly, the "graphe" or the act of writing has assumed great importance because it is through writing that the self and the life take a specific dimension and image. Lately many cognisance has been given to the "autos" or the "self" which the autobiographer discovers and creates in the process of writing. It is a case of self-examination, a discovery and an imitation of the self through the act of an inner assimilation. It ensures the revealation of the identity of the narrator in the work, where he happens to be the hero, and which covers a temporal sequence to allow the emergence of the contour of a life. However, the final product is "not life but an artful representation of life"[14]. The whole activity can also be a search for identity and a quest for self-definition, which could begin due to a feeling of alienation from one's surroundings, its socio-cultural and metaphysical background. Or the autobiography could be written because the individual thinks himself to be a unique person, who indulges in the exercise of self-exploration. In the latter case the autobiography is "perhaps by definition, the most narcissistic of literary genres"[15]. The fascination with one's own image is undoubtedly an important and an old concept: Narcissus viewing his own face in the depth of the fountain gives credence to this fact. Georges Gusdorf[16] is of the opinion that the invention of the Venetian Mirror in the Middle Ages made the image of man in the mirror a common, everyday reality. The human infant becomes aware of his reflection in the mirror from the age of six months. As he grows older he discerns the importance of his own identity and learns to distinguish the inner reality from the outer. The man of civilisation dwells in leisure in rediscovering himself and exults in the fascination of Narcissus. Georges Gusdorf says that the autobiography too is the mirror in which the writer reflects his own image. And with the global advancement in technology, the appeal of the reflection in the mirror boosts the tradition of self-examination not only in the West but in India too.

Autobiographies written by young men, says Roy Pascal[17] are not very satisfactory. Could it mean that the form demands its writer to be of a particular age? No other literary form has fixed an age limit for its writer to achieve recognition or even to indulge in creativity. But Philip Dodd[18] also thinks that the writers, who choose this mode of writing, should be of middle age. He further adds that Virginia Woolf confessed in her diary that she was forty when she found that she had a voice of her own. Dodd quotes Erik Erikson who says that autobiographies "are written at certain late stages of life for the purpose of re-creating oneself in the image of one's own method; and they are written to make that image convincing"[19]. An aging man tries to retrace the life, which he has lived in the literary genre:

> "Confession of the past realises itself as a work in the present: it effects a true creation of self by the self"[20].

The autobiographer who recounts his life's history is on a search for his self in the annals of history; it is not a "disinterested endeavour" but a case of personal explanation. Gerhard Stilz thinks that in order to bridge the gap "between past and present, the autobiographer borrows the models and devices of historiography which help him to show how the present, complicated state of affairs can be convincingly derived and explained by relating it to identifiable and well-arranged steps performed successfully in the past"[21]. It is the "bios" according to James Olney, which explains the historical course of a life, and a very complete relationship between the past and the present. An autobiography can never be complete, it can never have a conclusion like the other literary genres and as R.K. Narayan asks in his autobiography, *My Days* "how can an autobiography have a final chapter?". As long as the biological life of the writer continues, the autobiographical process remains unending.

> "Since no autobiography can be 'finished', the life or the progress through life that any such text-purports to represent can only be one that is in-the-making and therefore a fragment of a life"[22].

Autobiography has been claimed by Roy Pascal[23] to be a "distinctive product" of the Western "Post-Roman Civilisation" which has spread to other civilisations only in modern times. Georges Gusdorf too conforms to this view that it is "a late phenomenon in Western culture, coming at that moment when the Christian contribution was grafted onto classical traditions"[24]. Augustine's *Confessions,* the first example of a great autobiography, was written between 397 and 400 A.D. and provides an insight into the complexity of the soul; it is also a record of a great and powerful mind undergoing religious conversion. However, the form was not identified until the early nineteenth century when Robert Southey in 1809 coined the term "autobiography" in the Quarterly Review and thus established the credibility of the autobiography as a form of literature. The Western man discovered himself in a new way during the Renaissance and the Reformation. The obsession with the self was seen as a reaction to a widely discursive feeling that the days of the individual were numbered in the post-industrial, post World War II Western society.

> "Man is dependent on a community and is never isolated from it. But the life in a community demands that each man must play a role which had sometime or other been played by his ancestors and will also be played by his offspring, who would take on the names of their forefathers. Thus the community life helps in maintaining a continuity of the individual's self-identity. It, therefore, implies that the writing of an autobiography is not possible in a culture, which does not give prominence to man and to the self"[25].

It has been customary to distinguish the man of the East from the man in the West. Georges Gusdorf's remark that Gandhi's use of the autobiographical form to tell his story "is a Western mean to defend the East"[26] is quite presumptuous. Roy Pascal has endorsed Gusdorf's view:

> "Where in modern times, members of Eastern civilisations have written autobiographies, like Gandhi for instance, they have taken over a European tradition"[27].

It therefore, implies that the autobiography is purely a Western form of writing; moreover, it is argued that since the Eastern man in general, and the Indian in particular, is an introvert, he does not feel inclined to share his innermost secrets. This could mean that the Indian autobiographer in English has to use not only a language, which is not his mother tongue, but also a form, which is alien to his mentality. Writing in English has not been an easy task for an Indian writer when, as Raja Rao remarks, "one has to convey in a language that is not one's own the spirit that is one's own"[28]. He further adds that even though the English language is not a language of our "emotional make-up", it is very much the language of our "intellectual make-up."

We shall be discussing the use of the English language and the autobiographical form by the Indian writers in more detail later in the paper. At the moment to start with, it is essential to examine the concept of self in India during the Vedic and the *Upanishadic* times: the *Taitrya Upanishad* (600-500 B.C.), the *Manduka Upanishad* (500-400 B.C.) and the *Mahabharata* (1 A.D.) have exalted man and his self. Dr. S. Radhakrishanan in *The Concept of Man* says that the *Mahabharata* extols man as the highest creature in the chain of living beings on the earth.

> Guhyam brahama tadidam O-bravini
> na manust sresthataran hi kincit

Meaning thereby that "I tell you this, the secret of the Brahman: there is nothing higher than man"[29]. The *Upanishads*, says Dr. S. Radhakrishanan, also advice man to "know thy self" (*atmanam vidhi*), which is similar to the recommendation by Socrates "Know thy self". Philosophers all over the world instruct man to know himself before he tries to unravel anything else in the universe. The Indian philosophy gives importance not only to the "I", the inwardness of the physical body, but it also brings man in direct communion with God, who dwells in man as also in the external nature and unifies the world under His control:

> "But then, how can He control man, who has an inward mind? Can He do it by controlling only man's external circumstances? Here the inward - looking religion supplied an answer. He does it by controlling man's inward nature also. God controls man both from outside and from inside. The *Brhadaranyaka Upanishad* says that the light of the *atman* is the same as the light of the Sun, the self within is the same as the Sun without"[30].

The *Upanisads* conceive the *Atman* as the supreme self, *Brahman* being the true self. But man has to rise above the quagmire of everyday existence, inorder to discover and experience his real self. The form of writing, which can help man to interpret his real self, is autobiography.

> ".....Self-observation becomes an instrument of self-change. Letting thoughts take their course, they are brought under the magnifying glass of critical examination, being looked upon as other than the present individual, the energy frozen in them is broken and detachment reached"[31].

"*Atman*" says M. Hiriyanna[32], is "the inner self of man". His inwardness is his own private domain. The *Upanishads* say that the *realisation* of one's self is never lost, the duties in life have to be performed with the aim of self-realisation. Buddhism has a similar theory,

> ".....Buddhism overemphasized inwardness and said that man, if he is intent upon self-realisation, need not bother about pleasing Gods and ancestors. To a man of self-realisation, God themselves pay homage, as they did to Bhddha"[33].

Tagore in *Sadhana* emphasized the uniqueness of man:

> "I am absolutely unique, I am I, I am incomparable. The whole weight of the universe can not crush out this individuality of mine. I maintain it inspite of the tremendous gravitation of all things"[34].

Self, says Tagore, is like a lamp, which has to illuminate inorder to show its real nature. However, the self cannot realise its meaning by being alienated from God, and in this world the self is borning new every moment of its life.

The chief aim of this discussion is to present a critical survey of Indian autobiographies written in English. We have considered only those works, which have originally been written in Engligh. However, an exception has been made in the case of Mahatma Gandhi and Rabindranath Tagore, because both these works have become part of the canon, although they have been translated from Gujarati and Bengali respectively. The work does not aim to give a summarised account of the individual autobiographies; rather it has tried to trace the development of the genre in the Indian context through a historical survey of the autobiographies written down the ages.

In the course of preparing this paper, I received considerable assistance from R.C.P. Sinha's book *The Indian Autobiographies in Engligh*, for which I acknowledge my obligation.

Let us then review the Indian writings, which project the writer's 'I' and his self. An early example of self-presentation is found in India as early as 1500 B.C. in the *Rigveda* (10.34.2) in *Gambler's Lament*:

> "She did not quarrel with me or get angry; she was kind to my friends and to me. Because of a losing throw of the dice I have driven away a devoted wife"[35]

Here a Rishi turned gambler confesses his deeds and the misfortunes brought about by his gambling. It is a beautiful literary piece, but more than that it is a confession of the gambler's weaknesses and follies and is one of the earliest pieces of the portrayal of the self.

The inscription on pillars by Ashoka propagate not only *Dharma* but are also an examination of the emperor's self:

> "I scrutinise as to how I may bring happiness to the people, no matter whether they are my relatives or residents of the neighborhood of my capital or of distant localities. And I act accordingly...."[36]

Sanskrit literature has an important writing depicting the self in Bana Bhatt's *Harsha-Charita*, a historical romance of king Harsavardhan, written around 647 A.D. The first two chapters are devoted to an account of Bana Bhatta's life and family and a sort of self-portrayal. Bilhana, who according to A.B. Keith wrote the biography of his patron king Vikramaditya of Kalyan, wrote *Vikramanka-devacharita* before 1088. Bilhana attached his own life's account to it in which he discloses his scholarship.

These, writings cannot be termed as 'autobiographical works'; however, what they show is a self-portrayal of the Indian scholars, who were not so reticent in talking about their personal lives as the Western critics have make us believe. The practice of writing personal accounts or self-histories got a fresh impetus with the arrival of the Moghuls in India. The Muslim rulers and their officials were very keen to write their memoirs either themselves or got them written by others and by the end of 18th Century there were a number of such writings in the form of reminiscences or travelogues. The motive of these rulers in writing such works was self-glorification; nevertheless most of these books are important historical documents. An exception being *Babur-nama* which tries to come closer to the reader in an honest and truthful way. It has a confidential tone and reveals the sensitive nature of the man. In this work Babur (1483-1530) discusses his accession to the throne of Farghana, his departure from his native land, his years at Kabul and his life in India. Critics feel that the *Babur-nama* is incomplete, as the book has no description of the king's life of the first twelve years. Nonetheless it is a well-written document with a glimpse of the writer's life, his love for nature, animals, plants and flowers observed on his travels.

Tuzuk-i-Jahangir or *Memoirs of Jahangir* was written by the emperor till the 17th year of his reign. After that Jahangir (1569-1627) assigned the work to one Muhamad Khan till the nine-teenth year. The book contains a code of conduct for his servants, a list of appointments, promotions, pen-portraits of nobles, wars and conquests. However, the work fails to give an insight into the writer's personality.

In 1641, a Jain poet, Banarsidasa wrote the first autobiography in Hindi. He called it *Arddakatha* or the Half-story because it covered only fifty-five years of his life - the ideal life-span being a hundred years. Written in the form of verse it is an account of a man's life that was always in conflict with the people around him.

We have seen that though these works were in Sanskrit, Persian and Hindi, the practice of writing about oneself was not unknown in Ancient and Medieval India. However, the full development of the autobiographical form could take place only under the colonial influence. Gerhard Stilz is apprehensive in calling these writings as 'autobiographies':

> "While I find it most interesting to reconstruct such an early history of Indian memoirs from widely different documents like Emperor Asoka's rock edicts (dating from the 3rd Century B.C.), Bhavabhuti's dramatic prologues (written in the 8th Century A.D), or the reminiscences laid down by the great Mughals of the 16th and 17th Century, the question remains whether those self-presentations ever formed a productive tradition of autobiography and whether the generic concept of autobiography is at all applicable and reasonably useful for describing those early texts. It may be doubted that they ever stood in an effective relation based on comparable creative impulses and formative continuities"[37]

But after the end of the 18th Century, says Stilz, it is easier to trace the history of Indo-English autobiography, which was greatly influenced by the "English impact" as were all the other forms of Indian literature in English.

Taine, the French literary historian, says K.R. Srinivasa Iyengar[38], considered three factors to be important for any literary creativity. These were the race, the milieu and the moment; however, the social theory should not negate the importance of the individual writer. In the case of the Indians the 'race' bore the invasions and conquests of invaders for more than 4000 years. The 'milieu' comprised of the diversity of the Indian Sub-continent; and the 'moment' as far as writing in English is concerned, was the mingling of the English culture with the Indian, which throughout its history has shown "a genius for absorption and persistence"[39]. It suffered this infiltration too without altering its own indignity. William Walsh thinks that Indian literature in English is a product of the last hundred years, or if we want to be more precise, of the last fifty years, "when for the most part the British were no longer governing India"[40]. This literature expresses a keen sensitivity which is an embodiment of the Indian spirit and the Indian tradition. The use of the English language by the Indian creative writer makes him accessible even to the world's reader; it also brings into focus his thoughts and feelings, habits and experiences, perhaps even his taste, prejudice and value, which are typical of the Indian mind and the Indian ethos.

The period between 1835 and 1855 saw the British government advocating a policy in India which promoted the study of European literature and science. English books were sold in thousands and thus the Indians had an access to the Western thought and Science to suit their own motives. Gradually the Indians started techniques made the Indian give more importance to reason and experiment as the test of truth. Surendranath Banerjee felt that the Western education removed the cobwebs of ignorance from the Indian minds:

> "Our fathers, the first fruits of English education, were violently Pro-British. They could see no flaw in the civilization or culture of the West. They were charmed by its novelty and its strangeness ... Everything English was good - even the drinking of brandy was a virtue; everything not English was to be viewed with suspicion"[41]

Indian writing in English got a new boost particularly in Bengal; after which the rest of the country followed its example. Ram Mohan Roy was one of the earliest writers to write in English "a tradition in which Indians have found a peculiar intimacy with the English language, making it a natural second voice for the Indian mind and sensibility"[42]

It was a period of literary renaissance and the English influence encouraged the feeling of the self-expression among the Indians. However, the Indians were by and large considered to have plenty of inhibitions as far as revelation of their inner lives was concerned. Therefore, the autobiographical impulse had to be freed from the forces, which were smothering the projection of the individual's personality. Even so it has to be remembered that the rise and growth of the Indian autobiographies in English corresponds with one of the most forceful periods in the history of India. The spirit of inquiry, which is very essential for the rejuvenation of any form of literature, had infused the minds of the Indians. Coupled with this was the growing concern for the freedom of the country. It was thus an opportune time for the Indians to take up the writing of autobiography. But what was a more important achievement was the establishment of English language as a way of expression for the Indian intelligentsia in the modern world, which was very essential in a culture with a diversity of languages. However, it was in no way a deterrent to the rudimentary canons of the Indian tradition.

Ram Mohan Roy was an accomplished writer who could motivate the listless Indian mind into activity. India, he thought, had to acquire a new Western scientific discipline and integrate it with its age-old traditional values. This was the only way in which the country could become modern and strong to face the challenges. On the request of an English friend, one Mr. Gordon, Ram Mohan Roy wrote the first short autobiographical vignette, which was published in the **Athenaeun and the Literary Gazette** (1832). This was the earliest work, which later gave incentive to other Indian leaders like Mahatama Gandhi, Jawaharlal Nehru, Surendranath Banerjee and other to write their autobiographies in English.

Kasi Prasad Ghose (1809-1873) wrote yet another autobiographical sketch in the form of a letter to Rev. James Long. The letter contained details about his caste, its origin and his English education in 1821. In the postscript he wrote that he could express his feelings better in English than in his mother tongue, Bengali. What was most important in the letter was the remark which he made about an autobiography, "the most faithful representation of a person when made by himself is opt to betray him"[43]

In 1857 the first full-length the autobiography in English by Lutfullah was published. He had the English readers in mind when he wrote the book with whom he wanted to share his experiences. The autobiography described his escape from a tyrannous father into the hands of a thug. Later Lutfullah was employed as a post clerk in the East India.

Lal Behari Day wrote an account of his life between 1873 and 1876; titled Recollections of *My School Days,* it only covered the period of his school days. The book is important as it describes the new education system in Bengal in the nineteenth century. The campaign, which was transformed from "no education" to education through Sanskrit and Arabic and finally the modern education through the English language, is discussed vividly. Though the autobiography does not cover the full period of Day's life, it succeeds in revealing the true image of the writer.

By the year 1885 English language had been absorbed in the Indian way of life and the establishment of universities at Calcutta, Bombay, Madras and Allahabad further strengthened the need for education in English. The formation of Congress as a political party saw an epoch of meetings, conferences where the deliberations were in English. In 1909, N.C. Kelkar, who was the disciple of Bal Gangadhar Tilak, made the following statement:

> "I think I yield to none here in my admiration and appreciation of the English language and literature. And I think that we in India as a nation must be eternally grateful to the English language for opening to us endless vistas and beautiful avenues of Western thought,.... which has entirely revolutionised the aspect of things about the Indian ideals and Indian modes of thought ..... I like them only in so far as I can call them and make them my own"[44]

K.M. Munshi felt that the introduction of English led to a cultural upheaval in India. The language was used to its maximum benefit when in 1893 Swami Vivekanand used it to present his spiritual philosophy at the Chicago Parliament of Religions.

The emergence of the new Indian, who had received education in English and who was familiar with the Western thoughts and ideas, gave a new dimension to the autobiographical writing in India. Lala Lajpat Rai wrote a short account of his exile to Mandalay and called it *The Story of My Deportation* (1908), which revealed his personality. Later he wrote two fragmentary autobiographies, *The Story of My Life* (1914) showing his association with the Arya Samaj movement, and *Indian Revolutionaries in the United States and Japan*(1919).

Roy Pascal feels that in reconstructing the experiences of the past the writers with poetic talent do a better job than the other autobiographers, even though this "feel is always composite"[45]. The chief advantage that a literary writer has his command over the nuances of the language. However, having a sensitive nature and a "comprehensive soul" he can perceive even the minor details of his life and record them vividly in his work. His imaginative faculty makes the ordinary events acquire a new meaning and he succeeds in establishing a close bond with his readers. These autobiographies give a glimpse of the writer's mind as well as an account of the events of their lives, which perhaps shaped their destinies as creative writers. The works candidly display the portrait of these Indian writers in English, most of them having done their self-presentation quite objectively. For some writers the autobiography is an extension of the literary works, which they have been producing at regular intervals. These autobiographies also reflect the ebb and flow of the national consciousness.

Jiwansmriti (1911) is one such work which was written in Bengali by Rabindra Nath Tagore and later translated into English in 1917 by the Poet's nephew, Surendranath Tagore and was called *The Reminiscences*. He was the first

Indian poet to have written about his poetic career, which gave meaning to his life. W.B. Yeats described the English translation as "rich", which provided an insight into the complex Indian culture. The poet has tried "to talk of his past", to explore his picture chamber and has attempted "to gather a precise and logical story from memory's storehouse". He was enchanted in the process and thought that he would select some items from his life-story. *My Reminiscences* traces the growth of Tagore's poetic genius, in the background of the Bengal Renaissance, when the Raj was at its zenith. It is a beautiful mingling of the West and the East: there is Shakespeare in it as well as the *Mahabharata*; the songs of the Victorian England as well as the classical ragas of the Indian music. We see the streets of London as well as the mansions of the rich Bengalis in the city of Calcutta. The autobiography is in an episodic form and Tagore traces only those incidents of his life, which seem relevant in painting "memory pictures" and not to tell the history of his life, which as a child was very lonely. At age of eighty Tagore wrote another autobiography and called it Chelebela (1941). The English translation, *My Boyhood Days*, was published in 1943. Here the lonely child was no longer alone - storytellers, bangle-sellers, snake charmers, and women of the house surrounded him. He wrote about his sister-in-law with whom he had a scandalous relationship.

1919 saw the publication of *My Days with Uncle Sam* by Ras Behari Day and *Stray Thoughts on Some Incidents in My Life* by Bipin Krishna Bose. The leader of the "khilafat" movement, Maulana Mohamed Ali, wrote a short autobiography *My Life: A Fragment* in 1921-22.

The Autobiography of an Indian Princess (1921) is one of the earliest writings by an Indian woman. Sunity Devee, who became the Maharani of Cooch Bihar, lost her husband early in life. The book is an important landmark in the history of Indian autobiography because in it the writer has described certain aspects of her personality which were more or less peculiar to mostly all the Indian women of the time. Women were taught to accept male dominance over themselves either in the form of parental or filial supremacy. We shall be discussing the characteristics of women's autobiographies later in this paper.

Since the time of Ram Mohan Roy, Indian leaders had felt the need to be bilingual inorder to reach out to a larger reading in public. With the arrival of Gandhi on the national scene

> "Indian writing in English became recognisably functional. Gone were the old Maculayan amplitude and richness of phrasing and weight of miscellaneous writing. Gandhian writing was as bare and austere as was his own life; yet who will say that either the one or the other lacked the fullness of fulfilment"?[46]

Autobiographical writing in English too deployed simple, matter of-fact phrases and words. We can have an impressive account of the first quarter of the twentieth century from Surendranath Banerjee's *A Nation in Making* (1924). "The Thunderer of Bengal", as Surendranath Banerjee was popularly known, wrote this work to elucidate his political ideology. With the appearance of Bal Gangadhar Tilak and Gandhi on the national scene the policy of the moderates to co-operate with the British became anachronistic; their patriotism was being doubted. Hence to clarify the real motive of the moderates Surendranath Banerjee wrote his autobiography, which is significant for another reason too - it gives an account of the partition of Bengal in 1905. With the advent of Gandhi, Surendranath Banerjee's popularity started declining.

> "Gandhi", says K.R. Srinivasa Iyengar, "was no writer, properly so called, nor was he at any time particularly interested in the art of writing, but he had to write or talk a great deal (often in English), even as we have to walk or eat or breathe"47.

Gandhi's *"The Story of My Experiments with Truth"* (1927) written in prison at Yerauda and later in South Africa, appeared first in a Gujarati Weekly, *Navajivan;* the English translation was done around 1940 by his faithful secretary Mahadev Desai. C.D. Narasimhaiah[48] thinks that like Augustine's *Confessions, The Story of My Experiments with Truth* falls outside the domain of autobiography. The reason is being its pre-occupation with spirituality, which projects only "a part of the man when you seek to know the whole of him, his many-sidedness".

Gerhard Stilz[49] expresses almost similar views as Augustine "the accomplishment of religious life appeases the vital sting of autobiography". Stilz further adds that inorder to avoid the accusation of being under the Western influence Gandhi denied that he was writing a real autobiography. It was more of an attempt at "self-realisation" and "to see God face to face, to attain *Moksha"*.

> "I simply want to tell the story of my numerous experiments with truth, and as my life consists of nothing but those experiments, it is true that the story will take the shape of an autobiography"[50].

However, William Walsh[51] thinks that Gandhi's autobiography is purely an "Indian version" of the art, which brings forth not only the individual's characteristics but throws light on the society of his times too. The Gandhian era existed between the two World Wars, which was a difficult period for the country. The Montagu-Chelmsford Reforms had failed; the Muslims were not happy at the plight of Turkey during the Versailles Peace Conference. And at the top of it there was the Jallianwala Bagh massacre. The nation was in the spirit of agony.

Gandhi's greatness lay in his ordinariness, in his mantra of "Satyagrah", and in the concept of Truth. It is towards this idea of "truth", "universal love" and "God" that his autobiography moves and develops. Naturally there is not much of a self-revealation. Nevertheless Gandhi did follow the pattern of an autobiography and presented events in a chronological order, at least in the part covering the early years of his life. He did not saw the relevance of continuing the story of his life after the year 1920. He felt people knew every little detail about his life and his ideology and therefore it did not need any elaboration.

Gandhi's description of his visit to Southampton draws disapprobation from V.S. Naipaul, where the Mahatama was too conscious of arriving as the only person in "white flannels".

> "That is the voyage: an internal adventure of anxiety felt and food eaten with not a word of anything seen or heard that did not directly affect the physical or mental well being of the writer. The inward concentration is fierce, the self-absorption complete. Southampton is lost in that embarrassment (and rage) about the white flannels"[52]

Similarly his arrival in London, says Naipaul, has no description of the external reality which he saw around him. The scene in the capital of the world in the year 1890 is negated due to "his religious self-searching", his problems in learning English manners and his feeling of awkwardness at times due to his particular food habits. Gandhi, feels Naipaul, was so absorbed with his own self that he did not care to depict the landscape around him even on his visit to South Africa. The people are described but they were never shown as individuals. There were the people with whom Gandhi had spent twenty active years of his life.

Naipaul comes to the conclusion that the Indians never find it easy "to withdraw and analyze". He quotes a psychotherapist of Jawaharlal Nehru University, Dr. Sudhir Kakar, inorder to give credence to his theory. Kakar says that for the Indian the outside reality is useful only to "preserve the continuity of the self amidst an ever changing flux of outer events and things".

Therefore, says Naipaul, in an Indian autobiography

> "The outer world matters only in so far as it affects the inner. It is the Indian way of experiencing; what is true of Gandhi's autobiography is true of many other Indian autobiographies, though the self-absorption is usually more sterile"[53].

The effect of Western thoughts and English literature was strong on the minds of the Indian people right from the days of Ram Mohan Roy. K.R. Srinivasa Iyengar[54] mentions different movements and activities in India which benefited much from the Western influence; people and groups involved in religious awakening, social reform, the new education, women's emancipation, literary revival, political consciousness profited much from English education. A "new spirit" seemed to have possessed India and its people, which helped them in their diverse activities.

Bipin Chandra Pal, a contemporary of Surendranath Banerjee, wrote two volumes titled *Memoirs of My Life and Times*, published posthumously in 1932. His memoirs preach the policy of cooperation with the government; this could be due to the reason that Tilak's extremism had not entered the Indian political scene. The same year another important autobiography of a *sanyasi* or a monk was published. The work, *An Indian Monk: His Life and Adventures*, was written by Purohit Swami who defied the canons of autobiographical writing and did not reveal his past after he had renounced the world, wrote, His Life and Adventures. There could be a reason behind this inadequacy: it being the difficulty involved in an accurate communication of religious experiences, as the whole process can be intensely subjective. The book was written at the insistence of W.B. Yeats and is a moving account of the Swami's passion for the realisation of God, for which he undertook extensive travels. The spiritual experiences are narrated in a simple language and style. *Life and experiences of a Bengali Chemist* by P.C. Ray was also published in 1932. Ray was an Indian Scientist and played an active role in Indian politics.

Since this appraisal is going to include a number of autobiographies by women, it is imperative for us to know what the critics have to say about such writings. In Writing a **Woman's life** Carolyn G. Heilbrun says that a woman's life can be described in four ways:

> ".... the woman herself may tell it, in what she chooses to call an autobiography; she may tell it in what she chooses to call fiction; a biographer, woman or man, may write the woman's life in what is called a biography, or the woman may write her own life in advance of living it, unconsciously and without realising or naming the process"[55]

The first process of writing was termed "Autogynography" by Domna Stanton in her article titled "Autogynography: Is the Subject Different?"[56]. It could be defined as "writing by women about themselves".

The questions which are frequently raised by critics like Germaine Bree or Shirley Neuman or Carolyn G. Heilbrun are: is a woman's autobiography different from that of a man? Or is her autobiography different from her other writings? What were the conditions, which made a woman, use this genre of writing? These are compelling issues which have bothered the critics for a long time. An autobiography is a form, which reveals the inner being of the writer, it is a self-exploration which teaches the reader about the life of the writer in a way which a Bildungsroman would do. But can a woman, who is taught to be self-effacing, achieve such a goal? This problem is associated with the gender prejudice and has been very tersely put forth by Susan Stanford Friedman.

> "A.... man has the luxury of forgetting his ... sex. He can think of himself as an `individual'. Women..., reminded at every turn in the great cultural hall of mirrors of their sex ... have no such luxury"[57]

But there is nothing unnatural in a woman's literary creativity, which is an extension of her biological creativity. And given a room of her own, she can write her life's account quite capably.

There have been many women in India who has felt the urge to express their inner selves to the public reading. These women have been lawyers, political activists, women from royal families, literary writers and so on. According to Andre Maurois[58], autobiography is of two types: the first is "as interesting as novels and as true as the finest `life'". It possesses qualities like truth of tone, a "fidelity and impartiality in portraiture of a very high quality indeed". The other type is where the inner self of the writer is displayed. Most of the writing by Indian women autobiographers belongs to the first category. However, there have been a number of women writers who have been able to reveal the self as a powerful entity. Needless to say this second class of women has carved a niche for themselves in this field of life narrative.

There is a distinction to be noted in the writings of a woman and a man, which is discerned not only in India but everywhere in the world too. A woman's autobiography generally focuses on the various relationships like those with her parents, here siblings and later with her spouse, children and her mother-in-law. This last one is a typical characteristic of an Indian woman's autobiography. It is as if her identity is established and proved only on the basis of these relationships in her life. But a man's autobiography is mainly concerned with his success story, his achievements in his life, and very rarely does he give a vivid account of his wife and children.

George Henry Lewes says that a woman's literature "promises a woman's view of life, woman's experience: in other words a new element". But he further adds

> "Masculine mind is characterised by the predominance of the intellect, and the Feminine by the predominance of the emotions ... Woman, by her greater affectionateness, her greater range and depth of emotional experience, is well fitted to give expression to the emotional facts of life... [59]

Cornelia Sorabji's *India Calling* (1934) is the autobiography of a lawyer who raged a struggle against the suppression of women. Sorabji belonged to a Parsi-Christian family and was initiated into her job by observing the plight of women who visited her mother. Her book highlights the gender discrimination meted out to her not only in India, but in England too where she went to study on a Indian government's Scholarship. She emerged victorious from her ordeals and succeeded in becoming a lawyer.

In the foreword to the 1980 edition of Jawaharlal Nehru's *An autobiography* (1936), Indira Gandhi exalted it as "not merely the quest of one individual for freedom, but as an insight into the making of the mind of new India"[60]. However, Nehru as we know, was involved not only in "the making of India", but also, says C.D. Narasimhaiah, in

> "inaugurating in a major way the species called Indian writing in Engligh through half dozen masterpieces half of which became best-sellers, a privilege conferred on an Indian author for the first time in recent history"[61]

C.D. Narasimhaiah thinks that the autobiography is Indian not because of its description of Indian persons, places or the social scene but because it succeeds in depicting a sensibility which is typically Indian. And this is quite surprising because, he says, Nehru's English is much closer to "British English" than the English of Britain's great novelists.

Written in prison from June 1934 to February 1935, Nehru's main motive was to kill the boredom of those long hours behind the bars in isolation:

> "I began the task in a mood of self-questioning and, to a large extent, this persisted throughout. I was not writing deliberately for an audience, but if I thought of an audience, it was one of my own countrymen and countrywomen"(p.XV)

Nehru's attempt has been to trace his "own mental development and not to write a survey of recent Indian history".(PXV) Superficially, Nehru continues, the work might seem to the reader to be an account of India's history. But he warns, that it is only an egotistical narrative where many important events and persons have been excluded:

> "And so this 'autobiographical narrative' remains a sketchy, personal and incomplete account of the past, verging on the present, but cautiously avoiding contact with it".(p.XVI)

Nevertheless the book is a valuable chronicle of the historical events of the country as well as of the world. And therefore the result is, says Gerhard Stilz, that there is not much of "selfquestioning and self-analysis":

> "...the author is very occupied with himself and his own spiritual development. His emphasis is over-whelmingly on political life, on the welfare of his family, on achievements and disappointments experienced with political friends and antagonists, on life in prison"[62].

According to K. R. Srinivasa Iyengar[63] Nehru's autobiography has a beautiful blending of "personal history" with "national history" which reveals the evolution of writer's personality against the background of the country's struggle for freedom. Nehru's concern with the country's problems and the political activities prevented him from becoming too involved with his own self; however, there is a `triumph of the spirit':

> "I occupied myself with many activities and sought thereby to keep away from the problems that troubled me.... Action now was partly an attempt to run away from myself; no longer was it a whole-hearted expression of the self as it had been in 1920 and 1921"(p.104).

Gerhard Stilz thinks that his participation in the life of the country was absolute and therefore the self-analysis seems to have become secondary. According to C.D. Narasimhaiah the appeal of the autobiography lies in its idealism and disinterestedness of a life which was devoted wholeheartedly to action.

The epilogue of the autobiography has mentioned one of the few shortcomings of this genre, which has as its basic tenet, the recollection of the past events:

> "In writing this narrative I have tried to give my moods and thoughts at the time of each event, to represent as far as I could, my feelings on the occasion. It is difficult to recapture a past mood, and it is not easy to forget subsequent happenings. Later ideals thus must inevitably have coloured my account of earlier days, but my object was primarily for my own benefit, to trace my own mental growth. Perhaps what I have written is not so much an account of what I have been but of what I have sometimes wanted to be or imagined myself to be".(p.596)

Gerhard Stilz comes to the conclusion that *An Autobiography* is definitely a "self-presentation of the man of action, who was also a political leader and "who, by externalising and materializing his inward drives and feelings, tends to lose his own self in the overwhelming amount of *res gestae and gerendae* of things done and waiting to be done"[64]. In the words of M.K. Naik, "the book is essentially both a `discovery', of Nehru and a `discovery' of the India of the period roughly between the two world wars"[65].

In 1937, Subhash Chandra Bose wrote an autobiography *An Indian Piligrim* during his ten-day stay in Austria and described the period of his life from 1897 to 1920.

With No Regrets: An Autobiography (1943) says the writer Krishna Hutheesing, is "a book of memories and reminiscences"; but it fails to bring out the individuality of the writer, who is more concerned with her father, Motilal Nehru, and her brother, Jawaharlal Nehru. The autobiography is a record of the great Nehru family and the historical incidents of the country. However, the book does reflect her loneliness during the freedom struggle. Another aspect, which is revealed, is that even an educated and famous family, like the Nehrus, had inhibitions about women, in this case Krishna Hutheesing, taking up a job. It was Jawaharlal Nehru who argued with the parents in support of cause.

Seven Lives: Autobiography of Dr. Sir Harisingh Gour (1944) is the story of a successful lawyer of the country, who later founded the Sagar University in Madhya Pradesh.

Mulk Raj Anand's *Apology for Heroism*, written in 1945, was published in 1946, after his return from London in 1945, having lived there for nearly twenty years of his life. Thus the autobiography can be described as a search or a rediscovery of his Indian identity[66]. The book has a sub-title, "A Brief Autobiography of Ideas", which, Marlene Fisher says, hints at "the development of Anand's political and artistic consciousness, on the simultaneous evolution of his political and artistic selves and of a core of self-as-humanist which bound together his politics and his art".[67] Consequently the autobiography has no mention of his wife or child. Nearly all of Mulk Raj Anand's writings are autobiographical, which depicts "a voyage of discovery" and where he tries to answer questions put to himself: "Who am I? Where do I come from? Where am I going?".

In the preface to the first edition of the book, Anand describe his reason for this "confessional writing" which, he thinks, claimed that it was "a kind of worship of humanity". The second postscript to the autobiography has a title "There is No Higher Thing Than Truth", and Anand says that the work was meant to be "an essay in search of faith" which implied that his "search for faith was a search for truth". The statement does echo the Gandhian Philosophy and Gerhard Stilz says that through out the work there has been a continual stress on Gandhian Truth, "There is ... no higher thing than the search for truth". The second *Postscript* to the book ends with the words of the *Mahabharata* on Truth. This kind of contemplation, says Stilz, is not found in any of the earlier Indo-English writers. Written at the age of forty, *Apology for Heroism* is a recreation of the self of a younger Anand in the historical perspective.

The first autobiography of a Hindu Yogi was published in the year 1946; titled *Autobiography of a Yogi* it was work by Paramhansa Yogananda. It is an important book not only because it is written in English, but because it is "a book about Yogis by a Yogi". The autobiography highlights the laws by which "Yogis perform miracles and attain self-mastery". Yogananda obtained his graduate degree from Calcutta University and then went to live in the West for over thirty years. The book, which was credited as having brought about a spiritual revolution, was read in India as well as abroad.

India became a free country in 1947 - thenceforth "began a new era of challenges and changes in Indian life". The country withstood the trauma of partition and the subsequent bloodshed. The social scene went through a sort of revolution, which affected and inspired creativity of the Indian writer in English as well as in other regional languages. M. K. Naik feels that the Indian English writer gained much after the Independence.

> "It has given him greater self-confidence, widened his vision and sharpened his faculty of self-scrutiny ... Interest in Indian English literature has grown tremendously both in India and abroad, thus making possible a much larger readership than it could claim at any time earlier.... The post-Independence Indian scene with its curious criss-cross of rapid socio-political changes in a country where tradition still remains a strong force has presented a stimulating spectacle, which has naturally worked a variety of reaction from its writers, including nostalgic idealisation of the immediate past of the days of the freedom struggle, a strong desire to re-discover one's roots in the ancient Indian ethos as also to examine these ethos afresh in the light of Westernisation"[68].

Consequently the unraveling in the Indian mind found a reflection not only in fiction and poetry but also in the autobiographies which were written in the post-independence era. Earlier the autobiographical works had shown concern with the freedom movement of the country and had emphasized the external events more than the revealation of the self of the writers. Once the country became free and the society gained a stability, there was a scope to dwell on a self-analysis especially on topics which had been considered improper and had been unacceptable till now. The autobiographical genre developed and acquired a new meaning: it became more frank, straightforward and informal.

More and more women were feeling confident in taking up this form of life-narrative and had no inhibitions in telling the world about themselves. An unknown Khoja girl, Ishwani Pseud, wrote an autobiography titled *Girl in Bombay* (1947). The work reveals the development of the writer's personality by the forces of cultural canons and her own individuality. What becomes very evident in this autobiography is the denial of many privileges to a woman even in the rich and educated families of the time.

Savitri Devi Nanda's book *The City of Two Gateways: The Autobiography of an Indian Girl* (1950) is a case of the frustration of a woman. The significance of the sub-title cannot be overlooked and it does remind us of what Germaine Bree argued in her chapter titled *Autogynography* that why should there be a separate section for 'women's autobiography'?

> "I was somewhat puzzled by the implications of the title. We were not in any other section, invited to discuss 'Men's' autobiography".[69]

She further adds and enquires that did the title "imply that autobiography written by women constituted a subgenre." A lot has been written on women's autobiographies and their characteristics, which is beyond the purview of this paper. However, it can be said that autobiographical-writing both by women and men is determined by the socio-historical background of the age.

After Gandhi, Nirad C. Chaudhuri's *The Autobiography of an Unknown Indian* (1951) was the next work to catch the Western eye; or was it written with the Western reader in mind? Gerhard Stilz[70] says that the title may hint at the obliteration of the self of "an inconspicuous man-in-the street"; however, it can instantly be perceived that the writer is "brilliant, provocative and exceptional individual" who wants to shock the self-complacency of the country's leaders.

Nirad C. Chaudhuri, who is called "the cultural historian" by William Walsh confesses that his autobiography is "more of a national than personal history"; the autobiographical form is used as a device for getting the history started. The most notable aspect of the work is that it spans the story of the author's life up to the first twenty-four years and covers as many as 528 pages, roughly in a chronological order. Chaudhuri wrote this voluminous book in the "memory of the British Empire in India", emphasizing "All that was Good And Living within us was Made, Shaped, And Quickened By the Same British Rule". This dedication was enough to put the detractors of Chaudhuri on the defensive and they turned a blind eye to the revealation of Chaudhuri's development of mind, as also to the depiction of the milieu, the various customs and traditions prevalent in that part of the country, first in Kishorganj and then in Calcutta. Written at the age of fifty, the recollections appear as fresh as though observed at the time of writing. A record of the historical events presented in an autobiographical form may have seemed unusual in 1951, when the autobiography was considered a special variety of biography and as a sort of stepchild of history and literature with neither discipline granting it full recognition as an independent subject of study in itself. Today autobiography is no longer a handmaiden of history, theology, psychology or sociology.

The Autobiography of an Unknown Indian reflects the state of an old society, where the state was being encroached by the Western concept of nature, personality, nationalism and freedom all seen through the agency of the self.

> "The formation of Chaudhuri's character is the means by which we are enabled to observe the transformation of Bengal Society; and to watch the fundamental categories of thought"[71].

However, Gerhard Stilz feels that Chaudhury's 'split approach' to describe India and also to pass a judgment on its way of life created problems for him. The result was according to C.D. Narsimhaiah "an unreadable book".

> ".....an elaboration of the attitudinising so evident in the calculated choice of the title, the dedication, the preface characterised by the cultural cringe of an author who writes, of all things, an autobiography, not as others have done to see themselves naked, but with the conscious object of reaching the English-speaking world; indeed, everything is geared to that end"[72].

The autobiography exhibits the writer's intellectual energy, his courage and will and an unabashed interest in himself, defying its professed "objective" aim. Chaudhuri, says Gerhard Stilz[73], withdraws his own self from the world, which he describes quite impressively through "the act of describing it".

Brinda's *Maharani:The Story of an Indian Princess* (1953) is the story of a woman "trying to defy convention". Even in the royal family of the early twentieth century, male supremacy was predominant as is evident from this work. Here the father-in-law of Brinda abused and insulted her for not bearing a son. The autobiography is a tragic story of a helpless girl in a male-dominated set-up.

Another woman from the Nehru family who used the autobiographical form of writing was Nayantara Sahgal. *Prison and Chocolate Cake* (1954) is full of reminiscences from the family record, with emphasis on the political life of the family at Anand Bhawan in Allahabad. William Walsh thinks that it is a significant trend started by a woman that of bringing politics in her works. Nayantara Sahgal's writings have nothing very feminine about them; neither are they like the revolutionary writings of the Marxist writers. Her "dashing journalistic prose" exhibits her interest in the minute details of the political life.

Tenzing, the hero of Mt. Everest, narrated the story of his life to James Ullman and it was published as *My Public Life* (1954).

Ved Mehta's autobiographical writings are numerous; however, *Daddygi, Mamagi, Vedi* and *The Ledge Between the Streams* followed his first autobiography *Face to Face* (1957). The Indian family life provides plenty of rich material for any kind of writing. And autobiography is a genre, which thrives on personal life-account and benefits most from this kind of set-up[74]. Written at an early age of twenty three it invalidates Georges Gusdorf's theory that the task of writing one's account of life is undertaken by an "aging man" to appease "the more or less anguished uneasiness".[75]

Ved Mehta's work, autobiographical as well as the other, is exceptional and singular because it is the work of a blind man, who was gifted enough to conquer his disability. His "powerful memory and an extraordinary power of inference" provides his autobiography with richness. However, there is detachment in his writings even while describing things around him.

> "....Ved Mehta is the contemporary voice of a long line of Indian prose writers in English stretching back for two hundred years ... In all his work he has made the traditional view exciting and engaging. He has made the most of experience limited by handicap. Indeed he has made blindness itself a means of insight"[76].

Nayantara Sahgal wrote another autobiography *From Fear Set Free* (1962) which was a sequel to the first one. It is a revealation of the Gandhian influence on the writer. However, here the emphasis is on Sahgal's personal experiences and not on the political activities. The influence of Gandhian ideology is sadly missing in the autobiography.

There were many people writing the accounts of their lives between 1957 and 1968; prominent among them being diplomats, politicians, army personnel. Gen. B.M. Kaul's *The Untold Story* (1967) is a reply to the public criticism he received after India's defeat during Indo-China War in 1962.

Kamala Dongerkery wrote and published *On The Wings of Time* in 1968. In it there is an expression of the writer's determination and devotion towards medical profession. She succeeded in becoming a doctor against all odds. Sita Rathnamala's *Beyond the Judge* (1968) is a tribal girl's autobiography, who had to leave her home in the Nilgiri Hills and face disillusionment and discrimination in the world of the city. Pandit Ravi Shankar, India's international sitar mastero, wrote *My Music, My Life* also in 1968.

Dom Moraes' *My Son's Father* (1968), written at the age of 30, made him experience a catharsis of sorts in describing the trauma of his childhood and adolescence in the company of his mad mother. Moraes' feeling of alienation from his surroundings, his parents and at times even from himself forms a significant part of the autobiography. The work describes the solace he got from writing poetry, and in this way, Moraes' discovered of his vocation, it being "one of the traditional subjects of autobiography which criticism sees as originating with *Confessions* of St. Augustine"[77]. Being a poet for Moraes was more than a vocation, it was a compulsion which negated everything else.

My God Died Young (1968) by Sasthi Brata deals with his problems of adjustment not only in the Indian society, but in any society. Like Dom Moraes he did not seem to belong anywhere and thus at the young age of twenty-nine he felt an urge to write his autobiography inorder to give him some prominence.

In the Future that was (1972) Urmila Haksar recounts that her grandmother never forgave her sex, which made her rebel against the established norms of gender prejudice.

If we look back to the years after the country's independence, we will realise that autobiography had become a popular literary genre. The English language, which these Indian writers deployed to express their innermost feelings and urges, was slowly becoming a part of a particular Indian section's way of expression. Though a gift of colonialism and the Raj.

> "Its persistence, its increasing strength and expanding influence - long after the British had departed and in spite of a natural national hostility and the effort to develop in Hindi a universal national language - owed nothing to the British and everything to the capacities, the resources and the usefulness, national and international, of the English language itself[78].

India geared up to meet the challenges of modern technology and scientific discoveries and English no longer remained a 'link language' or a 'library language'. And autobiography too became a favourite literary form with Indians writing in English.

> "Everyone is an authority on himself; and, besides the success of the autobiographies of Gandhiji, Nehru and Nirad Chaudhuri has tempted many others also to spread themselves out on the printed page"[79].

R.K. Narayan is one of those novelists who, though they write in English, remain what K.R. Srinivasa Iyengar calls "recognisably autochthonous". His thoughts and feelings are all Indian. *My Days* (1974), "a set of autobiographical sketches"[80], has the disadvantage of not being a full-scale autobiography. Critics are of the opinion that his autobiography is very much like his novels just as his novels are very much his autobiography. Narayan in *My Days*, says William Walsh, appears like the hero of any of his novels. It is another work, which deals with the discovery of a vocation; Narayan knew, he says, that he wanted to be a writer. He was influenced by the events around him and created chatacters for his fiction. Malgudi's creation finds an expression in *My Days*. The work is suffused with a deep sense of melancholy.

India has had many autobiographies written by Princesses and Maharanis, which at the time of publication provided the much-needed revealation of the royal women. Most of them had lived behind the 'purdah' and thus the public read the accounts of their lives very avidly. Since mostly all of them were well educated, some of them had got their education in European countries too, writing in English did not pose a problem for them. They were also quite at home with the Western way of life, as a result writing an autobiography - a document of self-revealation - came naturally to them. Most of these autobiographies highlight the lives of these Maharanis in the shadow of their husbands; though they participated in social and political activities, they never appeared ambitious enough to hold independent positions. The main reason for this was the training given to them to be submissive and do their duty.

Gayatri Devi's autobiography *The Princess Remembers* (1976) is one work, which shows the active role, she played in the welfare of her state of Jaipur. She gave up 'purdah' to join politics and won every election. But her autobiography concentrates more on the personal events of her life than on politics.

One of the bold, uninhibited self-revealations seen in recent times is found in Kamala Das' *My Story* (1976) with which she has been able to carve a niche for herself in the annals of this genre. *My Story* is an attempt at redefining the male-female relationship; it is also a challenging account of the writer's experiences, not necessarily of her life only, but of the life of everybody as well. Through these experiences, which were sociological, psychological and spiritual, she has redefined her personality. It is an account of a woman's life who tries to live traditionally but is forced at times to break the rules inorder to satisfy her inner urges, which are very much part of her personality. She could not be bound by the formal constraints of a role, which the society wished to impose on her, generally as a woman and particularly as a wife.

Till the arrival of Kamala Das on the scene the women writers who revealed their lives had been either political leaders, social workers or women from royal families. The accounts of their personal history had traced the development of their personalities in the socially defined slots for them. A couple of them had revolted against the predetermined life-patterns; but by and large a woman's autobiography was a definition of her subjectivity as seen against the backdrop of the country either before independence or in a free India. But in Kamala Das we have what Shaw would call a "New Woman": a woman conscious of her femininity and determined to vindicate it against male supremacy. The autobiography defines the personality of Kamala Das as it has been made by the dictates of the society. Thus a `good' girl is made to rebel against the established social, cultural and traditional norms to fulfil her psychological needs. Her narration breaks down all the cultural barriers of feminine modesty, which at times shocks the conservative readers. Vrinda Nabar says that what is surprising in the autobiography is that there are no dates, "may be because the writer wishes to avoid sounding like a chronicler, and would prefer to be artistically factual"[81].

There have been many other women who have written their autobiographies. Prominent among them have been: Shudha Mazumdar, *A Pattern of Life* (1977); Dhanwanti Rama Rau, *An Inheritance* (1977); Vijayraje Scindia, *Princess, The Autobiography* (1985), Kamala Devi Chattopadhya *Inner Recesses Outer Spaces* (1986) to name a few.

Eminent personalities in the country had been indulging in writing their memoirs concerning the times during which they had played an active role either on the political platform or the social scenario. V.V. Giri's *My Life and Times* (1976) is one such book written with the aim of letting the world know about the events concerned with India's Independence which he had the seen. His contribution to the establishment and development of the trade union movement also forms a major part of the work.

Indira Gandhi appears to be the only woman from the Nehru family, apart from her mother, who did not want to write an account of her life and times. Her aunt, Vijay Lakshmi Pandit's *The Scope of Happiness* (1979) is an important work as it reveals not only the affluent life style of the Nehrus, which changed dramatically once the family came under the influence of Gandhiji, but also for the prejudice prevalent in the family against the birth of a girl child, in this case Indira. What is uncovered through her writings is the personality of a powerful woman who fought for the inheritance rights of the women of India and got the Hindu Code Bill passed in their favour. Her political career spanned many years, in which she served as India's ambassador in many countries.

Another woman of substance was Durgabai Deshmukh, who was awarded a Padma Vibhushan for her achievements. Her autobiography *Chintaman and I* (1980) is significant, as it depicts not only her husband C.D. Deshmukh (the title is significant), but also for highlighting her successful career in the service of the country.

Dr. Karan Singh's reminiscences were written in two parts: Heir Apparent (1982) and *Sadar-i-Riyasat* (1985). The first part describes his birth in 1931 and covers a period of twenty-two years of his life upto 1953. It refers to Kashmir's accession to India as the state of Jammu and Kashmir. The second part discusses the wars with China and Pakistan and the period of political history at the time of Nehru and Gandhi. Dr. Karan Singh also reveals his spiritual quest and inner development.

Nirad C. Chaudhuri, "India's famous but controversial NRI", published his second book *Thy Hand, Great Anarch!* in 1987. The work, which covers some thousand pages, is a sequel to *The Autobiography of an Unknown Indian;* however, the writer was no longer unknown. Released on his 90th birthday, it is a brazen version of the decline and fall of the British Empire in India. The history of the times is presented in Chaudhuri's inimitable style together with a self-portrait of the ideas. An unemployed Chaudhuri, the "scholar gypsy" gives his own life-story against the backdrop of India's freedom movement from 1921 to 1952.

Commenting on the publication of the book, *The Daily Telegraph* wrote: "Here is energy, courage, honesty and intelligence; pugnacity, too, and scorn for venality, hypocrisy, and cowardice". William Walsh thinks that the lengthy autobiography does not have the descriptive power or the penetrating analytical style seen in the earlier one. However, what Chaudhuri does present is his

> "defence of the nature and purpose of the British Raj, the utmost scorn for the British in India, who were incapable of forming human or even humane relationships with Indians, and severe contempt for the ones he has lived among for the last eighteen years as an exile in Britain. The former he detests for their inhumanity, the latter for their illiteracy"[82].

Chaudhuri explains in the Introduction the three motives involved in the writing of *Thy Hand, Great Anarch!:* he has made his personal life a framework for the history of the period; there is an expression of his thoughts and feelings about the public and historical events through which he passed; and lastly, the book is an account of the political and cultural activities of the period between 1921 to 1952. An important observation has been made by Chaudhuri in the Epilogue, after passing through an age of decadence he concluded:

> "At the end of my life I have come to the conclusion that civilised human existence all over the world is completing the latest cycle of its history by descending into its natural awareness. I think our times are

comparable to the fifth century of the Christian era when St. Augustine saw the Graeco-Roman world crumbling all around him"[83].

Thy Hand, Great Anarch! can be termed as a "historical autobiography" where the discovery of the self is not contaminated by the mess of history.

With the fast developing technology, television has acquired new dimensions. Therefore, today we have the visual autobiography and its telecast gives a chance to the viewer to interpret the autobiographer's hitherto unexplored possibility of arriving at accuracy. Doordarshan's telecast on 25th April 1993 of a film by Rajiv Mehrotra gave Nirad C. Chaudhuri an opportunity to talk directly to the viewers, who had been till now his readers. But the film did something more: it took the viewer right inside Chaudhuri's house, into his study, his kitchen, to watch him read and eat his breakfast. Clad in a dhoti and kurta, Chaudhuri showed a great agility in his movements to beguile his old age. He could be seen listening to Bengali music, which reminded him of his life in Bengal. His aestheticism makes him love his garden with an "earthly passion".

There is one danger in a visual autobiography, which could lead to a disaster. If two famous people sit opposite each other, the discourse could become meaningless. However, in this film Rajiv Mehrotra kept a low profile and apart from putting some questions to Chaudhuri, he let the famous man do all the talking. The camera followed every movement of Nirad C. Chaudhuri.

'N' For Nobody: An Autobiography of an English Teacher was published in 1991. Written by C.D. Narasimhaiah, an eminent personality on the Indian literary and critical scene, the book is dedicated to his family and to his students. The significance of the title cannot be overlooked; it may have been selected inadvertently, but, says Mulk Raj Anand, the

title does reveal the "traditional Indian attitude, which is against abetting one's ego. So he uses a stray incident as the reason for calling his autobiography *'N' for Nobody*"[84].

The life revealed is that of a poor village boy and his transformation into an urbane teacher of English literature. His aim in writing his autobiography was firstly to obey his "urge to write" and secondly to oblige his friends who asked him to reveal his life which, as a teacher, was linked with English studies in India. The English language, he feels, has enabled the Indians to think globally while living locally. *'N' for Nobody* reveals how CDN (as the writer is popularly known) established the "Dhvanya loka", a kind of Gurukul Ashram, inspired by the Institute for Advanced Study at Princeton. In the traditional norm of the genre, the autobiography traces the development of the writer from childhood in pursuit of knowledge in various educational institutes, in India as well as abroad, culminating in the role of an English teacher. His autobiography, therefore, answers and exemplifies the question "How did I become what I am?"

Knowing CDN's views on Nirad C. Chaudhuri's *The Autobiography of an Unknown Indian,* he must have been shocked when Bidhubhushan Das while reviewing *'N' for Nobody* for the journal *Indian Literature* (Sahitya Akademi, NO. 149, May-June, 1992) placed it in the same category as the autobiography by Chaudhuri! C.D.N had called book "unreadable" and had said,

> "The man was no writer, at least when he wrote his Autobiography...He is singularly lacking in self-awareness as you would see when he modestly claims that his Autobiography will live as long as the English language lasts, not realising writers like him are just the one's who contribute to hastening its undeserved decline"[85]

He further adds:

> "I shall stand by it until I am proved wrong, provoked by its reputation I have thrown out the challenge frequently and no one has cared to contradict me".

And then we have Bidhubhushan Das putting the two autobiographies in the same class. Writing about *'N' for Nobody* he quotes that part of the book which shows CDN's attachment for England!

> "It is here that one remembers another eminent Indian, Nirad Chaudhuri, who migrated to Oxford to settle down there for this reason. The resemblance of this book to *The Autobiography of an Unknown Indian,* cannot be missed. All of which points to one singular aspect of the minds of both authors, their adumbration of intellectual aristocracy which still receives recognition in England, not in our country, generally speaking, although that has been prominently our cultural tradition"[86].

Lessons (1991) by P. Lal is called a "strange amalgam of a book: an `autobiography', almost a `self - obituary'". However, it is an account of P. Lal's life only of a very short period, from 1989 - 1991 when he faced a `Near Death Experience' in a hospital in the U.S.A. and learnt a few "lessons".

Dom Moraes wrote a sequel to *My Son's father* and called it *Never At Home* (1992); starting from where he had left off in the first autobiography Moraes covered a period of his life between 1974-1990. The title is significant and depicts the spirit of this particular work - Moraes traversing the whole world as an investigative journalist in search of a home. It was a period of anguish for him and a search for identity; alienation from his mad mother, his country and his first wife had made him a wanderer. His misery increased with the Muse of poetry deserting him. The account of the loss of his poetic inspiration is a painful refrain in the autobiography, which reveals Moraes as a restless traveller, as a globe-trotting journalist. His quest for a home ended in India, with the stirring of his poetic prowess.

Up At Oxford (1993) is termed as "The latest installment of Mehta's long-running autobiography"[87]. The title tells the reader that the book deals with Ved Mehta's student days at Oxford during the 1950s. In the course of narration he wishes many times that he "had been born an Englishman". The style of writing shows an aptitude for aestheticism with "well-formed sentences" which are "to borrow Barthes' expression, very white writing"[88].

R. Venkataraman, India's eighth President from 1987-1992, wrote an autobiographical account concentrating on his tenure in the office of the President. Hence *My Presidential Years* (1994) cannot be termed as an autobiography in the real sense of the genre, where it is imperative to trace the years of one's life right from the beginning. However, the book does reveal the personality of the former President and gives a purely subjective account of the various issues of his times. It also expresses the "Chilling Unpredictability of a Political System", as it contains an account of political activities which were never revealed to the general public. The book discusses thorny issues like the Sri Lankan crisis, Bofors Gun deal, assassination of Rajiv Gandhi and Stock Scam.

My Years Through Raj to Swaraj by T.N. Kaul was published in 1995 and spans seventy-five years of his life. Such autobiographies by people in the administrative service of the country are important for revealing the diplomatic way of life. The major events covered in the book are: the partition of the country in 1947; the two wars with Pakistan in 1965 and 1971 and Indo-China conflict of 1962. Referring of the Kashmir issue to the UN by Nehru, he says, was done at the insistence of Lord Mountbatten. Other issues discussed are the Panchsheel agreement, the Tashkent Agreement and the Shimla Pact. He has lauded Indira Gandhi for improving relations with China, U.S.S.R and Bangladesh and criticised her for emergency and for mishandling the Punjab problem.

Kushwant Singh, the naughty, old man who has always been in the limelight more for his uninhibited views on sex and the female form rather than for any other kind of writing, finally published his autobiography in 1995 and named it *Truth, Love and a Little Malice*. He calls it his "swan song" and feels that now there is not much of creativity left in him.

Singh always moved in the powerful circle of India's capital and was also the editor of *The Illustrated Weekly*. As such he became friendly and intimate with people who carried clout. Thus it is not surprising at all that the autobiography reveals the private lives of these important people like Indira Gandhi, Maneka Gandhi and other notable personalities and his associations with them. He confessed in an interview given to *Saturday Times* (June 25, 1994), "I have not spared anyone".

Journalistic writing has always been Singh's forte and it accounts for more than seventy books written by him. The autobiography shows this characteristic hallmark of his writing, where he has also discussed his student life in England. It was as a diplomat at the Indian High Commission in 1947 that Singh discovered his flair for writing. He confesses that he himself is responsible for creating the image of a man in "lurid colours", a man who is forever enamoured of beautiful women, loves to be inebriated most of the time. His controversial reputation made him a cult figure in the country.

> "At the heart of Singh's work lies the paradox of serious scholarship and tomfoolery"[89].

Looking back on this historical survey of Indian Autobiographies in English, we can come to the conclusion that the 'autobiography' was introduced in the country during the Indian Renaissance; after that it gradually developed as a genre in the Western sense and followed its own natural trend to display the "Indianness" of the writers. However, it will not be wrong to point out that the progress of autobiography - writing in India is associated with the extraordinary expansion of English in India "which proved itself capable of expressing the innermost, as well as the strongest and subtlest, feelings of members of a culture immensely remote in history and distance".[90] The English language has been used beautifully and perfectly by the writers of autobiography for over the last sixty years or so as this survey has revealed. These writers have displayed a richness of diction in their life - narratives which have also reflected the changing social framework, individual struggle, "tradition and morality, aspiration, injustice, tragedy and comedy"[91] of the individual self. Today the groundwork is much stronger than it was at the time of Independence for the talented Indian writer to take up this form of writing.

Coming to the point whether autobiography is suited to the Indian temperament or not, it can be cogently assumed that the Indian writer has shown a great proficiency in following all the concepts of this genre and has succeeded in answering the fundamental question of 'autobiography': "How did I become what I am today?" Many of the autobiographies have succeeded in revealing the inner self and the private life of a man or a woman behind the role they adopted to display their public image or for their social commitments. The major demand of the genre is not a depiction of the external accomplishment, but an expression of the writer's private, intimate assessment. And we have seen that most of these authors have achieved a remarkable success in doing just this; the autobiographers have also come to terms with their own individuality and the world. They have also provided an insight into their private selves, by doing a review of their lives and by indulging in a kind of soul-searching and self-examination. The reader too has benefited by having the privilege of reading the autobiographies of some famous men and women, drawing incentive from those who have served as role-models of lives lived bravely, even in adverse circumstances.

In the end we can say that autobiography has been successfully, even brilliantly, indigenised by the Indian writers in English, and in this enterprise the Indian writers exposed to English literature have played a prominent role. We cannot but agree with what C.D. Narsimhaiah had said at the Seminar on *Commonwealth Autobiography* organised at Dhavanyoloka in November 1995:

> "It is often glibly argued in the West that Autobiography is an alien form to the Indian mind because of its constant preoccupation with the other world - I wish it were true for the sake of our self-respect, for the truth is the Indian of today is the most philistine animal one can think of. Granting for arguments sake the Indian is other-worldly I should have thought precisely for that reason he should feel better qualified than others to write an Autobiography because of his constant engagement in an uninhibited dialogue between the self and the Soul — that is what `other worldly' means to me. Autobiography, especially, must give evidence of a writer self-wrung, self-strung, self against self-grinding in introspection"[92].

REFERENCES

1. Roy Pascal, *Design and Truth in Autobiography*, Harvard University Press, 1960, p. 7.
2. "Autobiography and the Cultural Moment", in *Autobiography: Essays Theoretical and Critical*, ed. James Olney, Princeton University Press, 1980, p. 4.
3. "Criticism and the Autobiography", in *Modern Selves, Essays on Modern British American Autobiography*, ed. Philip Dodd, Frank Cass, 1986, p. 2.
4. *Design And Truth in Autobiography*, p. 9.

5. Ulric Neisser, "Self-narratives: True and false" in *The Remembering Self* ed. by Ulric Neisser and Robyn Fivush, Cambridge University Press, 1994, p. 1.
6. *Ibid.*
7. A.O.J. Cockshut, *The Art of Autobiography in 19th and 20th Century England*, Yale University Press, 1984, p. 16.
8. *Ibid.*, pp. 5, 17.
9. *Design and Truth In Autobiography*, p. 184.
10. Ulric Neisser, *The Remembering Self*, p. 1.
11. Michael Sheringham, *French Autobiography, Devices and Desires*, Clearndon Press Oxford, 1993, p. vii.
12. Susanne K. Langer, *Feeling and Form*, Routledge & Kegan Paul Ltd., 1967, p. 396.
13. "Autobiography and the Cultural Moment", *Autobiography: Essays Theoretical and Critical*, p. 6.
14. John Sturrock, *The Language of Autobiography*, Cambridge University Press, 1994, p. 25.
15. Martin Stannard, "In Search of Himselves: The Autobiographical Writings of Graham Greene", in *Modern Selves*, ed. Philip Dodd, Frank Cass,1986, p. 141.
16. "Conditions and Limits of Autobiography", in *Autobiography: Essays Theoretical and Critical*, p. 32.
17. *Design and Truth in Autobiography*, p. 10.
18. "Criticism and the Autobiography", in *Modern Selves*, p. 21.
19. *Ibid.*
20. George Gusdorf, "Conditions and Limits of Autobiography", *Autobiography: Essays Theoretical and Critical*, p. 41.
21. Gerhard Stilz, "Experiments in Squaring the Ellipis: A Critical Reading of the Autobiographies of Gandhi, Nehru, Chaudhuri and Anand," in *New Perspectives in Indian Literature in English*, ed. Yaravintelinath, Balaram Gupta, Venugopal, Amritjit Singh, Sterling Publishers, 1995, p. 164.
22. Marlene Fisher, "Mulk Raj Anand As Autobiographer", in *New Perspectives in Indian Literature and English*, p. 127.
23. *Design and Truth in Autobiography*, p. 180.
24. "Conditions and Limits of Autobiography", p. 29.

25. Meena Sodhi, "Autobiography: An Agency of Man and His self", *Occasional Papers*, Vol.IV, No.1,1995-96, p. 26.

26. "Conditions and Limits of Autobiography", p. 29.

27. *Design and Truth in Autobiography*, p. 22.

28. Foreword to *Kanthapura*, Delhi, OUP, 1989, p.V.

29. *The Concept of Man*, Indus, Harper Collins Publishers, 1995, p. 9.

30. P.T. Raju, "The Concept of the Indian Thought", in *The Concept of Man*, p. 216.

31. Hans Jacobs: *Western Psychotherapy and Hindu Sadhana*, London, George and Unwin Ltd.,1961, p. 118.

32. *Outlines of Indian Philosophy*, London, George Allen and Unwin Ltd., 1951, p. 55.

33. "The Concept of the Indian Thought", *Concept of Man*, p. 256.

34. "The Problem of Self", *Sadhana*, Macmillan, 1988, p. 57.

35. *The Rig Veda*, translated by Wendy Deniger O'Flaherty, Penguin, 1994, p. 240.

36. Pillar Edict VI, from Pillar Edict II, *Incriptions of Asoka*, Delhi, 1967.

37. "Experiments in Squaring The Ellipsis", *New Perspectives in Indian Literature in English*, p. 162.

38. *Indian Writing in English*, Sterling Publishers Limited, 1993, p. 22.

39. William Walsh, *Indian Literature in English*, Longman, London, 1990, p.1.

40. *Ibid.*

41. As quoted in *Indian Writing in English*, p. 41-42.

42. *Indian Literature in English*, p. 32.

43. As quoted in *The Indian Autobiographies in English*, by R.C.P. Sinha, S. Chand and Co., New Delhi, 1978, p. 48.

44. As quoted in *In Indian Writings in English*, p. 550.

45. *Design and Truth in Autobiography*, p. 14.

46. *Indian Writings in English*, p. 272.

47. *Ibid.*, p.248.

48. *The Literary Criterion*, Vol.XXXI, 1996, No. 1 & 2, p. 2.

49. *New Perspectives in Indian Literature in English*, p. 166.

50. As quoted in *New Perspectives in Indian Literature in English*, p. 166.
51. *Indian Literature in English*, p. 39.
52. V.S. Naipaul, *Indian: A Wounded Civilization*, Penguin Books, 1977, p. 98.
53. *Ibid.,* p. 101.
54. *Indian Writing in English*, p. 520.
55. *Writing a Woman's Life*, The Woman's Press, London, 1988, p. 11.
56. Germaine Bree, "Autobiography", *Studies in Autobiography*, edited by James Olney, Oxford University Press, New York, 1988, p. 17.
57. As quoted in *Autobiography and Questions of Gender*, ed. By Shirley Neuman, Frank Cass & Co.Ltd., 1991, p. 2.
58. Cassell's Encyclopedia of Literature, Vol.I, London, 1953, p. 63.
59. George Henry Lewes, "The lady Novelists" in *Women's Liberation and Literature*, ed. By Elaine Showalter, Harcourt Brace Javanovich, Inc. New York, U.S.A., 1971, p. 174.
60. *An Autobiography*, Jawaharlal Memorial Fund, OUP, 1980, p.vii.
61. Essays in *Commonwealth Literature, Heirloom of Multiple Heritage*, Pencraft International, Delhi,1995, p. 46.
62. "Experiments in Squaring the Ellipsis", *New Perspectives in Indian Literature in English*, p. 168.
63. *Indian Writing in English*, p. 303.
64. "Experiments in Squaring the Ellipsis", *New Perspectives in Indian Literature in English*, p. 170.
65. *A History of Indian English Literature*, Sahitya Akademi, 1995, p. 73.
66. Marlene Fisher, "Mulk Raj Anand as Autobiographer', *New Perspectives in Indian Literature*, p. 182.
67. *Ibid.,* pp. 182-183.
68. M.K. Naik, *A History of Indian English Literature*, p. 191.
69. Germaine Bree, "Autobiography", in *Studies in Autobiography*, p. 171.
70. *New Perspectives in Indian Literature in English*, p. 170.
71. William Walsh, *Indian Literature in English*, pp. 51-52.
72. Essays in *Commonwealth Literatureb,* p. 61.

73. *New Perspectives in Indian Literature in English*, p. 172.
74. *Indian Literature in English*, p. 57.
75. George Gusdorf, "Conditions and Limits of Autobiography", *Autobiography: Essays Theoretical and Critical*, p. 38.
76. *Indian Literature in English*, p. 766.
77. Philip Dodd, "Criticism and the Autobiographical Tradition", *Modern Selves*, p. 4.
78. *Indian Literature in English*, p. 124.
79. *Indian Writing in English*, p. 766.
80. William Walsh, *Indian Literature in English*, p. 55.
81. Vrinda Nabar, *The Endless Female Hungers, A Study of Kamala Das*, Sterling Publishers Pvt. Ltd., New Delhi, 1994, p. 1.
82. *Indian Literature in English*, p. 53.
83. Nirad C. Chaudhuri, *Thy Hand, Great Anarch!*, Addison-Wesley Publishing Company, Inc., England, 1988, p. xxiii.
84. *LITTCRIT,* Vol.18, No.1&2, June, December,1992.
85. *The Literary Criterion*, Vol.XXXI, 1996, No. 1 & 2.
86. *Indian Literature*, Sahitya Akademi Bi-Monthly Journal, No. 149, May-June, 1992.
87. *India Today*, Nov. 30,1993.
88. *Ibid.*
89. *Saturday Times*, June 25, 1995.
90. William Walsh, *Indian Literature in English*, p.124.
91. *Ibid.*
92. *The Literary Criterion*, Vol. XXXI, No. 1 & 2.

CHAPTER 5

Autobiographies by Indian Women Writers in English : Life with a Difference

What should an autobiography written by a woman look like? Before we are able to answer this question, we will have to answer a number of queries put forth by Carolyn G. Heilbrun on the essentials of a woman's autobiography:

> "Where should it begin? With her birth, and the disappointment, or reason for no disappointment, that she was not a boy? Do we then slide her into the Freudian family romance, the Oedipal configuration; if not, how should we view her childhood? .... What, in short, is the subject's relation - inevitably complex - with her mother? The relation with the father will be less complex, clearer in its emotions and desires, partaking less of either terrible pity or binding love. How does the process of becoming, or failing to become a sex object operate in the woman's life; how does she cope with the fact that value is determined by how attractive men find her? If she marries, why does the marriage fail, or succeed?"[1].

These are compelling issues which must be probed and answered if we have to understand the life of a woman. Though Carolyn G. Heilbrun's questions aim to analyze the life of a Western woman, which is very different from that of her Indian counterpart, they can very well be applied in the Indian context too. The Indian women autobiographers, and here we are concerned only with those who have written about their lives in English, feel differently about these issues and they have presented them in a different way; this difference in attitude has been inevitable due to the diversity in the socio-economic and cultural background of the Western and the Indian way of a woman's life. Anyone who studies these autobiographies by the Indian women in English is bound to feel that some more relevant questions, peculiar to our culture, need to be raised: what was the writer's household set-up? Did she get a proper education? What was her age at the time of marriage? How was her relationship with her husband? Does her autobiography focus on the mother-in-law syndrome? Is the Indian woman autobiographer able to establish her identity, which is the real purpose of this form of writing? The answers to these questions form the groundwork of the present paper; an effort has been made to present a cogent, systematic and analytical review of all the queries mentioned earlier.

The Indian panorama of women's autobiographies in English is undoubtedly rich with some exceptional writings by outstanding women of the country. Since many of these women autobiographers have written their books during the period of the Indian struggle for freedom, there are bound to be some political leanings too. However, it is essential to see whether these writers have consciously or unconsciously secured their "sense of self". The autobiography reveals the "hidden forms of inwardness" and the writer's self succeeds in establishing the writer's portrait in the public eye. So, can a woman reveal her unique self and indulge in self-exploration, which educates the reader about her life, much as a Bildungsroman would do? A woman is taught to be selfless, self-effacing and is only either a daughter, a wife or a mother. But the same concept, seen from another perspective, shows that a man is a man only because he has been pampered and made a God by a mother, a wife and a daughter. And sometimes all three rolled into one like Candida, who shatters the complacency of a smug Morell when she says:

> "Ask me what it costs to be James's mother and three sisters and wife and mother to his children all in one.... I build a castle of comfort and indulgence and love for him, and stand sentinel always to keep little vulgar cares out. I make him master here, though he does not know it, and could not tell you a moment ago, how it came to be so."[2]

A woman is naturally creative and thus if she has a room of her own, she can very well write not only fiction but can also defend her selfhood and narrate the story of her life. There is nothing unnatural in her literary creativity, which cannot be a rival to her biological creativity; the radical feminists are right when they consider it to be a superior endowment:

> "... the literary professions were first to be opened to women, the status of the women writer has long served as an index of a society's views on female abilities and rights. Although writing has never been regarded as an unfeminine accomplishment, women writers have always encountered more critical resistance than men."[3]

All the autobiographies from Sunity Devee's *The Autobiography of an Indian Princess* (1921) to Kamaladevi Chattopadhya's *Inner Recesses Outer Spaces* (1986) begin confessedly and each woman starts on a search to find her life's work. What they lack is an authoritative voice to speak and till the nineteenth century could speak only of family or religion:

> "Although each author has significant, sometimes dazzling accomplishments to her credit, the theme of accomplishment rarely dominates the narrative ... Indeed to a striking degree they fail directly to emphasize their own importance, though writing in a genre which implies self-assertion and self-display."[4]

The establishment of identity by women autobiographers is based on the relationship with some chosen ones, without any affiliation; they feel constricted to write candidly and unreservedly about themselves. Most of the Indian women autobiographers reveal their tendency to treat their culture that is women's culture, as a "sub-culture": men's culture being the main culture, with the women conforming mainly to it. Elaine Showalter[5] feels that denouncing of "female self-assertiveness" was one of the methods used by the women of "feminine" culture to expiate for their literary and public activities. Autobiography, says Andre Maurois[6] is "a prolonged speech for the defense" and is of two types: one is where the writing is "as interesting as novels and as true as the finest 'life'." It has truth of tone and a "fidelity and impartiality in portraiture, of a very high quality indeed." But the best autobiographies are those which elaborate the inner self of man and depict the movement of his inner life. Majority of autobiographies by Indian women belongs to the first category; nevertheless there have definitely been a few which reveal the progress of the self as a coherent and powerful identity. These writers have established a permanent place for themselves in the realm of literature, because they have written as women and have not initiated the male manner of writing. Genuine female experience expressed in writing will always have a universal value. I shall be dealing with this distinction later in the paper.

The birth of a female child is still not a very joyous event in many of the Indian families, where the arrival of a girl child is announced as "It has arrived". Many of the women autobiographers have not elaborated upon it, but some have discussed the attitude of the other family members at the time of their birth. What is interesting to note is that Vijaya Lakshmi Pandit's *The Scope of Happiness*[7] (1979) gives a detailed account of the birth of a girl in the Nehru family. Kamala Nehru was expecting a child and all the family members waited anxiously outside the room. Sometime later Swarup Rani announced, "Hua...", at which Motilal Nehru laughingly asked "Baccha Hua?". When his wife did not reply, he knew that a girl had been born and announced it to the whole family:

> "Mother had not said a son is born but `it' has been born. In the traditional way she could not bring herself to announce the birth of a daughter!"[8]

It was another matter that the girl child, who was not given any identity at the time of her birth, went on to become India's first woman Prime Minister! But if such was the bent of mind of the emancipated, educated, wealthy Nehru family, what could one expect from the country's lesser-known clans?

Savitri Devi Nanda's autobiography *The City of Two Gateways*[9] (1950) has a sub-title, *The Autobiography of an Indian Girl,* which demands the reader to put it into a specific category and to expect certain particularities in it. The discrimination meted out to her from the moment of her birth, made her long "to be a boy", even a poor dirty boy would have been better than girl. The work clearly shows the frustration of the girl. She aspired to know more about the world with a "longing so great that all else was swept aside"[10]; her discontent at being a girl made her father dress her in a boy's clothes. The same frustration is evident in Brinda's Maharani: *The Story of an Indian Princess* (1953)[11], who was filled with "black rebellion" at the injustices which girls had to suffer. The rebellion burning in her heart made her "defy convention". Urmila Haksar's grandmother, and that too the maternal one, could never forgive her for her sex. *The Future That Was* (1972)[12] opens with an anguish at being born a girl, in a family which already had the first born as a girl. Hence the second girl child did not make anyone very happy.

In many of these autobiographies, it is seen that a sense of failure, despite having achieved success, continues through out the lives of these women. They felt discrimination against them in their childhood and, therefore, as Carolyn of Heilburn says:

> "Nostalgia, particularly for childhood, is likely to be a mask for unrecognised anger."[13]

Surprisingly childhood for these women has often been projected as the happiest of times in their writings; it could be because by the time they had understood that their births were not very happy events for their families, they had already enjoyed the best part of their lives, their childhood:

> "For women, adulthood - marriage or spinsterhood - implied relative loss of self. Unlike men, therefore, they looked back fondly to the relative freedom, and power of childhood and youth."[14]

However, the childhood memories are often secondhand; parents and grandparents narrate incidents from early life and therefore, what is offered as recollections of childhood are generally no more than what the writers have heard about themselves from others. These are then the 'edited' versions of childhood memories, written by adults. But there can be instances of genuine, first-hand memories of childhood and these can give the notion of being really true.

Most of these girls were allowed to play with the boys of their own age, with a freedom, which was restricted later in life as they grew older. What is significant is

> "that accounts of childhood were somehow freed from the terrible anxieties induced by adult female ambition and encounters."[15]

Sunity Devee's *The Autobiography of an Indian Princess* (1921)[16] narrates her childhood by describing how young girls were made to worship "symbolic figures made of flour" to have a good husband and wealth. She belonged to a Brahmo Samaj family and studied in English medium schools; she was lucky to have a liberal father who saw to it that all his three daughters received a proper education, which helped Sunity in getting a good marriage proposal from Cooch Bihar.

An autobiography by India's first woman lawyer, Cornelia Sorabji, deserves special mention. *Her India Calling* (1934)[17] tells the story of her relentless struggle in the male-dominated society to establish a place for herself. The plight of a woman who visited her mother made her decide in favour of her profession. Being a woman she faced many hardships in her career, even though she had been awarded the Government of India scholarship to study law at an English University. The situation was no different in England and at Oxford. She was told that no woman could study law. After much effort she was allowed to attend lectures; but her troubles did not end there. Just prior to her final examinations, her London examiner informed her that since she was a woman he would not examine her answer-books. It was after the intervention of the Vice-Chancellor that she was allowed to appear for her examinations and obtain a degree. On returning to India she started her practice at law; it became essential for her to take the helpless women under her shelter. Her autobiography deals mainly with her concern for improving the sad condition of the women in the Indian society.

Nayan Tara Sehgal's *Prison and Chocolate Cake*[18] (1954) does not give much of an insight into her childhood, except that when she was three years old and having chocolate cake for tea, her father was taken to prison; thus for her prison was always associated with chocolate cake.

Savitri Devi Nanda's father always encouraged her to be a tomboy; since her mother did not appreciate her daughter's behaviour, she was sent to her grandparents' house for a disciplined upbringing. Her autobiography reveals the training she received in domestic chores; however, she was not allowed to enjoy a carefree childhood, but was taught to be a docile, cute girl like all her cousins. Her father was the only one who understood her aspirations and 'stole' her from her grandparents' home. She was put in a school where she would always aspire to become an achiever in life; while other girls would dream of getting a prince charming for a husband, Savitri would aim at conquering glorious heights. She had a great 'hunger' for gaining knowledge. She foiled all the attempts of her relatives to force her into marriage and joined the London School of Medicine. Unfortunately the autobiography does not provide any further details.

Another girl who loved dressing like a boy was Shoilabala Das. *A Look Before and After* (1956) does not reveal any feeling of inferiority at being born a girl. Shoilabala's determination to achieve success made her a "born fighter", "a blunt woman". She received high education, often in boy's colleges, which contributed a lot towards moulding her personality. She was an adopted child of Madhusudan Das, who was an important political leader of Orissa. He sent her to Cambridge to take Teachers' Training Course; on her return she helped him in the affairs of the Orissa State. Her bold attitude and forthright manner got her an honorary post of a Magistrate in Orissa. She later became a member of the State's Public Service Commission and held many public posts later in life.

An autobiography with a difference, *Beyond the Jungle* (1968)[19], is written by Sita Rathnamala, who, as a tribal girl, lived in the jungles of the Nilgiri Hills. She had a happy and protected childhood with an indulgent father. There are vivid descriptions of her childhood escapades into the jungle with her friends. The memories of her easy, happy-go-lucky days are a counter-view to her description of the city life she encountered later; a chance accident took her from her secure world in the jungle to the metropolitan 'jungle' where she learnt to speak new languages. She was later given a scholarship by the Department of Education, Government of India to study in the Dodo Boarding school. Here she encountered class-consciousness of the civilised and sophisticated society. The innocence, which had nurtured her, was replaced by a sense of inferiority. However, she excelled in sports and established a place for herself in her school.

Urmila Haksar's childhood was not a happy one and it is revealed in *The Future That Was;* she was a girl and not as beautiful as her sister, which made her mother quite indifferent towards her. However, she always excelled in her studies and outshone her sister easily. She cut her hair short, dressed like a tomboy and felt more comfortable in the company of boys. It has been observed that in many of these works, the women have pictured the father as a representative of patriarchy; he is the focal point on which a new awareness, generally in memory, is formed. Urmila Haksar's father encouraged her to be her true self. What is heart-rending about her autobiography is her mother's behaviour towards her in her childhood, who did not make her aware of the biological truths about her female body. This nurtured hatred in her towards the categorisation of woman, who was seen only as a future wife and a mother. She hated the changes taking place in her body, and wanted to deny herself the right to procreate.

Women started telling their stories in a frank manner, which not only enlightened the readers but also shocked them. Kamala Das's *My Story* (1976)[20] is one such exceptional, bold self-revealation in the whole category of Indian women's writings. Her childhood was spent like that of any other girl; her mother was from the Nalapat royal family, and her father was a peasant Nair, who later became a Managing Director with a British concern. The parents were indifferent towards Kamala and her brother:

> "They took us for granted and considered us mere puppets, moving our limbs according to the tugs they gave us. They did not stop for a moment to think

that we had personalities that were developing independently, like sturdy shoots of the banyan growing out of crevices in the walls of ancient fortresses."[21]

However, her closeness to her grandmother is revealed through her writings. She also gives a detailed account of the customs and traditions in the Nair family; the performances of Ottanthullal dancers; the theatre group which she and her friends established. She received a proper education, first at Nalapat and then at Calcutta. Her childhood was full of laughter and happiness and its account covers more than half the length of her autobiography.

Dhanwanti Rama Rau was the sixth child of her parents. An Inheritance (1977)[22] describes the domestic training which was given to the girls of the family from the childhood. They were taught to inculcate the womanly virtues of Sita and Savitri. And all this was done to conform to the conservative male outlook! Dhanwanti's mother was much concerned about the well being of her daughters and therefore, she wanted them to be highly educated. She had been a mute witness to much maltreatment of the women in her family by her mother-in-law. Dhanwanti, despite the opposition from the family, but with the support of her mother, was admitted to the Presidency College of Madras in 1909. It was a "brave decision" in those days and braver still was her mother's approval to take up a teaching job for economic independence.

Shudha Mazumdar's father considered her birth to be an important moment in 1899 and had noted it down. Her childhood was spent in keeping 'vratas' to get a good husband and little Shudha was taught that it was "a sin to displease one's father", and naturally the same applied to the husband also. She describes in *A Pattern of Life* (1977)[23] how the women of the house lived in the inner rooms of the house while the father occupied the outer rooms. He followed a western style of life and gave Shudha a good education in a

Christian School. Shudha's autobiography expresses her awareness of being a female as she narrates that as a child she was taught that the female was inferior to the male. Hence her mother did not allow her to eat meat even though her brothers ate it and her father did not disallow her. As it was considered a sin to revolt against the husband, Shudha's mother did not object to anything; but she did tell her husband that if he wanted a trouble-free future for his unorthodox child, he should leave a part of his estate in Shudha's name. When she found that he did not heed her advice, she withdrew the girl from the school.

The picture of a remarkable and awe-inspiring childhood is presented by Durgabai Deshmukh in her autobiography *Chintaman and I* (1980)[24]. Her father taught her to be selfless and to have a humanitarian approach towards life. Her autobiography reveals her being unaware of womanliness. It is only natural that the account of her childhood does not include any personal descriptions, and she elaborates her deeds in public life, which she indulged in from the age of twelve. Instead of reprimanding her for her outspoken behaviour, her parents encouraged and aided her. Thus Durgabai, with the help of women's organizations took out protest marches against wife beating and other women's causes like the 'purdah' system, the 'Devdasi' culture. She belonged to a traditional Hindu family and was married at the age of eight to the son of a 'zamindar'. But she refused to live with her husband and later divorced him so that he could marry again. This was in 1930. When she was twelve years old, she organised a meeting for the women of her town to be addressed by Gandhiji, so that they could be inspired to abandon 'purdah'. She was also an active member of the nationalist movement. As literacy was bound to lift the veil of ignorance, Durgabai's autobiography reveals keenness for the women to be educated. Hence she founded the Andhra Mahila Sabha in 1940. She did her Matric from the Banaras Hindu University and her B.A. from Andhra

University in 1939; she also studied law and became a criminal lawyer of Madras.

Kamaladevi Chattopadhya, whom Raja Rao calls "the most august woman on the Indian scene today" in the Preface to the autobiography, emphasizes the encouragement she received as the girl child by her `nani' and her mother to become emancipated and to develop aesthetic skills. They in their turn had been influenced by Annie Besant. Inner Recesses Outer Spaces (1986)[25] reveals her familial background which aided her development. She was allowed to do whatever she desired, her father was her `closest companion' and she felt a vacuum in her life after his death. She realised the apartheid against women, when, after her father's death, his property was taken over by his step son; being girls, she and her sister were not allowed any share in inheritance:

> "But it was Mother's self-esteem as a woman that was deeply hurt ... All the vast property the largesse to no part of which we, the girls, qualified because of our sex, all went to a stepbrother ... "[26]

She became bitter and was "transformed into a responsible woman" who had to fight for women's rights. Helped by reformists like Gopal Krishna Gokhale, Justice Ranade and Annie Besant, she joined the national movement. The work does not throw much light on her personal life.

The next point of discussion centres around marriage, which is the most persistent of myths which imprisons a woman; and with it the relationship with the husband; the mother-in-law syndrome is another important and related matter of the discourse. The present-day woman may decline marriage or may opt for dual-career marriages; they may even decide to have a live-in relationship. But the times when most of these women autobiographers lived, either before Independence or just after the country gained freedom, marriage was both conventional and mandatory. Therefore, most of these women hoped for a perfect marriage, and the media encouraged it by showing a happy ending in the movies, with the marriage of a hero and a heroine, flashing the sign, "And they lived happily ever after", little realising that the trouble would start only after marriage. Women willingly referred to themselves as Mrs. so-and-so, they still do, not knowing the servitude represented in that nomenclature. Women even today exchange their surname for that of their husbands', not perceiving the confusion it might create in case of a marriage ending in a divorce:

> "Women have long been nameless. They have not been persons. Handed by a father to a another man, the husband, they have been objects of circulation, exchanging one name for another."[27]

A common and absurd practice, which is highlighted in some of these autobiographies, is the change of the first name after marriage.

George Henry Lewes[28] says that it would not be wrong to regard literature as "the expression of the emotions", because women generally take part in "emotions, the whims, the caprices, the enthusiasms". Thus the women's literature "promises a woman's view of life, woman's experience: in other words, a new element". On the other hand it is not possible for men to express life otherwise than as they know it, which again is according to their own experience. He further distinguishes between the two and says that the masculine mind is characterised by the

> "Predominance of intellect and the Feminine by the predominance of the emotions ... Woman, due to her greater affectionateness, her greater range and depth of emotional experience, is well fitted to give expression to the emotional facts of life."[29]

This is well illustrated when we see that autobiographies of the male writers do not give a vivid account of wife and children but mostly concentrate on their career development and their search for vocation. Female autobiographers have almost always discussed their parents, their marriages, their husbands, and their in-laws in detail. For the male autobiographers their success and achievement have been more important than their relationships in life. Hence there is bound to be a thematic difference in the writings of male and female:

> "We are proud of the female culture, of emotion, intuition, love, personal relationships ... It is our male colonisers - it is the male culture - who have defined essential humanity out of their identity and who are 'culturally deprived'."[30]

Sunity Devee reveals that she got married at the age of fourteen to the Maharaja of Cooch Bihar. Belonging to a Brahmo Samaj family, her father was not in favour of her marriage in a royal family, which gave much license to the men. However, he agreed to the alliance on the condition that the marriage be performed according to Brahmo Samaj rites. She says that she was the first woman from the royal family to travel abroad with her husband in 1913. She became the mother of four sons and two daughters. Her autobiography unfolds her willing submission to her husband, though he was only two years older to her. And when he died her "world seemed empty". This was the general feeling of most of the Hindu widows. Sunity Devee lived under the shadow of men all her life; after her husband's death her son looked after her.

Engaged at the tender age of ten, Brinda was taken under the guardianship of her future father-in-law to be taught the etiquette of the future Maharani of Kapurthala. She was sent to Paris, where she became acquainted with the Western ways of life and fell in love with a French man; she did not want to return to the Indian way of life and adapt herself to the old customs and traditions once again.

It was a paradox that she had been sent to France to learn to be a sophisticated, modern woman and was then expected by her husband and father-in-law to conform to the ideal of a docile, timid, obedient Hindu wife. She started defying her husband; the drift between the two widened when she gave birth to three daughters in a row. Her father-in-law was full of contempt for her and restrained her from doing social work for her state. He insisted that she undergo a painful surgery to rectify the fault in her system for not producing a son. Her husband was the obedient son of an autocratic father; she was full of contempt for the two men in her life. The operation failed and her husband was forced to take a second wife.

The women from the Nehru family had quite a happy marriage. Most of them married for love as did Nayantara Sehgal and led a contented, married life. Vijaya Lakshmi Pandit had an arranged marriage at the age of twenty and she willingly changed her maiden name "Sarup Kumari,"which she had never liked, to "Vijaya Lakshmi- the conquering goddess Lakshmi". Later both the husband and the wife became actively involved in the freedom struggle. Once when she was imprisoned for sixteen months, she found her daughters, specially the older Tara, in a gloomy state:

> "I was shocked to see how she must have suffered, and now I suffered because of what I had done to the children."[31]

Even though she felt guilty for neglecting her domestic duties, she did not sacrifice her career. What is significant about her autobiography is that she reveals the inheritance rights for women of that time, which Kamala Devi Chattopadhya has also emphasized in her autobiography:

> "As the widow of a man who died intestate and was the member of the joint Hindu family, and because I had no 'offspring', meaning son, I was not entitled to any part of the joint immovable property."[32]

She fought legal battles through social organisations and got the Hindu Code Bill passed. She had a successful political career and was India's ambassador to Russia, U.S.A. and England. She was also elected the President of the eighth session of the General Assembly of the United Nations. Later she was made the Governor of Maharashtra. Her political achievements did not negate her womanly qualities.

Sita Rathnamala had been treated by a doctor during her illness in the city, with whom she fell in love, as she grew older. The doctor, a Brahmin, had reservations about his relationship with Sita. Her autobiography reveals the pathetic condition of the woman, who ultimately decided to end her relationship on a Diwali day. Trained to be a nurse she returned to her village in the Nilgiri hills, among the tribals.

Kamala Dongerkery, in *On the Wings of Time* (1968),describes some prevalent customs and traditions in the country in her writings. She had received good education and was married at the age of eleven. But what helped her in her in-laws' house was her capability to adjust in the large family. She had been trained to respect patriarchy and to believe that the male child was the primary supporter of the family. One of the main concerns of the women autobiographers has been the mother-in-law syndrome, a part of the Indian culture since times immemorial. Kamala Dongerkery discusses the dictatorial behaviour and the acerbic tongue of her mother-in-law, on whom she depended financially too, as her husband handed over his salary to his mother. The old lady tortured her more because she was childless. What is remarkable about this work is that the writer brings out a sense of achievement, even while living in adverse circumstances. She established her identity by becoming a social worker in Maharashtra; she also achieved success as a handicraft critic and later published many books on Indian handicraft.

After fulfilling the promise made to herself to be successful in life, Urmila Haksar married Shri P.N.Haksar. What is paradoxical to the whole vein of her autobiography is that no where in her work does she mention her maiden name "Urmila Sapru", but calls herself by her married name. Perhaps she did it to gain respectability and immunity for saying some bold things in her autobiography.

Kamala Das's childhood account reads like any other autobiography by any other woman. It is only after marriage that her "self-revealation" becomes bold and she bares it all to her readers. She was married to a relative working in the Reserve Bank, after the country gained Independence. Her romantic ideas of life with a man were shattered soon after her betrothal; there was no tenderness in her fiancé who only wanted to maul her body. After marriage his behaviour was insensitive and purely physical and she calls it a kind of rape; in the process she suddenly grew up:

> "A coldness took hold of my heart then. I knew then that if love was what I had looked for in marriage I would have to look for it outside its legal orbit. I wanted to be given an identity that was lovable."[33]

Her experiences as a mother have an endearing quality; she was happy looking after her son. Her husband, however, used to feel irritated with the baby around the house; his callous behaviour made Kamala Das decide to be "unfaithful to him, at least physically". No other woman autobiographer has dared to reveal such intimate details about her physical body, her sex-relationships or her extra-marital affairs. Kamala Das describes her disgust at her husband's homosexual activities and says that she often contemplated suicide. Eventually, however, she reconciled to her plight and decided to mould herself into a new being. She resolved not to live a loveless life and began looking for a right man to love her. She met men of different ages and of various types and most of them loved her to satisfy their own needs. A serious illness made her write her autobiography to meet the doctor's bills; she had become a writer of repute. People could not understand her unnatural yearnings to look for happiness outside marriage. Her narration breaks down all the cultural barriers of feminine modesty, which at times shocks the conservative readers. There is no mother-in-law to torture her, no customary family responsibilities to hinder her progress; it is only the conflict within her, which does not allow her to be at peace with herself. Her own hopes and aspirations to gain something more out of life bring about the turmoil in her existence.

Dhanwanti Rama Rau was married to an ICS officer in a registered marriage, which, she explains, allowed her the freedom later in life in case of lack of adjustment, to divorce her husband. She was given the new name of "Sita" after marriage, but she never encouraged her in-laws to call her by this name. However, her Cambridge-educated husband did not call his wife by any name and showed no intimacy towards her in public. He did not appreciate her interaction with people; but his behaviour did not deter Dhanwanti from developing into an individual in her own right.

Shudha Mazumdar was married at the age of thirteen to a man who was in Bengal Civil Service. At his insistence, she gave up "purdah" and learnt to read and write in order to become a perfect wife. She also became a social worker, adapted new ways of life, but never abandoned her traditional values learnt at her parents' home. After husband's death she defied the social norms and wore coloured sarees and attended meetings abroad.

Despite all her education, Durgabai states that, she remained "almost a rustic" and was, therefore, hesitant to accept the marriage proposal of C.D.Deshmukh, the then Finance Minister in the Nehru Ministry. However, the marriage proved to be happy and successful as the two individuals respected each other. Both cared for one another "and found a kindred soul in each other" and Durgabai had no hang-ups in looking after the needs of her husband:

> "When I look back over the twenty-six years of our married life, I cannot find even a single instance where we differed significantly. Thus, there was no question of adjustment because adjustment and compromise arise only when one differs basically from the other on a significant matter. We are assimilated in one another and were integrated as a whole like Parvati and Parameshwar."[34]

Vijayraje Scindia, who was "Lekha" before marriage agreed to the change of her name. In *Princess: The Autobiography of the Dowager Maharani of Gwalior* (1985) she says that her husband was her God and to please him she became a non-vegetarian. She was a broken woman after his death. Due to differences in political ideology, she suffered alienation from her only son. Her autobiography is an account of the plight of a woman, her pain, her sorrow and her sacrifice.

Kamala Devi Chattopadhya's marriage to her friend Sarojini Naidu's brother was a failure. And hence her autobiography does not discuss much of her married life.

Virginia Woolf had recorded in her diary that she was forty years old when she found that she could talk freely about her life. It is quite possible that women feel that they can indulge in the act of self-creation, which is also confessional and self-revealing, when they have reached the middle age. In order to confront the society one needs either the dare devil attitude of youth or the shrewd, cold and calculating mind of the middle age. Erik Erikson has observed that autobiographies

> "are written at certain late stages of life for the purpose of re-creating oneself in the image of one's own method; and they are written to make that image convincing."[35]

Woman's involvement in her early life in responsibilities, duties, preoccupation, living life day to day make her forget her right to be called a woman. But as she was becoming older, "She may well for the first time be woman herself."[36] Hence it is no great surprise that women are "well beyond youth when they begin, often unconsciously, to create another story".[37]

Let us therefore, review the ages of some of the women autobiographers who found courage to tell the story of their lives. Sunity Devee wrote *The Autobiography of an Indian Princess* at the age of fifty; Dhanwanti Rama Rau's *An Inheritance* was written when she was eighty years old. *A Pattern of Life* by Shudha Mazumdar was written when she was thirty-one, but the book was published only when she was seventy-eight years old. Shoilabala Das wrote *A Look Before and After* at the age of eighty-two. Vijaya Lakshmi Pandit's *The Scope of Happiness* was written by the time she was seventy-five years old.

A woman is expected to be petite, demure, passive and attractive; she is not encouraged to be active, assertive, competitive and unattractive. Most women writers do not write "about the condition of being born homely". It is something, which is important for every woman from the moment she becomes conscious of her physical appearance:

> "Every girl who lacks beauty knows instinctively that she belongs to an underprivileged group, and that to climb up and out she will have to be cleverer and stronger and more ruthless perhaps than she would choose to be."[38]

This is particularly true of Urmila Haksar who was conscious not only of her uncomely looks but also of the winsome looks of her sister. Hence, she concentrated more on her studies and, being intelligent, excelled in her student-life. Kamala Das says that her grandmother was anxious for her dark skin and would rub the turmeric on her body and would oil her curly hair regularly to make her more beautiful. On the other hand, attractive women like Dhanvanti Rama Rau, Vijaya Lakshmi Pandit or Nayantara Sehgal have not tried to highlight their good looks.

Georges Gusdorf[39] observes that each person thinks himself to be a special being, worthy of special interest"; this makes him write about himself and his life in an autobiography. The individual narrates his life because he thinks that his existence is significant to the world, and his death, in all probability, would leave the world incomplete. It, therefore, implies that the individual thinks himself to be a "unique self" with a special identity; the process of writing then becomes, *thorough* self-*revealation*, a "quest for identity." It can be affirmed, that the autobiographical work develops as the author develops.[40] Related to this process of development is a question which a true autobiographer, according to A.O.J.Cockshut[41] has to answer, "How did I become what I am?" It is this process of conversion, which was first seen in Augustine's *Confessions*. How many of these women autobiographers have been able to establish their identity through their writings? How many of these women autobiographers can answer the crucial question put forth by Cockshut? There are not many, but undoubtedly some women autobiographers have accomplished the task of revealing their true self quite successfully.

Most noteworthy for self-expression and for writing and divulging her own point of view, to establish her distinctive personality is ofcourse Kamala Das. The society, with its conventions and taboos, puts some barriers for women, which restrain them from rising above a certain level. But women have proved, through a latent consciousness that they can ably break all the hurdles of conventions fixed by society for them and can liberate themselves and also establish their identity. My Story is one such work, which reveals the individuality of Kamala Das. Other names, which can be added to the list, are of Cornelia Sorabji, Sita Rathnamala,

Shudha Mazumdar, Urmila Haksar, Dhanwanti Rama Rau, Brinda, Durgabai Deshmukh and Vijaya Lakshmi Pandit. In the Foreword to Mrs. Pandit's book The Earl Mountbatten wrote:

> "Nan Pandit's charming, well-written and informative autobiography gives an insight into a remarkable woman."[42]

It is true of all these women who have been remarkable in every sense of the word, have not been deterred by the prevalent customs and traditions in achieving their goal in life and have affirmed their identity through their writings. They have all been achievers in their own social fields and have risen above the "collective consciousness" of women at large. Coming from different socio-cultural backgrounds, they refused to play second fiddle to male supremacy. "Tolerance is a virtue that has always appealed to me", wrote Durgabai Deshmukh in the "Summing up" of her autobiography. And this appears to have been true of each one of these Indian women autobiography writers. They have not been cowed down by the adverse situations in life, but phoenix-like have risen with a new vigour, a new determination and a new perspective to fight against the odds of circumstances. They have been achievers in life:

> "It implies that each found in a public role the chief purpose of life; and thus they came to understand themselves mainly through the reflection of themselves that they saw in the reaction of others."[43]

Writing an autobiography for each of them has been a novel experience where a woman's

> "own gender status and her female models (mother, grandmother, mentor friend) contribute to a concept of self and quality of writing voice that are distinctly of women."[44]

REFERENCES

1. *Writing a Woman's Life*, The Woman's Press Ltd.,1989, p. 27.
2. Bernard Shaw, *Candida*, Orient Longmans,1957, p. 79.
3. Elaine Showalter, ed., *Women's Liberation and Literature*, Harcourt Brace, Iovanowich, Inc., New York,U.S.A.,1971, p. 3.
4. "Selves in Hiding", *Women's Autobiography*, ed., Estelle C.Jelinek, Indiana, U.P.,1980, pp. 113-14, 131.
5. *A Literature of Their Own*, Princeton Univ., Press, 1977, p. 13.
6. *Cassell's Encyclopedia of Literature*, Vol. I, London, 1953, p 63.
7. *The Scope of Happiness*, Vikas Publishing House Pvt., Ltd.,1979.
8. *Ibid.,* p. 57.
9. The City of Two Gateways, *The Autobiography of a Girl*,, London, George Allen and Unwin Ltd., 1950
10. *Ibid.,* p. 273.
11. *Maharani: The Story of an Indian Princess*, New York, Henry Holt,1953.
12. *The Future that Was*, New Delhi, Allied Publishers, 1972.
13. *Writing a Woman's Life*, p. 15.
14. Patricia Spacks, "Stages Of Self: Notes On Autobiography and the Life Cycle", in *The American Autobiography*, ed. Albert E.Stone, p. 48.
15. Carolyn G. Heilbrun, "Woman's Autobiographical Writings: New Forms", in *Modern Selves*, ed., Philip Dodd, Frank Cass, 1986, p. 18.
16. *The Autobiography of an Indian Princess*, London, John Murray, 1972.
17. *India Calling; The Memories of Cornelia Sorabji*, London, 1935.
18. *Prison and Chocolate Cake*, London, Victor Gollanez, 1954.
19. *Beyond the Jungle*, London, William Blackwood and sons Ltd., 1968.
20. *My Story*, New Delhi, Sterling Publishers Pvt. Ltd., 1976, Reprint 1991.
21. *Ibid.,* p. 74.
22. *An Inheritance*, New Delhi, Allied Publishers Pvt., Ltd., 1977.
23. *A Pattern of Life*, New Delhi, Manohar, 1977.

24. *Chintaman and I*, Allied Publishers Pvt. Ltd., 1980.
25. *Inner Recesses Outer Spaces, Memoirs*, New Delhi, Navrang, 1986.
26. *Ibid.,* p. 25.
27. *Writing a Woman's Life*, p. 121.
28. "The Lady Novelists," *Women's Liberation and Liberation*, ed.,Elaine Showalter, p. 171-183.
29. *Ibid.,* p. 174.
30. Barbara Burris, The fourth world manifesto', in *Radical Feminism*, ed., Anne Koedtl et all. Quadrangle Books, 1973, P.355, as quoted in *Contemporary Women's Fiction*, Paulina Palmer, Harvester Wheatsheaf, 1989, p. 20.
31. *Scope of Happiness*, p. 114.
32. *Ibid.,* p. 178.
33. *My Story*, p. 95.
34. *Chintaman and I*, p. 76.
35. Life History and the Historical, New York, W.W.Norton, 1975,P.125 as quoted in *Modern Selves*, Essays on Modern British and American Autobiography, ed. by Philip Dodd, Frank Cass & co. Ltd., 1986, p. 21.
36. Carolyn G. Heilbrun, *Writing a Woman's Life*, p. 109.
37. *Ibid.,* p. 131.
38. Catherine Drinker Bowen, Family Portrait,as quoted in *Modern Selves*, ed., pp. 18-19.
39. "Conditions and Limits of Autobiography," *Autobiography: Essays Theoretical and Critical*, ed.James Olney, Princeton University Press, 1980.
40. Peter Abbs," *Autobiography: Quest For Identity*", The Present, Vol. 8., The New Pelican Guide to English Literature, ed., by Boris Ford, 1983, p. 521.
41. *The Art of Autobiography in 19th & 20th Century England*, Yale University Press,1984, p. 16.
42. *The Scope of Happiness*, p. 39.
43. *The Art of Autobiography in 19th. & 20th. Century England*, p. 120.
44. Julia Watson, "Shadowed Presence: Modern Women Writers' Autobiographies and the Other", *Studies in Autobiography*, edited by James Olney, Oxford University Press, 1988, p. 181.

CHAPTER 6

The Female Voice : A Quest for Self-definition

Literature, a means of socio-cultural reforms, intends to expedite the proper and predestined outcome of class struggle. It also helps in bringing about a change of those established norms and traditions, which may be detrimental to the general development of an individual. Writings in English in India have always echoed this quality whether it be in fiction, poetry or the articles in newspapers. There has been another form of writing which has of late started getting recognition as an independent genre of literature not only in the West but also in the Indian sub-continent. The autobiography, which is an expression of self, depicts an individual's quest for self-definition or identity. For a man this poses no problem as no one questioned his journey of self-discovery.

> "Academically autobiography has been a male creation. Riding the tide of New Criticism, critics were quick to establish the literary respectability of the genre-to-be, quick to consider autobiography made in the name of the Father. Autobiography became the story of the male self constructed by himself and creating the metaphors of his life. The more the male dominated autobiography the better the genre."[1]

Traditionally a woman writer, anywhere in the world, and this includes India, was expected to deal only with the romantic narrative concentrating on romantic love leading to conventional marriage. Such form of writing was not only desirable and unobjectionable, but was thought to be the metier of a woman. Consequently for a woman there have been many hurdles on this "voyage of inner-discovery". Thus the initial obstacle which had to be overcome by a female writer on this quest for identity was her encroachment on this hitherto male-dominated stronghold of autobiographical writing. An autobiography is expected to reveal the "hidden forms of inwardness". So the question often asked is can a woman, who is marginalised and is taught from her birth to be self-effacing and selfless, indulge in the luxury of self-exploration which should provide an answer to the question "How did I become what I am?" This problem has been associated with gender prejudice and has been very tersely put forth by Susan Stanford Friedman:

> "A ....man has the luxury of forgetting his .... sex. He can think of himself as an 'individual'. Women ....reminded at every turn in the great cultural hall of mirrors of their sex ......have no such luxury."[2]

Women have revolted against these established prejudices and have been successful autobiographers. Infact recent feminist critics have indicated an antipathy towards this nomenclature i.e. autobiography and have suggested alternatives like autogynography, liflines, personal narratives.

There is nothing unnatural in a woman's literary creativity, which is an extension of her biological creativity. And given a room of her own, she is quite capable of writing her life's account. There are some very interesting dissimilarities to be noted between the writings of a woman and a man, not only in India but elsewhere in the world too. A woman's autobiography generally focuses on the various relationships like those with her parents, her siblings and later with her spouse, children and her mother-in-law. This last is a typical characteristic of an Indian woman autobiographer. It is as if her identity is established and proved only on the basis of these relationships in her life. But a man's autobiography is mainly concerned with his success story, his life-achievements; very rarely does he give a vivid account of his wife and children. George Henry Lewes finds that a woman's literature "promises a woman's view of life, woman's experience: in other words a new element." He further adds that

> "Masculine mind is characterised by the predominance of the intellect, and the Feminine by the predominance of the emotions ....Woman, by her greater affectionateness, her greater range and depth of emotional experience, is well-fitted to give expression to the emotional facts of life ...."[3]

A number of Indian women have felt confident of taking up this form of life-narrative and have not been inhibited in telling the world about themselves. Prominent among them have been Sunity Devee with *The Autobiography of an Indian Princess* (1921); *With no Regrets: An Autobiography* (1943) by Krishna Hutheesingh; *Girl in Bombay* (1947) by Ishwani Pseud; Savitri Devi Nanda's *The City of Two Gateways: The Autobiography of an Indian Girl* (1950); *Maharani: The Story of an Indian Princess* (1953) by Brinda; *Prison and Chocolate Cake* (1954) and *From Fear Set Free* (1962) by Nayantara Sahgal; *The Scope of happiness* (1979) by Vijaylakshmi Pandit; Kamala Devi Chattopadhya's *Inner Recesses Outer Spaces* (1986); Yamini Krishnamurthy's *Passion for Dance* (1996) to name a few down the years.

What is noteworthy as well as surprising in some of these works is that their writers have felt the need to specify their genderic attributes in the titles of their autobiograohies. Germaine Bree puts a very valid question in this regard:

"…..did the title imply that autobiographies written by women constituted a subgenre? Or a different genre – in which latter case perhaps they should acquire a different label?"[4]

The prevailing pattern in these life-narratives is of their writers being very conscious of being born as females. Subsequently they reveal the discrimination against them since their childhood. A few retaliated by dressing and behaving as a boy. Since marriage, generally an arranged one, was thought to be the ultimate goal of a girl's life, she was taught various domestic chores. Her married life was not always a happy one but the woman did not have the courage and the inclination to revolt; this was due to the teachings instilled in her from her very young days that a woman always needed the support of a man. However, certain autobiographies highlight the emancipation of women – so we have Cornelia Sorabjee, Vijaylakshmi Pandit, Kamala Devi Chattopadhya, Durgabai Deshmukh, who helped in bringing about a change in the society and in its norms towards women.

Virginia Wolf had recorded in her diary that she was forty years old when she found that she could talk freely about her life. It is quite possible that women feel they can indulge in the act of self-creation, which is also confessional and self-revealing, when they have reached life's middle age. In order to confront the society, one needs either the dare devil attitude of youth or the shrewd, cold and calculating mind of the middle age. A woman's involvement in her early life in responsibilities, duties, the preoccupation of living life day to day make her forget her right to be called a woman. But once as she staets ageing, "she may well for the first time be woman herself"[5]. Hence it is no great surprise that women are "well beyond youth when they begin, often unconsciously, to tell another story".[6]

The women autobiographers mentioned above were generally the princesses, political activists, and social workers.

But their autobiographies were very "traditional" and provocative as they delineated the women and their lives lived in the socially defined slot for them; their roles were well defined on the basis of their relationships with others. A couple of women had revolted against the pre-determined life-patterns; but by and large a woman's autobiography was a definition of her subjectivity as seen against the backdrop of something more powerful. However, with the publication of *My Story* by Kamala Das in 1976 there emerged a new kind of woman's writing, which was not only bold, daring and tantalising but also self-assertive. Here is a writer who defies all conventional models to retaliate against the worn out social values and traditions which forever hinder and retard the development of a woman's personality, emotionally as well as intellectually.

The autobiography aims at redefining the male-female relationship and is not only a challenging account of the writer's experiences of her life only, but of her body as well. In Kamala Das we have what Shaw would call a "New Woman" – a woman conscious of her femininity and determined to vindicate it against the male supremacy. The autobiography defines the personality of Kamala Das as it has been made by the dictates of the society. Thus a "good" girl is made to rebel against the established socio-cultural barriers of feminine modesty which at times shocks the conservative readers. The frank and confessional language, which helped in transcending her "marginal self", prompted her critics to brand her as an exhibitionist.

The essence of *My Story* is its authenticity about the autobiographer's feminine sensibility. In it she introduces herself as a daughter, a mother, a wife, a poet; but what is more important is that she is conscious of her woman's identity which is an amalgam of all these personalities. Identity to Kamala Das did not mean fitting in a predefined slot;

> "Dress in saris, be a girl
> Be a wife, they said. Be an embroiderer, be a cook,
> Be a quarreler with servants, Fit in, oh,
> Belong, cried the categorisers"
>
> (An Introduction)

Kamala Das learnt to defy these pre-established canons of feminine identity; for her it was important to be a woman and a lover with a body and a soul. The autobiography becomes a vehicle for voicing an "inner privacy", and a protest against the senseless restrictions which force a sensitive woman to lead an insipid life.

A significant and important aspect of *My Story* is the description of such experiences, which only a woman can have. These are the personal accounts of childbirth which, Cynthia Huff[7], in her essay "Delivery: The Cultural Representation Childbirth" observes that it is the characteristic of a cultural phenomenon; it also embodies metaphorically physical as well as external creation. Kamala Das's autobiography has three such textual accounts of physical creations, narrated probably for the first time in the history of Indian women writings in English.

The writing was started to distract her mind, to help her recover from a grave illness and also to take care of hospital bills. The time had come when Kamala Das found a voice of her own, but it was only when she realised that she was face to face with Death.

> "I wanted to empty myself of all the secrets so that I could depart when the time came, with a scrubbed-out conscience"[8]

Autobiographical writing can prove to be cathartic as it can help the writer in coming to terms with herself. In the case of Kamala Das, *My Story* gave her "the courage to move forward into as yet unnarrated and unexplored ways of living"[9]. It also gave her abundant happiness in the process.

> "I have written several books in my lifetime, but none of them provided the pleasure to me as the writing of *My Story* has given me. I have nothing more to say."[10]

We read a woman's autobiography for other reasons than we read her novels, diaries, and letters or edited papers. We read these feminine writings to hear from, learn from some specific historical figures about how they found their own voice not only in these autobiographical writings but as a product of historical forces. These works also elucidate how the author acquired or came to do without a room of her own; how she came to command an audience "rhetorically, ideologically and socio-economically"[11]. The story illuminates the correlation between the act of finding a voice and of using it too. This is what makes an autobiography a privileged form of historical agency for a woman.

The writing of an autobiography involves the process of reinventing one's self. Kamala Das did it when she wrote *My Story;* she has done it again by her conversion to Islam. Kamala Das has kicked up "yet another storm with her conversion to Islam". A retired Professor and a CPI(M) activist, Nabeesa Ummal, has observed, "I challenge her to write a book like *My Story* now. She will face the same fatwa and fate as Bangladeshi writer Taslima Nasreen"[12]. But Kamala Das nee *Suraiya* could not care less. For her the "burqa" is a symbol of "protection" and at the age of sixty-five she needs it more than ever! The freedom, which she enjoyed as a Hindu, will not be allowed to her now. "Who needs freedom?" retorts *Suraiya*. In an interview given to Times of India (19 December 1999,) she *tells* that she was wary of freedom:

> "I don't want freedom. I had enough of it thrust on me. Freedom had become a burden for me ......I want a master to protect me. I wanted protection and not freedom. I want to be subservient to *Allah*"[13]

The Kamala Das of earlier days, the swallow, which resisted from being tamed, had been undergoing a metamorphosis of sorts even earlier to her conversion:

> "Before I was the rebellious type I used to move around a lot, involve myself in various activities; most of the time taking risks and living dangerously. Now I have changed. I have become a virtuous, clean woman. A puritan in all senses who prays daily, wears white clothes and is conservative in thinking".[14]

However she had been transformed into a woman who said she loved the orthodox lifestyle of Muslim women:

> "I want guidelines to regulate and discipline my life. I want a master to protect me .... My husband died seven years ago and I am now a lonely widow who is 67 years old. When he was there he provided me with protection. I had not to bother about getting tickets, passport, visas and such other things. I just had to follow him".[15]

It is apparent that the swallow had really been tamed and now it missed the master and was lonely. But can the conversion also be viewed as an evolution of a woman who had come full circle? She found freedom an encumbrance and needed the solace of a protective religion like Islam and a merciful God like *Allah*. Her comments in her other writing seems to suggest that she might have longed for a more circumscribed existence for some years then. Nevertheless what needs to be questioned is the sincerity of her decision not only now but in her earlier life too. How genuine were her expressions in *My Story* and how sincere are they now? They may be "bold" and "unconventional", but somewhere in the mind of the reader there lurks the doubt to regard all her statements and actions, flamboyant gestures as publicity gimmicks. Nevertheless we cannot but agree with Dom Moraes's recent remark "much may be forgiven those who write well" and we realise that the female voice of Kamala Das continues to define itself.

REFERENCES

1. Cynthia Huff, "Delivery: The cultural Representation of childbirth", in *Autobiography and Questions of Gender*, ed. Shirley Neuman, Frank Cass & Co. Ltd.,1991, p. 108.
2. Susan Stanford Friedman, as quoted in *Autobiography and Questions of Gender*, p. 2.
3. George Henry Lewes, "The Lady Novelists", in *Women's Liberation and Litrature"*, ed. Elaine Showalter. Harcourt Brace, Iovanowich, Inc., New York, USA, 1971, p. 171-83.
4. Germaine Bree, "Autogynography" in *Studies in Autobiography.* ed. James Olney, Oxford University Press, New York, 1988, p.171.
5. Carolyn G. Heilbrun, *Writing a Woman's Life*, Woman's Press, London, 1988, p. 131.
6. *Ibid.*
7. Cynthia Huff, "Delivery ....childbirth", p.108.
8. Kamala Das, *My Story*, Sterling Publishers Pvt. Ltd., 1991, Preface.
9. Carolyn G. Heilbrun, "Women's Autobiographical Writings: New Forms", in *Modern Selves, Essays on Modern British & American Autobiography*, ed. Philip C. Dodd, p. 21.
10. *My Story*, Preface.
11. T.L. Broughton, "Women's Autobiography: The Self at Stake in *Autobiography and Questions of Gender*, p. 79.
12. *India Today*, December 27,1999.
13. http:www.timesofindia.com/191299/19conim3.htm
14. *Ibid.*
15. *Ibid.*

Dom Moraes's Never at Home : Alienation and Search for Identity

While trying to finish his second autobiography, Dom Moraes had given strict instructions to his household that no matter what happened he was not to be disturbed during any part of the day. On finishing the book, he revoked the orders and immediately had a phone call from a friend:

> " 'Where in hell have you been?' he asked. `I have been phoning you all day for a week. I've even phoned you at night, and they say you're somewhere else, they don't know where. Are you never at home?'"[1]

Dom Moraes found in this outburst the title of his autobiography, which somewhat accidentally emphasised Moraes's feeling of being rootless and restless. The loss of identity, which he had faced, and which had made him take up the job of a globe-trotting, investigative journalist, had alienated him more and more from his poetry, from the land of his birth and also from England, where he had decided to settle after leaving India. His search for roots, for a permanent home and for the rejuvenation of poetry in 1982 form the backdrop of his second autobiography appropriately called *Never At Home*.

Moraes wrote his first autobiography *My Son's Father* at the age of thirty and was called presumptuous to write his life's history at such an early age. The autobiographical practice is a process of inner assimilation and is generally undertaken much later in life. Though his first book was more revealing and more ruminative, the second book does depict a self-portrait of distinction. *Never At Home* picks up from where *My Son's Father* left off. It moves at a fervent speed and as we accompany Moraes on his journey across the globe we see the world through his eyes; we meet dozens of leaders and statesmen. As a writer he covered events like the Eichmann trial in Israel; travelled in Asia, Africa, the Americas; made television documentaries for the BBC, wrote for a number of foreign newspapers and worked for the UN. As an investigative journalist, he rushed around the world in pursuit of stories, like perhaps no other Indian journalist has ever done. Therefore it is not merely a case of name-dropping, which is seen in the book, Moraes has done serious reporting too. "A poet, a restless pilgrim, and a keen observer of the world around, Dom Moraes is remarkable as a writer and a commentator on man's struggle for survival. His life-story is both fascinating and poignant."[2] This account is filled up with numerous incidents and anecdotes which are described distinctly. The book has the best prose that we can find written today by an Indian writer, even though Moraes frequently stresses that he does not want to be merely a prose writer.

Never At Home covers the period between 1974-1990 in Dom Moraes's life : a period of anguish, search for identity, and of alienation from his mad mother, his motherland and his first wife. The Muse of poetry, feeling neglected, had suddenly deserted him after he had won accolades as a poet. He felt disconsolate and experienced the symptoms of withdrawal. The autobiography as a genre is a search for identity, which begins due to a feeling of alienation from one's surroundings. In the case of Dom Moraes, it is a withdrawal from the mother, from the country, its sociocultural and metaphysical background. It resulted in a forceful severing of his tellurian moorings. Alienation is one of the ailments of the modern world. Superficially the malady is purely a subjective feeling of unease, dissociation or exile.

It would be wrong to say that alienation is a catastrophe, which strikes a human being externally. Fundamentally, it is a perverted, malignant and self-destructive manifestation of human creativity. People suffering from it find it difficult to "identify" with the social and spiritual conditions of their existence. Alienation makes the individual feel oppressed and though he may not know, the feeling is of his own making. "Ultimately it implies that modernity is the loss or disruption of an original unity, and may also suggest that a day of reconciliation in a `higher unity' is about to dawn."[3]

Dom Moraes's identity lay in his capability to write poetry which he had done ever since he was a pimple-pocked adolescent and had blurted out to Stephen Spender: "I want to be a poet."[4] He wrote a poem called "French Lesson" at the age of sixteen which won him the praise of Nissim Ezekiel, who had remarked, "This is a good poem. It's a first poem you have ever written." After that there was no looking back and he became the youngest and the first non-English writer to win the Hawthornden Prize in 1958.

The account of the loss of his poetic inspiration, though written indirectly, is a painful refrain in the autobiography. It nags Moraes quite frequently, even when he is at the peak of his career as a journalist. The search for identity is a persistent theme which is explored in modern Indian literature: "Indian poets in English have failed when they have forgotten that a sense of identity is a perennial sustaining creative force in a poet and that the loss of identity is the root cause of all his problems."[5] What we miss in *Never At Home* is Moraes's grappling the problem; we wish he had paused to describe it vividly and elaborately. Instead we have a full account of his vagrant life as "an international nomad".

Existence to most people achieves significance due to a sense of belonging to some place, with relatives and even a permanent home. But it did not happen to Moraes: he was born in India when it was ruled by the British; he and his family learnt to speak only English:

> ".....I only spoke the English language; the Indian languages were foreign to me. So were Indian traditions, Indian customs, and an entire style of life. This alienation was added to, because, through much of my childhood and adolescence, my mother was mentally ill, and this affected my emotions and attitudes considerably. I blamed India for my mother, and my mother for India. Very early on, I started to write poetry in English." (P. viii)

He left for England at the age of sixteen, because he thought it to be his real home and felt that he had taken root. He lived there for the next fifteen years. The prose and poetry, which he wrote, were acclaimed by people and he had a sense of belonging to that country. But there was an inherent uneasiness in him, perhaps because everyone in Britain had not accepted him:

> "I had not been fully accepted in India because I did not seem Indian, though by birth I was. I realised that I was not fully accepted in England because the colour of my skin said I wasn't English, though because of my upbringing and conditioning, I had assumed a nationality." (P. viii)

Dom Moraes's quest for identity is the reflection of any modern man who is without roots of any kind : social, spiritual, personal or any other. But Moraes is different from his counterpart in his loss of vocation and also of nationality. "Poetry cannot exist in a vacuum;" writing poetry was important to him: it was an escape from the task of facing a mad mother. She was an obsession with him, but at the same time he longed for the old mother, one who was not insane and whom we meet in My *Son's Father*. In place of a woman who was "radiant, a rustle of scent and silk," he now encountered a maniac who would shout at the slightest provocation, smash crockery and furniture, He was alienated from her and *Never At Home* opens with Dom Moraes's feeling of horror and considering his mother to be a problem. She was the reason for not returning to the country of his birth:

> "One of the reasons I had travelled 7,000 miles was to obviate the possibility of seeing her. Before I left India, I felt nauseated, and went into a cold sweat every time I saw her." (p. 7)

She was the "albatross" round his neck; the very sight of her made him feel nauseated and though he hated himself for it, there was very little he could do to alleviate the feeling. Her death in 1989 rejuvenated him:

> "As we took the corpse out of the morgue and to the crematorium, the undertaker's men holding handkerchiefs to their noses, it struck me that all this might represent for me the shedding of an obsession, and some kind of belated rebirth." (p. 3)

Moraes shocks us with a vehement hatred for his mother; social norms require a repression of such negative feelings for one's parent; but a good autobiography needs its expression especially if it gives a better insight into the author's personality. Most of his adult life had been an escape from his mother as she had turned his childhood and adolescence "into a macabre kind of purgatory". But life does not stop at death and Moraes forgot his mother and his famous father, Frank Moraes, as he continued his life's journey.

In 1961 Pandit Nehru ordered the Indian forces to take over Goa, the place which made Moraes feel almost euphoric and gave him a sense of belonging on his occasional visits to India. The conquest of Goa by the Indian army made him feel ashamed to be known as an Indian and while the English press lauded his stance, the Indian government withdrew his passport. He applied for a British passport which was issued to him quite easily:

> "But if I had had a subconscious desire to alienate myself from the country of my birth, I couldn't have chosen a better way to do it." (p. 42)

The act uprooted him altogether from the country of his birth:

> "I felt English; my attitudes to life were English; whatever sense of humour I had was English; I thought myself accepted in England for whatever I was. It was not that, like a gem in Diaspora, I had to disguise my difference. The colour of my skin was not English, but my mind was." (p. 43)

It was very important for Moraes to be accepted by the British society and therefore his anger knew no bounds when once a policeman frisked him up because he looked like an immigrant. Later he realised that he was in reality an immigrant and knew very little about the way of life of the other immigrants. (P.94) Moraes decided to do a film on the Asian immigrants with the BBC. Part of the film dealt with his own life and its approval by the British society.

By 1965 Moraes had published three books of verse and felt that he could have written much more. His anthology of *Poems* 1955-1965 was brought out by Macmillan. Commenting on the book, the poet-critic Hayden Carruth felt that the poems did not have any literary value and Moraes, with his talent for poetry, should write about India and its innumerable problems. Moraes was shocked and hurt at his suggestion and felt that the comment was uncalled for. In his opinion, he was incompetent to write about India, "except as a foreigner". (P.66) He did not know the Indian languages and had not travelled extensively in the land of his birth: he was paranoid about re-visiting India. But no one could understand these negative feelings of the man.

With this kind of perspective about India and himself, Moraes plunged into a dark period of his life, which he terms as "wholly barren". He failed to write any poetry. R. Parthasarthy says that aphasia or loss of poetic speech inflicts every poet sometime in his life and he should be ready for it. But Moraes was unable to reconcile with his state of being and inability to write a poem nagged him constantly. The melancholy deepened as many of his friends were poets and did not have his problem:

> "Things had never been like this before. I had had breaks in my poetry, but never such a block as this. My whole intention in life had been to write good poetry, but now, not very satisfied with what I had already produced, I was unable to continue." (p. 92)

By the time Moraes was thirty, he had written six books of verse and one book of prose. He was commissioned by his English and American publishers to write his autobiography, *My Son's Father,* which largely dealt with his childhood, his arrival in London and ended when he was twenty two years of age. The death of poetry bothered him even when he was busy with the film on immigrants in the summer of 1968. He had never "experienced this crippledom, this matyrdom." So much so that he could not read the verses of other people. The relationship with his first wife had "fallen apart" and only the embrace of his son, Francis, gave him a sense of security.

His publisher suggested that he should write a book on Indira Gandhi's India. The BBC too liked the idea of Moraes going back to India and decided to make a film on the country. While in India, he clung to his English friends, as they were the true representatives of the life he knew and felt frightened of India and its people. Its villagers "were alien and incomprehensible" to him (p. 103) and he was convinced that he could never really understand India. His wife and son were attacked with stones on the beach in Bombay and he felt it was another instance of mindless violence which characterised the Indian behaviour.(p. 113) He later realised that they were very friendly people and he should have mixed with them : "I felt sympathetic towards India."(P.109) The sense of alienation from the country of his birth was predominantly due to its association with his mother. "It was not a question of out of sight, out of mind."(P.108)

However, on this visit he did go to meet his mother with his wife and son and found that she was after all "an inoffensive old lady".(P.112) Her room had an air of sadness and he felt sorrow and pity "for a world in which there was so much personal loss".(P.112) The feeling of nausea, always associated with his mother, came sweeping back when he saw dozens of rats "with red and evil eyes" on the raftered roof of the room. (p.112)

After Bombay the family went to Bhutan; on the way to a Monastery on a mountaintop, Moraes felt a strong urge to surrender himself to the chasm below. Had it not been for his son, whom he clutched in his arms, he would have hurled himself from the slopes of the mountains. Such was the effect of the "very bad days"(P.147) on him:

> "My attempts to write poetry were completely futile. The old excitement, the thrill in the blood that produced a poem, the rhythms that had sung themselves in my head, the complete lines that came out of nowhere, none of these visited me any more, nor could they be compelled to do so. I could not put their absence out of my mind".(p. 147)

This trip to India was fateful in another sense too; his wife left him and Moraes toured Rajasthan, Calcutta and East Pakistan with his friends. But he still did not want his Indian passport back. He had been away from England for more than two years and knew that he would not get lucarative assignments either in England or in America. He felt anathematic and "claustrophobic" at the idea of settling down in India, even though he was aware that the subcontinent offered him a far more interesting life than was to be found elsewhere. But since he had made a great endeavour to establish himself outside India, he thought it to be a better idea to go back. What bothered him more than anything else was the "writer's block":

> "Most writers I know have suffered from it, particularly novelists. None of them are really able to understand why it happens. Allen Tate, as he once told me, had a block very similar to mine; his block, like mine, was only for poetry".(p. 187)

A person's identity gives him the strength to survive in the world; to correlate with his fellow beings, to know his social rank. An artist has to create an identity, which Balchandra Rajan defines as "the process of creative self-realisation". He says:

> "A sense of nationality can grow out of the discovery of identity and it is important that this should happen frequently, if one is to establish a tradition that is both distinctive and rooted".[7]

For Moraes the constraints of identity and its loss became irredeemable. Every person, he says, wears a mask, which he allows the world to see; it is not a difficult thing to do. Moraes's mask was that of a casual person, unconcerned and unaffected by the worldly affairs: he was a poet, a war correspondent:

> "I could respond to the demands of my mask, and offer its smile, with some confidence, to others. Behind this mask, I thought, lay my identity, which was not to be exposed. It was by keeping the identity, not the mask, that I remained alive. The identity contained all the experiences the mask had, but experienced them differently. A great part of my identity lay in my ability to write poetry, and also in knowing exactly what world I belonged to." (p. 310)

Now that he did not write poetry, he did not know to which world he belonged to. It was a new problem for him as he wore a mask without an identity. He was more or less living in exile from England and had married again.

Early in 1982, the Muse of poetry visited him in the city of Bombay as he walked "by the polluted sea":

> "A peculiar shiver ran down my spine, and at first I thought I must be ill. Then I recognised my own symptoms. I had not felt like this for seventeen years."(p. 328)

Words and phrases came tumbling into his mind and on returning home he wrote a poem and felt the purity of power pouring out of him. He forgot the world, his surroundings and was conscious only of himself and his writing. He called the poem "Absences". He was not very confident about the permanence of rejuvenation of his poetic powers and felt euphoric when he could write another piece of poetry, "Visitors". Feeling more confident about his attainment he wrote to people in Universities in England and America for a job. But he was turned down by all of them. He did not feel particularly discouraged and knew that it was the opportune time for him to decide his future plans. He wrote occasionally for the Indian newspapers and though he was paid the highest fees in India, it was a lot less than what he got in the West. But Moraes had mellowed and had come to terms with himself:

> ".....after fretting for the best part of twenty years about not being able to write poetry, shifting my abode once more might be a mistake now that the gift had returned. I resolved to try and make the best of where I was".(p. 331)

In 1987 Penguin India published his *Collected Poems 1957 - 1987*, which had his old poems as well as some of his new ones. Moraes decided to follow his own path, which the sages in India said, was predestined. While not forgetting the past, he waited eagerly for any poetry in his native surroundings: full of dust and heat, rain, which would be polluted and very, rarely the winter winds, which came down from the Himalayas.

Moraes is still waiting to be at home as India continues to appear like an alien land to him. The only change that has taken place in him is that he does not feel too comfortable even in England. He has painfully realised that "The best thing to do is to preserve some form of balance on the constantly ground tectonic plates of this planet".(P. 341)

Never At Home is a work of art and of enlightenment. We encounter the very private Moraes, not as he really is but as he believes and wishes to have been. Dom Moraes, the hero of his story, wants to expound his past, so that he can find out the essence of his being in time. The secret of the intrinsic nature is the absolute state of all kinds of knowledge. "Confession of the past realises itself as a work in the present: it effects a true creation of self by the self".[8] Recollection of one's life is not an easy process; but in a work of art, it takes the form of a revealation of the inner realm into the exterior where it becomes conscious of itself.

"Writing", said Sainte Beuve, "is liberation". This could not have been truer than in the case of Dom Moraes. He is no longer the same man after writing *Never At Home*. Written when Moraes was almost fifty-two years old, it depicts the autobiographical spirit and answers the question "How did I become what I am?" But it is not the end, the process of self-realisation, of search for identity is still continuing. George Gusdorf has very pertinently remarked:

> "Autobiography is therefore never the finished image or the fixing forever of an individual life: the human being is always a making, a doing....."[9]

Moraes very relevantly ends his second autobiography with an ambiguous remark "I am waiting". Perhaps he will let us know more about his life, its mysteries and his search for a home in the third book of his experiences.

REFERNCES

1. Dom Moraes, *Never At Home* (Viking, Penguin India Ltd. 1992), p. 341. All subsequent references to the work are from this edition and have been absorbed in the text by giving page references.
2. P. Tharyan, The Hindustan Times, 20.2.'93.
3. *The Concise Encyclopedia of Western Philosophy and Philosophers*, ed. by J.O. Wurson & Jonathan Ree (Unwin Hyman, London, 1989), p. 6.
4. Dom Moraes, *My Son's Father*, (Penguin, India, 1990), p. 76.
5. R.S. Pathak, ed., *Quest for Identity in Indian English Writing*, vol. II, (Bahri Publications, NewDelhi, 1992), p. 2.
6. R. Parthasarthy, *Ten Twentieth Century Indian Poets*, (OUP, Delhi, 1983), p. 11.
7. "Identity and Nationality", in Meenakshi Mukherjee (ed.), *Considerations* (Allied Publishers, Bombay, 1977), p. 1.
8. Georges Gusdorf, in James Olney (ed.) *Autobiography. Essays Theoretical and Critical*, (Princeton University Press, Oxford,1980), p. 45.
9. *Ibid.*, p. 7.

CHAPTER 8
The Nature of Homesickness in V.S. Naipaul and Dom Moraes

One of the maladies afflicting the modern writer is the feeling of alienation or of not belonging anywhere. In the case of some authors, the historical, social or personal factors have so intensified the sensibility that their sense of alienation has become a major preoccupation. It may ultimately lead to an uneasy state of mind where the personal life of the writer no longer remains at the centre. Unknowingly the feeling is created by the writer and like V.S.Naipaul he can become interested in his former community in search of his roots. Or as in the case of Dom Moraes, the exile may have the feeling of homesickness even in his own country.

> "Exile is a process of becoming, in between origins and destinations, and because the exile is in-between, his journey can be a two-dimensional movement."[1]

Julia Kristeva[2], in her book *Etrangers a nous-memes* (Strangers to Ourselves), treats the "stranger" or "foreigner" psychologically. She analyses the process of alienation and the response of the stranger "within" to the stranger "without". It is, therefore, essential to recognise the "stranger in ourselves" to live peacefully in a multicultural and multiracial society. This kind of exile, as we shall see in Naipaul and Dom Moraes, gives extensive opportunities for creativity. It also offers, if we can borrow a phrase from Todorov "the epistemological privilege" to the writer, who suddenly becomes a stranger to himself. He indulges in self-examination because he discovers new things about himself. The exile or the homelessness creates in him a potentiality of "exotopy", a word coined by M.M.Bakhtin to signify "outsideness", which is further explained by Todorov as "finding oneself outside"[3].

Homelessness creates a pain in the heart, yet it makes the writer move forward in search of new possibilities. It becomes an unprecedented source of creative energy and the writer can learn to know much about himself, the world and its people. It signifies a break from the life at home, a break with the centre; the writer is always travelling, is always a stranger wherever he goes and is living at the margin in alien lands amongst alien people. As he is always a stranger wherever he goes, he is constantly trying to understand himself and the world around him:

> "The perception operates in two directions: the exile understands the self through the lens of strangers, and understands strangers through the lens of the exiled self."[4]

The exile makes the familiar fade away and be replaced by the new or the strange and of having a feeling of not belonging. It makes the person live in isolation and can either disintegrate the self or it can enable the self to reconstruct itself. Exile or homesickness can make him feel as if he is "Never at Home" or take him on a voyage across the world in "Finding the Centre" to end in an "Enigma of Arrival". He carries his past forever with him even though he tries to escape from it: it is the Albatross around his neck, which threatens to strangulate him.

Exile can be of two types: it can be a voluntary exile or a forced exile. Dom Moraes's exile, as seen from his autobiographies *My Son's* Father (1968) and *Never at* Home (1992), is of the first kind, and we find his deep anguish due to a feeling of withdrawal from a mother who was slowly becoming insane; alienation from the country of his birth, its socio-cultural and metaphysical background. It resulted in a forceful severing of his tellurian moorings; he left India for England at the age of sixteen, in his search for a 'home':

> "It is something, which most people I know were born with, and I wasn't: a sense of belonging somewhere, of possessing roots and relatives and even a permanent home."[5]

In Naipaul the distinction between the types of exile is not so well defined. He is an Asian living in Trinidad, a former British colony, a part of the English world and consequently a place superior to India. Yet he is precluded from it, to dwell perpetually on the margins. His outlook, unlike that of Dom Moraes, is western, because he was born in a society, which was a part of the western world. This Asian-Indian-Trinidadian has his "grandroots" in India, with which he enters into a relationship by living in the country for sometime. What he sees in India fills him with disgust, more so because, in one way or the other, India is attached to him. His feeling of homelessness separates him from the Indian Hindus in Trinidad, from the natives of that country, from the English in London, from the Indians in India. He is incessantly an observer, who lives in "a kind of limbo", feels like "a refugee" because he is always "peripheral".[6] His writings reveal his distress in living in Trinidad, without any rights, knowing that his mother country was probably in a worse condition.

Books particularly like *An Area of Darkness* (1964), *India: A Wounded Civilization* (1977) express true autobiographical processes of self-exploration. *Finding The Centre* (1984), containing two narratives, mainly deals with "the process of writing". The first essay "Prologue to an Autobiography", he says is not an autobiography. However, it does confirm that though he entertains the feeling of being rootless, travelling has been "a necessary stimulus" which liberated him from his "colonial shell".

Naipaul is at pains to refute that his writings are in any way autobiographical or a revealation of the self:

> "Do you keep asking, who I am? I never ask that question. I always knew who I was. My search was for knowledge. My writings have been my discoveries. I have no problem about identity. None at all. My work is not exploration of the self. No. It is the exploration of the world. Not the exploration of my mind."[7]

His writings may be "the exploration of the world", but they are also his reactions to the places and the inhabitants of the world. He may have gathered knowledge from his extensive travels, but the readings of his books unmistakably reveal an assessment of the self in search of its identity. He has confessed in an interview that he was conscious of his Indian identity right from his childhood:

> "As a child, I was surrounded by people who had come from India. When I was born, it was so much a living presence. What came first was the realisation that India was a dependent country. That was very shocking to me, very shameful. The local cruelty was a later discovery."[8]

Naipaul's idea of the past, like his idea of India, was a dream. It was "an area of darkness", of "undated time, historical darkness":

> "Our own past was, like our idea of India, a dream. Of my mother's father, so important to our family, I grew up knowing very little. Of my father's family and my father's childhood I knew almost nothing."[9]

He "lived easily with that darkness" till 1972, when he turned forty. His grandfather had abandoned India and had denied Trinidad. But Naipaul could not deny the island or its ways. Neither could he deny India, which was the country from which his grandfather had come: a country, which never seemed real to him, which existed beyond the "dot of Trinidad":

> "To me as a child India that had produced so many of the persons and things around me was featureless, and I thought of the time when the transference was made as a period of darkness, darkness which also extended to the land...."[10]

Naipaul's frequent examination of his own "malady" and his "wound" of colonialism and exile reveal that his anxiety was a "neurosis". However, at hindsight he was compelled to assess his impressions about India:

> "The poverty of the Indian streets and the countryside was an affront and a threat, a scratching at my old neurosis. Two generations separated me from that kind of poverty; but I felt closer to it than most of the Indians I met."[11]

Nevertheless, his exile in India became twofold: he was quite distinctive as an outsider in Trinidad; but in India, even though he was an immigrant, he was not singular because he looked like an Indian:

> "It was like being denied part of my reality. Again and again I was caught. I was faceless. I might sink without a trace into that Indian crowd. I had been made by Trinidad and England; recognition of my difference was necessary to me, I felt the need to impose myself, and didn't know how."[12]

His books on India continually describe his encounter with his "Motherland", where he is a stranger, as he tries to establish his roots in the country ; at the same time these writings also emphasise Naipaul's difference with the Indians, which he is at pains to illustrate, together with the decay of the country; in the absence of any change, Naipaul equates the condition to a "wounded civilisation". Despite his disillusionment with India, a country which he constantly affiliates with his grandfather, he tried to associate himself with it but not with its people. He always felt like "an intruder". His myth about India is shattered when he saw Indians defecating everywhere: on the railway tracks, on the beaches, on the hills, on the riverbanks, on the streets. It left him feeling disgusted with the country and its people. This antipathy was developed in his travels through the country and was in direct contrast to the empathy with the Indian things which he saw in his house at Trinidad:

> "....in a string bed....in plaited straw mats; in innumerable brass vessels...in books...in one ruined harmonium."[13]

The confession brings the self of the writer into prominence and accentuates his feeling of living in exile. On the last leg of his journey to India, he visited his grandfather's village in Uttar Pradesh, which proved to be "an unlikely adventure". He was forced to leave abruptly:

> "We drove off. I did not wave...so it ended, in futility and impatience, a gratuitous act of cruelty, self-reproach and flight."[14]

He left India after spending a year in the country to arrive at Beirut, a part of the world with which he thought he was familiar; India receded into a "dead world" and "became part of the night". Later he went to London to live a glamorous life and to make it the centre of his world, a dream of all the West Indians:

> "And I was lost. London was not the centre of my world. I had been mislead; but there was nowhere else to go. It was a good place for getting lost in...."[15]

His encounters with what he termed as the negative aspects of the Western way of life made him feel "physically lost". He was forced to review his position in the context of the Hindu view of life:

> "The world is illusion, the Hindus say. We talk of despair, but true despair lies too deep for formulation. It was only now, as my experience of India defined itself more properly against my own homelessness, that I saw how close in the past year I had been to the total Indian negation, how much it had become the basis of thought and feeling. And already with this awareness in a world where illusion could only be a concept and not something felt in the bones, it was slipping away from me. I felt it as something true which I could never adequately express and never seize again."[16]

Naipaul had pursued the journey to India to confirm his idea about the country of his grandparents. But it increased his feeling of worldlessness and made him realise that he had become more of an exile:

> "I was not English or Indian; I was denied the victories of both."[17]

Existence to most people achieves significance due to a sense of belonging to some place, with relatives and even a permanent home. But it did not happen to Moraes: he was born in a colonial India, where he and his family learnt to speak only the English language:

> "...I only spoke English language; the Indian languages were foreign to me. So were Indian traditions, Indian customs, and an entire style of life. This alienation was added to because, through much of my childhood and adolescence, my mother was mentally ill, and this affected my emotions and attitudes considerably. I blamed India for my mother, and my mother for India. Very early on, I started to write poetry in English."[18]

Since Dom Moraes had no real consciousness of a nationality, he left India at the age of sixteen to settle in England for various reasons: it was the country which had most of the poets, with whom he felt he had an affinity; but mainly because it was an escape from the ordeal of facing a mad mother. She was an obsession with him, but at the same time he longed for the old mother, one who was not insane, smelt of perfume and dressed in silks and whom we meet in *My Son's Father.* One of the reasons he travelled seven hundred miles was to escape from her. He thought England to be his real home:

> "...Indian society as I had seen seemed to me narrow and provincial, and I wanted to escape it."[19]

Moraes wanted to be himself, which was to be a writer and a Poet; he exiled himself from India, which was never a 'home' to him and the country to which he did not want to return. He lived in England for the next fifteen years, wrote extensively both in prose and verses and was acclaimed by the people there. He had a sense of belonging to that country and thought that he had taken roots in England. He felt homesick on his infrequent and short trips to India. But he became confused when he experienced many conflicting emotions on such visits. His new life in London together with its milieu, which he understood more than that of his motherland, beckoned him in an opposite direction. Moraes had left India to free himself from his mad mother and to search for his own identity; we get an account of his accomplishment as a Poet in his first autobiography, *My Son's* Father (1968).

The conquest of Goa in 1961 by the Nehru Government made him take a stance against India; the English Press lauded him, while the Indian Government withdrew his Indian passport. The act uprooted and alienated him altogether from the country of his birth:

"I felt English; my attitudes to life were English; whatever sense of humour I had was English; I thought myself accepted in England for whatever I was. It was not that, like a gem in Diaspora, I had to disguise my difference. The colour of my skin was not English, but my mind was."[20]

It was very important for Moraes to be accepted by the British society and his anger knew no bounds when once a policeman frisked him up because he looked like an immigrant. He later realized that in reality he was an immigrant in England. It was at this time that he discovered that he could not write poetry; it was a "wholly barren" and dark period and his restlessness increased as he was failing in the very purpose of his visit to England. His vocation as a poet had made him feel closer to England and its people; but with his poetic prowess deserting him, he felt more of an alien in the British society. He had not been accepted in India because he did not seem Indian; neither was he accepted in England where he was a foreigner. He lost his nationality as well as his vocation. An artist has to create an identity, which Balchandra Rajan defines as "the process of creative self-realization". He says:

"A sense of nationality can grow out of the discovery of identity and it is important that this should happen frequently, if one is to establish a tradition that is both distinctive and rooted."[21]

Dom Moraes's "centre" had fallen apart as Naipaul's had never done. He became a globetrotting, investigative journalist for BBC and the UN and rushed around the world in pursuit of stories. *Never at Home* gives a full account of his vagrant life as "an international nomad". What we miss in the autobiography is Moraes's grappling the problem of alienation and exile and discussing it all-inclusively.

Moraes's publishers suggested to him to make a film on Indira Gandhi, for which he planned a trip to India with his wife and son. He toured the country extensively and though he was aware that the subcontinent offered him a more interesting life than was to be found elsewhere, he felt anathematic and "claustrophobic" at the idea of making a home in his Motherland. On this fateful trip Moraes's wife left him and he felt all alone in the world. He still suffered from the "writer's block" and it made him feel not only homeless but "faceless" too - without any identity. A person's identity gives him the strength to survive in the world; to correlate with his fellow beings, to know his social rank. For Moraes the constraints of identity and its loss became irredeemable. Every person, he says, wears a mask, which he allows the world to see; it is not a difficult thing to do. Moraes's mask was that of a casual person, unconcerned and unaffected by the worldly affairs: he wore the mask of a poet and his identity lay behind it:

> "It was by keeping the identity, not the mask, that I remained alive. The identity contained all the experiences the mask had, but experienced them differently. A great part of my identity lay in my ability to write poetry, and also in knowing exactly what world I belonged to."[22]

Now that he did not write poetry, he did not know to which world he belonged. It was a new problem for him as he wore a mask without an identity. He was more or less living in exile from England and had married again.

Early in 1982, the Muse of poetry visited him in the city of Bombay as he walked "by the polluted sea". Words and phrases came tumbling into his mind; he forgot the world, his surroundings and was conscious only of himself and the thrill of being able to write again. He applied for job in the universities of England and America, but was turned down by all. Not feeling discouraged, he knew that it was the opportune time for him to decide his future plans. He had mellowed and had come to terms with himself:

> "...After fretting for the best part of twenty years about not being able to write poetry, shifting my abode once more might be a mistake now that the gift had returned. I resolved to try and make the best of where I was."[23]

The main difference, which can be construed, between Naipaul and Dom Moraes is that the Trinidadian was able to have an uninterrupted career as a writer. He did not have to face a barren period in his life, a period when he could not write whatever he wanted. Although the feeling of homelessness predominated in most of his travel writings, Naipaul, as a writer, had at least discovered his centre. L.K.Sharma in his interview with Naipaul for The Times of India (10.7.94) says:

> "Naipaul has achieved most of what could have been achieved as a writer competing in the western world, in a society which allows and enables him to write."

Even though his "instinct was towards fiction"[24] he wrote a number of travel books which disclose his impressions of the various places of the world, its people with whom he formed new relationships. He was however uncertain about the way he should treat the "traveller's 'I' " because in 1960 he identified himself as a colonial writer, writing about other colonies of the world:

> "His early travel books show an author struggling to define a method of selection and emphasis of material - should he emphasise facts or impressions? Should he be sociological or autobiographical? - and his position as a colonial and exile writing about a transitional, colonial and post colonial world."[25]

Naipaul's desire to travel and to leave Trinidad was not only because he wanted to travel, it was because he wanted to understand other societies as well. Perhaps what was more important to him was his desire to know his roots and himself. Thus he goes forward in time to understand his past; through art he has tried to show his ordeal of exile:

> "To become a writer, that noble thing, I had thought it necessary to go back. It was the beginning of self-knowledge."[26]

His homelessness gave him a tension, which tried to pull him in opposing directions; writing provided him with a "centre" or a "home":

> "...it was that fear, a panic about failing to do what I should be, rather than simple ambition, that was with me when I came down from Oxford in 1954 and began trying to write in London. My father had died the previous year. Our family was in distress. I should have done something for them, gone back to them. But, without having become a writer, I couldn't go back."[27]

His Indian sense of duty urged him to return to Trinidad, but the western influence dominated him, urging him to give importance to the individual, the writer in him. To go back would be to prove to himself and to his people his incapability in becoming a writer. His exile is thus a synthesis of distress and a restrained sense of guilt. Naipaul's predicament gives vent to autobiographical writings mostly in his travel books and in *Finding the Centre. The Enigma of* Arrival (1987), his most autobiographical book, where the story partly allowed the growth of the writer's life, Naipaul showed had he has created himself by his own creations. He had bridged the gap between the "man" and the "writer": both unite in the act of creation and through it exorcise the "evil spirits" in order to create a new self and a new world. He also began to have a sense of belonging to the world.

In *Etrangers a nous-memes*, Julia Kristeva writes about the "secret wound" which compels a person to wander all over the world as a stranger. Naipaul was forced by the circumstances of his family, in a colonial society, to become an exile. In India: *A Million Mutinies.* Now (1990) he indicated that he had inherited his exile from his grandfather and "had carried in my bones that idea of abjectness and defeat and shame".28 Dom Moraes, wounded by his mother's insanity, fled to England and then wandered across the world in search of a home. Both Naipaul and Dom Moraes felt the need to write in order to live; writing helped them to comprehend their selves in the post industrial social framework. Their creative activity enabled them to understand the reality, the people around them and also to create a home.

REFERENCES

1. Timothy F. Weiss, On the Margins, *The Art of Exile in V.S. Naipaul*, The University of Massachusetts Press, 1992.
2. Julie Kristeva, *Etrangers a nous-memes*, Paris, Fayard,1988.
3. On the Margins, p. 229.
4. *Ibid.,* p. 15.
5. *Never At Home*, Viking, Penguin, 1992, P.viii.
6. On the Margins, P.230.
7. The Times of India, 10-7-94.
8. *Ibid.*
9. *Finding the Centre*, Penguin, 1984, p. 53.
10. *An Area of Darkness*, Penguin, 1968, p. 30.
11. *India: A Million Mutinies Now*, Minerva, 1991, p. 8.
12. *An Area of Darkness*, p. 3.
13. *Ibid.,* p. 29.
14. *Ibid.,* pp. 262-263.
15. *Ibid.,* p. 42.
16. *Ibid.,* pp. 266-267.
17. *Ibid.,* p. 98.
18. *Never At Home*, p. viii

19. *My Son's Father*, Penguin, 1989, p. 100.
20. *Never At Home*, p. 43.
21. "Identity and Nationality" in Considerations, ed. M. Mukherjee, Allied Publishers, Bombay, 1977, p.1.
22. *Never at Home*, p. 310.
23. *Ibid.,* p. 331.
24. *Finding the Centre*, p. 10.
25. *On the Margins*, p. 160.
26. *Finding the Centre*, p. 40.
27. *Ibid.,* p. 72.
28. *India: A Million Mutinies Now*, p. 517.

R.K. Narayan : His Life into Art

Susanne K. Langer in her book *Feeling and Form, The Theory of Art* makes the following observation:

> "...... the main business of all poetic art is to create an 'illusion of life', which shifts the attention from actuality to fiction. People listen with rapt attention to stories just as they keenly look at pictures".[1]

Let us first understand what Langer means by the word "life". Ignoring the assorted, abstruse connotations, she says "life" has two distinct meanings: one is "life" in the biological sense, where it is antithetical to the word "death"; the second signification, that is the social application of the word "life" means *what happens* or what the living being encounters and copes with. The second definition of "life" belongs to the realm of poetic art that is to its primary illusion. What she means by "illusion" we shall discuss later in this paper.

Now the question "what is art?", says Morris Weitz in *Problems in Aesthetics*[2], is perhaps as old as the history of aesthetics. It is a query which numerous philosophers and critics from Plato to the present times have tried to answer in their own different ways. DeWitt Parker[3], while discussing "The Nature of Art" is able to arrive at a conclusion of sorts and says that "what we call a work of art is on the one hand a thing; on the other hand, an experience". It has value, is part of the history and culture of a people and provides pleasure not in privacy and in silence but through communication. This aspect of a work of art, that is its ability to communicate, as Kant also emphasized, is its most important feature. The artistic beauty can not be enjoyed in isolation; on the contrary it becomes valuable only when it is appreciated and shared by everyone. It therefore implies that art is not only for the artist but for the whole society as well.

A work of art can have the image of the experienced events of life, which Susanne K. Langer terms as "the illusion of life". The writer, she says, employs various modes, tricks too, in order to produce this "illusion of life", one of them being the assertion that is what one is writing is actually a memoir or history:

> "If you can get people to take your fiction as fact, it seems that "the air of reality" must have been achieved".[4]

What is an integral part of the whole artistic process is its "sense of life", the "livingness" which has a close relationship with life. It is, however, lacking in newspaper reports, which are also always based on facts. It is the "livingness" of a story which is valuable, infact it is much more important than the actual experience.

> "Life itself may, at times, be quite mechanical and unperceived by those who live it; but the perception of a reader must never fall into abeyance. People in the book may be dull and dreary, but not the book itself. Virtual events, however subdued, have character and savour, distinct appearance and feeling - tone, or they simply cease to exist. We sometimes praise a novel for approaching the vividness of actual events; usually, however, it exceeds them in vividness".[5]

However, like T.S. Eliot, Langer does not recommend a slavish copying or a blind imitation of actual Life: "blind or timid adherence" to actuality is to be discouraged. There should be no confusion between a work of art and its model, even though the primary illusion in the artistic creation has been a semblance of "real life". Though the central character has been identified with the writer, and the events in the novel are supposed to be his own experiences, actual or imagined, art is very different from its real life model.

A story, though told in the first person (if it is a literary piece), is totally transformed by the writer's imagination, which David Daiches[6] says in *The Novel and the Model World*, always creates and never records, so that the "I" of the story becomes simply a character. Any event in the story may have an archetype in the author's actual memory. But just as even an actual self-portrait is not the sitter, in the same way events observed in real life are not literary elements but materials for literature.

David Daiches illustrates his argument by giving the example of James Joyce's *Portrait of the Artist as a Young Man:*

> "It is fiction in the sense that the selection and arrangement of the incidents produce an artistically patterned work, a totality in which there is nothing superfluous, in which every detail is artistically as well as biographically relevant. Joyce, in fact, has given us one of the examples in English literature of autobiography successfully employed as a mode of fiction".[7]

There are very few writers in whom the autobiographical gift is intently associated to that of fiction; mere autobiography moulded to the narrative forms of fiction will not suffice. What more is needed is the imaginative faculty of a real artist, to whom his own life is a theme among many other themes. A true writer knows the difference between his own story and fiction: one provides the raw material for the other, in which every thing appears in a new light. In Indian writing in English, R.K. Narayan, is one of those few writers who has used his autobiography, the experiences of his life, which include the people who come into his life, in an organised form in his fiction. He was an artist who took his craft of writing seriously, trying constantly to achieve perfection. Therefore, for Narayan his life provided him the raw material for his novels, and if we compare his autobiography *My Days* (1974) with *Swami and Friends* (1935) and *The English Teacher* (1945) (these being the two novels discussed in this paper) we will see the truth of the matter.

These three works have used the same background of the Indian past, and the crowd, which forms a part of the family life, is also the same. "A profound and unmitigated loneliness is the only truth of life" wrote Narayan in *The English Teacher.* While reading Narayan this is what we are conscious of in *My Days* is an autobiography or any fictional work. However, the diversity between his autobiography and the two novels is absolute.

Rene Wellek and Austin Warren, while discussing the relationship between Literature and Biography, feel that there is a great difference between an autobiographical statement and the employment of the same leimotif in a work of art. Many times the writer's work is a mask, "a conventionalisation of his own experiences, his own life". They further add:

> "The whole view that art is self-expression pure and simple, the transcript of personal feelings and experiences, is demonstrably false. Even when there is a close relationship between the work of art and the life of an author, this must never be construed as meaning that the work of art is a mere copy of life".[8]

The yearning to write an autobiography is displayed everyday in the stories we tell about ourselves. A human being's life can be the best material for writing a story. It is then no longer only a focus on the life of the author, but a work of art, with its own narrative form. This transformation gives it gravity and the life history no longer remains a disorganised, erratic recollection of the past, but is converted into personal history. The art of autobiography helps the writer in examining the events of his past, in selecting and arranging them systematically; the whole process gives a new meaning to the life recollected and converted:

> "A life storied is a life made meaningful, and any life, however vapid, is at least storiable. I begin therefore from the assumption that whoever narrates his or her life is willing its transformation from a lived farrago into a thought whole".[9]

The autobiographer converts the story of his life into literature, and by the means of narration is able to establish a close relationship with his readers. He may or may not reveal all the little details of his life, but he does make a contract with the reader that the autobiography is not life, but an artful representation of it, which is analogous to the life lived, not a transcription of it. Dante's *Vita Nuova* applied the autobiographical form to his writings inorder to trace his liberation from life into art.

It is not only that everyday life can become literature, but a literary work can also take events directly from life :

> "The formalists themselves know that everyday life can become literature, and literature can become life. They also know that, at the same time, literature does not cease being literature, and life does not stop being life, that in changing places these areas retain their identity."[10]

As the two forms of writing, autobiography and fiction, employ the narrative techniques, they may readily borrow from one another. We have seen that *Sons and Lovers* borrows techniques from autobiography, but no one can deny that it is ultimately only fiction. However, what brings fiction closer to autobiography are various designs used by the novelist like the first person narrative, some historical facts, some local colour. But even though both novel and autobiography are bound together by certain common narrative techniques, critics and readers can never forget that one is different from the other.

James Olney says that the fundamental difference lies in the aim of the two types of writing: whereas an autobiography is at great pains to reveal that "this happened to me", fiction has no such motive as its ultimate goal. Sometimes an autobiographer has a definite edge over the novelist, as he can very often introduce the real world into his story. At the same time a novel can be more revelatory of its author than a formal autobiography as "we identify ourselves in the names we give others".[11]

Fact and innovative rendering of fact mingle together to produce a personal understanding of experience. Good books can be written in which the writer has made extensive use of his experience as well as his imagination.

R.K. Narayan's fiction, says William Walsh, is "unusually close to and intimate with his personal life" That like Katherine Mansfield, Walsh says, Narayan is predominantly autobiographical, and utilises the experiences of his life to organise them in his work of art:

> "The personal past, the known place, the home, the physical context and chores of the household, family relationships, and in particular the friction and harmony of young and old, these are the points through which the line of her art goes. And much the same might be said of Narayan".[12]

Narayan's personal life in *My Days* is like any of his novels, with his emphasis on the Indian domestic scene, the middle class, especially the small segment of the agricultural community, and the personal relationships. The Indian middle class, which Narayan says, is the only class he understands, is beautifully represented not only in his autobiography, but also in ***Swami and Friends*** and ***The English Teacher*** - the two novels which have drawn heavily from the facts of Narayan's life. Though it makes Narayan limited in his scope of art, he is content, as K.R. Srinivas Iyenger says, "like Jane Austen, with his little bit of ivory, just so many inches wide".

Whether it be a young boy like Swami or an older person like Krishna , Narayan in his autobiography resembles any one of the heros from his own novel. And this we feel, is nothing unusual because

> "we are all each other's fictional creation, not only in how we see each other, but in how we induce others to see us".[13]

Susanne K. Langer[14] does not recommend a "slavish transcription of actual life" which, she says, would appear dull beside "the world-created experiences of virtual life". In such a case the final product would be as uninteresting as a plaster mask which though made from "a living subject is a dead counterfeit" when compared to even the most "conservative portrait sculpture". This problem invariably crops up in an autobiographical study, which may at times lack "the quality of being completely felt-livingness". But this malady does not inflict the writings of R.K.Narayan where the difference between biography and fiction is clearly marked. The novels portray the biographical events in new combinations; they are selected, altered and imbued with the brilliance of the various themes to suit the particular framework and ambience of the stories. Narayan's art is a blending of explicit realism with poetic myth, experience with imagination. Narayan's "serious comedies", as William Walsh calls his novels, depict the rebirth of the self and the revealation of his most intimate experiences through the recomposition of other personalities, his characters, who live their day to day life quite happily.

"The effect on the reader is twofold. The world - or worlds - dealt with in the stories strikes him as enjoying an objective existence independent of the contribution of the author. On the other hand, the attitude of the author is modest and unobstructive. It has the air of being dependent on, and responsive to, things outside himself. Actuality, one feels, is not being bullied or tricked into false positions. Nor is it being sucked up into some dominating and abstract symbolising system".[15]

This is a major concern of literature, which is correlated with maintaining "the air of reality" in the work. The writer who utilises the facts of his life in his fiction has to vindicate the fictional quality of his work. The reader can easily perceive the various devices, which Narayan is able to attain a life likeness; but he can also discern the means by which the writer validates the dissimilarity between art and life. Narayan's image of life becomes anomalous to its prototype. Style, says Susanne K. Langer, is the device, which helps a writer in taking care of these two basic requirements. Narayan's style gives a "slant" to the events of his life, and makes them more interesting. "Recall and hearsay turn fact into fiction".[16] And Narayan's fiction, say his biographers Susan and N. Ram, is "deceptively simple and seemingly innocent of literary technique." At the same time it mingles the comic with the sad and provides a philosophical insight to life. A "lean, lucid and wonderfully expressive" style of writing is typically characterise by a "lightness of touch."[17]

When Narayan wrote *My Days* in 1974, he was already well known as a novelist. As such his literary autobiography "forms a part of an oeuvre". Born in 1907 in a Brahmin family at Madras, Narayan's earliest memories are of his childhood companions - a peacock and a monkey (p. 3). *My Days* opens with the town of Madras in the background, and its various problems; then there is the family circle, the central framework of the autobiography, which operates its main sensibility. And in its midst is Narayan, the hero, one of those middle class men,

> "who are psychologically more active and in whom consciousness is more vivid and harrowing".[18]

The quiet city of Mysore of his personal life, where he spent a major part of his life, becomes the Malgudi of his novels (p.174), a small town in south India; and in the larger context it represents the whole of India.

On an 'auspicious' day of Vijyadashami in September 1930 Narayan's grandmother initiated him into becoming a writer; after writing the first line "It was Monday morning", he could visualise a small railway station. Such was the birth of Malgudi in *Swami and Friends,* which grew and developed over the years. The railway station, where Swami went to watch the trains, needed a name-board. Narayan was not keen to take any name from the railway timetable:

> "I wanted to avoid that, because some busybody was likely to say, 'this place is not there, that shop he has mentioned is not there'. If it's a real town it's a nuisance for a writer.
>
> And while I was worrying about this problem, the idea came to me – Malgudi just seemed to hurl into view. It has no meaning. There is a place called Lalgudi near Trichy and a place called Mangudi near Kumbakonam or somewhere. But Malgudi is nowhere. So that was very helpful. It satisfied my requirement".[19]

Malgudi, since its inception, has been central to Narayan's literary achievement. "I am a treacherous writer when I move out of Malgudi," was his remark in a 1995 conversation.

Susan and N. Ram do not think that Malgudi is essentially Mysore, Narayan's home of seven decades. They feel that Malgudi does not have either the size or the "princely trappings of Karnatak's second city".

> "It is also a place whose inhabitants are clearly, although not obtrusively, Tamil. It is said, it is evident that Mysore has made significant inputs into what is the quintessential South Indian district town. Elements from Narayan's Madras childhood can also be detected along with impressions of Coimbatore and other urban settings ....which he visited as a young man."[20]

However Narayan in *My Days* (p.174) emphatically stated that "the river side forest, village, and crowds, granite steps and the crumbling walls of a shrine" of Mysore "combine to make up the Malgudi of my story". This fictional town is essentially Indian with a unique identity.

> "After having read only a few of his books it is difficult to shake of the feeling that you have vicariously lived in this town. Malgudi is perhaps the single most endearing 'character' R.K. Narayan has ever created".[21]

Malgudi is a place far from the madding crowd of metropolitan India, where life is lived easily and unhurriedly. It is near a jungle and the town has plenty of colour and a variety of Narayanesque characters:

> "Swami, the undistinguished, cricket-loving school boy; Savitri, the put-upon and briefly rebellious housewife; Krishna, the college lecturer traumatised by the loss of his wife; Nataraj, the printer with his proofs delayed into posterity; Margayya, the 'financial expert' at his questionable business beneath the banyan tree; Raju, the tourist-seeking guide ... Through these South Indian characters and the moral predicaments in which they find themselves, the writer reveals the universal in the particular."[22]

Malgudi in *Swami and Friends* is not presented as a village or city, but as a town of small size. The hero of the novel, Swaminathan or Swami, is an average schoolboy; in him Narayan has captured all the essence of his own boyhood days. The writer's own childhood experiences find a reflection in Swami. So we have Swami watching a small piece of tin skimming gently along in the gutter of Vinayaka Mudali street (p.32) which is reminiscent of Narayan training the grasshoppers in *My Days* (p.35). Childhood, according to A.O.J. Cockshut is "often the most important time of all. Parents and Siblings are often central, friends are sometimes important".[23] Childhood forms a substantial part of *My Days;* probably inorder to accentuate the significance of this part of his life, Narayan wrote a full novel on a child. Graham Greene, who was compelled to read *Swami and Friends* by Krishna Rahavendra Purna, a young neighbour of Narayan in Mysore, and who eventually recommended it to British publishers, "took instant liking for the novel that changed decisively Narayan's literary career".

> "Incidentally, Greene knew, as only an insider could, the difficulties inherent in writing about children, and he greatly admired those, who had successfully written about – or even for – children"[24]

Swami, who likes Narayan, hates school and education, loves to spend time with his friends and lives with his grandmother. The most lovable person of Narayan's family was his grandmother, with whom he spent his childhood in Madras. She looked after his needs, taught him multiplication, the Tamil alphabets, Sanskrit shlokas in praise of Goddess *Saraswati* (p.11). What was most important was that granny kept a strict watch on his behaviour.

> "My grandmother's preoccupations were several and concerned a great many others, she was a key figure in the lives of many". (*My Days*, p. 29)

> "My grandmother was an abiding influence. Grandmothers were in those days very important. They are no longer so – have disappeared."[25]

Not only was she "a key figure" in the Narayan household, but she became an epitome of all the grandmothers in the novels of Narayan. Swami's granny was a benign and ignorant old lady, who lived in an "ill-ventilated dark passage between the front hall and the dining-room" (p.21). She was an important part of Swami's life:

> "After the night meal, with his head on his granny's lap, nestling close to her, Swaminathan felt very snug and safe in the faint atmosphere of cardamom and cloves" (p. 21)

Swami used to share every little secret of his school with his granny; and she would narrate stories of Harishchandra to him. Swami's grandmother is the prototype of nearly all the Indian grannies, who uphold the traditional values of the Indian society.

The old lady finds a reflection in *The English Teacher* in Krishna's mother. The novel, claims Narayan in *My Days*, is heavily autobiographical, "very little part of it being fiction", (p.134). Krishna is a fictional character, who lives in the fictional city of Malgudi; but his experiences of life, especially those after the death of his wife, Susila, are those of Narayan's. M.N. Srinivas states that the loss of Narayan's wife shattered him.

> "I remember accompanying Narayan on a few of his walks around this time. They were not walks through the city but brooding, sad walks on the roads, skirting Kukkarahalli Tank to the West of the town. Narayan talked about death and after-life, and incidentally, his preoccupations expressed themselves in a few ghost stories. Sometime later he went to Madras and

> there met the medium through whom he was able to contact Rajam. All this is narrated elegiacally in *The English Teacher.*"[26]

In the novel Krishna's mother comes to Malgudi to set up the house for the young couple:

> "House-keeping was grand affair for her. The essence of her existence consisted in the thrills and pangs and the satisfaction that she derived in running a well-ordered household. She was unsparing and violent where she met slovenliness".(p.29)

She demanded the same perfection in the household chores which Narayan's mother had expected from his wife, Rajam:

> "Rajam was less than twenty, but managed the housekeeping expertly and earned my mother's praise".(*My Days,*p.110)

Both Rajam and Susila got typhoid and died after a prolonged illness. The second part of *The English Teacher* is "spiritual" and it becomes very difficult for the reader to know where fact and fiction diverge:

> "...... in a world without beliefs where there are only individuals, the writer, perhaps like all of us, stands face-to-face with himself".[27]

The English Teacher is by and large an attempt to bridge the gulf between the "man" and the "writer". Krishna in the novel tried to accept the death of his wife, even while living his every day life. And Narayan, through the act of writing, gave meaning to his grief and learns to come to terms with it. The act of writing proves to be a cathartic therapy as it helped him to overcome the grief and the subsequent upheaval in his life by submitting it to the orderliness of art.

When Narayan wrote *My Days* almost thirty years after having written *The English Teacher,* he was unable to give direct expression to his personal grief. Why did Narayan need the mask of Krishna to give vent to his grief? Why did he think it necessary to talk about the death of his wife through a persona? And why he did not write in detail the death of Rajam?

> "I have described this part of my experience of her sickness and death in *The English Teacher* so fully that I do not, and perhaps cannot, go over it again. More than any other book *The English Teacher* is autobiographical in content, very little part of it being fiction" (p.134)

Maybe we can guess the reasons behind this distancing of a tragic episode in his life. It could be because the death had given him so much anguish that he could not bear repeating it in the naked form of an autobiography. He had already described it in the fictive form, and had immortalised the fact. Secondly, Narayan has been able to establish a link between fiction and autobiography. By mentioning the novel, ***The English Teacher***, he expects the reader to fill this gap in his autobiography by reading his fiction! Perhaps Narayan can provide better clues; we can only conclude:

> "Through his recollection and its transformation into art (the narrator's writing about it) the deceased ... is honoured and grief dispelled".[28]

This is the relationship between art and life and inorder to be a writer, Narayan must bring his life into his art.

However, "spiritual" experience of Krishna does find a reflection in *My Days*, which is described by Narayan without any inhibitions. Narayan was able to have a contact with Rajam through one Raghunath Rao. Later he was able to attain a "philosophical understanding" (p.135). In the same way Krishna too made adjustments with the grief in his life and finally overcame the sense of decay:

"Thus I reconciled myself to this separation with less struggle than before. I read a lot, I wrote a lot, I reflected as much as I could ... My mind was made up. I was in search of a harmonious existence and everything that disturbed that harmony was to be rigorously excluded, even my college work". (pp. 178-179)

Hence we see how art and life permeate each other:

"This extrinsic reality is reflected in the novel, and thus the extrinsic is in a sense the intrinsic as well, and vice versa".[29]

Narayan mentions a mystic friend in *My Days*, who after the death of Rajam, had hinted at the therapeutic value of art:

"you will write a book which is within you, all ready now, and it is bound to come out sooner or later, when you give yourself a chance to write".(p.136)

He wrote *The English Teacher* and found solace.

There are some minute details, which find a reflection in *My Days* as well as in *Swami and Friends*. An autobiography is not only an account of the writer's inward journey from childhood to maturity; it is also a unique representation of the social scenario of the writer's time. And so we have in both the works a picture of the life and times of the pre-independent India, that is India in the early 20th century. There is a detailed account of the lighting of the street-lamps by the lamp-lighter, which Narayan had seen as a child on a visit to the street of shops with his uncle (*My Days*,p.7). The man in khaki coat, with a can of oil, rags and matches, lighting the lamps impressed the child's mind so much that as a writer he incorporated the lanterns with their smoldering wicks in *Swami and Friends* (p.151). Similarly the turbulent times of the freedom struggle also find a reflection in both the books. However, Narayan was not keen to include the political events of his time in his novels or autobiography. His role during the freedom movement was that of a mere spectator. Narayan's meeting with Nehru in Teen Murti House in 1961 finds no mention in *My Days*, whereas his friend, K. Natwar Singh, who had arranged the meeting, had been refereed to in the autobiography. On being questioned by the latter about the absence of any reference to Nehru, Narayan calmly answered,

> "'It never occurred to me to give publicity to it, and in any case I could not weave it into the narrative. *My Days* is a literary work, not a political tract'. At that time, I thought this was carrying modesty too far, but now I realise how right R.K.N was. There is a time to include and a time to exclude."[30]

The lampooning of the Hindus in Narayan's Lutheran Mission School was also a done thing in Swami's school. In *My Days* Narayan says:

> "The scripture classes were mostly devoted to attacking and lampooning the Hindu Gods, and violent abuses were heaped on idol-worshippers as a prelude to glorifying Jesus. Among the non-Christians in our class I was the only Brahmin boy, and received special attention; the whole class could turn in my direction when the teacher said that Brahmins claiming to be vegetarians ate fish and meat in secret, in a sneaky way and were responsible for the soaring price of those commodities". (p.12)

Swami's scripture master was also a fanatic who abused the Hindus for their idol-worship:

> "'Oh, wretched idiots!' the teacher said, clenching his fists, why do you worship dirty, lifeless, wooden idols and stone images? Can they talk? No. Can they see? No. Can they bless you? No. Can they take you to Heaven? No. Why? Because they have no life". (p.5)

Swami and his friends formed the M.C.C. team to play cricket matches (p.129). Narayan and his schoolmates were addicted to football and their team was called "jumping stars" (p.47). While choosing names for their cricket association Swami and the other boys also mention "jumping stars" as one of the proposed names (p.111)

Edwin Muir in his *Autobiography* says:

> "Children live in two worlds, in their own and that of grown-up people. What they do in their own world seems natural to them; but in the grown-up world it may be an incomprehensible yet deadly sin".[31]

Swaminathan too lived in his own private world, which did not include the restrictions of school. He always looked for some plea or other to miss school: sometimes it would be feigned headache and fever (p.131). It would win him the sympathy of his granny and mother, but not of his father, who knew his son's tricks too well:

> "Father stood over him and said in an undertone, 'you are a lucky fellow. What a lot of champions you have in this house when you don't want to go to school!' Swaminathan felt that this was a sudden and unprovoked attack from behind. He shut his eyes and turned towards the wall with a feeble groan".(p. 132)

Examinations were very unnerving for Swami and studying for them was an ordeal. Looking at the crooked map of Europe he would often wonder how people lived in it. He had mixed feelings of exaltation as well as uneasiness when the exams were over:

> "With dry lips, parched throat, and ink-stained fingers, and exhaustion on one side and exaltation on the other, Swaminathan strode out of the examination hall, on the last day.

Standing in the veranda, he turned back and looked into the hall and felt slightly uneasy. He would have felt more comfortable if all the boys had given their papers as he had done, twenty minutes before time".(p.61)

We have more or less the same kind of distaste for education in *My Days:*

> "My outlook on education never fitted in with the accepted code at home, I instinctly rejected both education and examinations, with their unwarranted seriousness and esoteric suggestions. Since revolt was unpractical I went through it all without conviction, enthusiasm, or any sort of distinction. Going to school seemed to be a never-ending nuisance each day, to be borne because of my years. At Madras, in my Lutheran mission days, my uncle was strict and would not allow me to stay home, however much I tried. When I lay in bed groaning with a real or feigned headache, he would merely say, "Get up, get up, I'll myself take you to the school and speak to the teacher to treat you lightly". (p.53-54)

Narayan's strict uncle and father, the latter was a headmaster of a school, found reflection in the autocratic rule of Swami's father:

> "Much to Swaminathan's displeasure, his father's courts closed in the second week of May, and father began to spend the afternoons at home. Swaminathan feared that it might interfere with his afternoon rambles with Rajam and Mani. And it did. On the very third day of his vacation, father commanded Swaminathan, just as he was stepping out of the house: 'Swami, come here".(p.82)

Narayan's theory that "fiction outlasts fact" finds a mention in *My Days* (p.122). Perhaps this was the reason why he mingled incidents, both major and minor, from his life in the stories, which he wove in his fiction. The artistic motive is to immortalise his life-experiences by giving it the form of a story. Undoubtedly it gains a kind of richness by being transformed and transmuted. When he wrote *Swami and Friends* in 1935 and *The English Teacher* in 1945 he had been too young to think about writing his autobiography, which he eventually did in 1974, at the ripe old age of sixty-seven. And in order to eternalise the many events and the people of his life, he included them in these two novels as in many others. This practice is not confined only to *Swami and Friends* and *The English Teacher*: his printer, Mr. Sampath, became a character in one novel and two film stories (*My Days,* p.154). An incident about someone "suffering enforced sainthood in Mysore offered a setting for.... a story" (p.167). The story concerned a drought-hit region, where in desperation the municipal council organised a prayer for rains. A group of Brahmins prayed and fasted, to the accompaniment of the chanting of *mantras* on the dry bed of Kaveri and brought rains to the region on the twelfth day: "This was really the starting point of *The Guide"* (p.167).

Mysore provided plenty of subject matter to Narayan for writing stories as he ambled along the streets of Mysore and he was "always willing to listen to someone who had a story or an incident to narrate. And he knew many of the people he ran into during his walks."[32]

> "At every turn I found a character fit to go into a story", and on "returning home, sat at my desk and wrote till the evening". (***My Days***,p.151)

Narayan's long-time friend M.N. Srinivas saw those walks as "ethnographic forays" as they provided him

> "with material for his stories or column. He also enjoyed his encounters with idiosyncratic acquaintances and friends .....Extremely important and urgent matters had to await a chance encounter on the streets of Mysore for discussion, if not resolution. If this is not the essence of Malgudi, what is?"[33]

Realism in art form, says Marjorie Boulton, is selective because it has to maintain a sense of proportion. This, according to Boulton, is the principle of art:

> "The first and most necessary and unbreakable convention of every art is that the artist chooses those aspects of the subject he wishes to treat in detail, ignores or almost ignores everything else, and suits the details of the treatment to the chosen matter".[34]

Narayan's writings are about the people and about the life itself; critics observe a "karmic dimension" in his writing, which is Indian and yet universal with an essence of timelessness.

> "Graham Greene who was instrumental in introducing Narayan to all of us, writes that without Narayan he would never have known 'what it is like to be are Indian'. No body can know Narayan like Greene does. Yet I beg to differ from Greene in his opinion. True Narayan writes about this fictitious Southern Indian town called Malgudi. True his cultural backdrop is very Indian, very Tamil in fact. Yet if you change the backdrop and set it in Modern day Los Angeles, you could invent the very same characters, their schemes, their petty machinations, their struggles with life. Narayan's theme is very universal. Its about people, people with plans in life, people with aims and aspirations. If there is any way to describe Narayan's writings, it is this 'Life goes on'"[35]

R.K. Narayan selected and organised the raw material, which became available to him in the city of Mysore according to the thematic constraints of his various books. In them the routine of ordinary life was transformed into a rich experience. The data is not presented in a photographic way; the exclusion of certain episodes from his life makes the writer emphasize certain other events. His literary talent helped him to meet the requirement of a true novelist, to whom his own life or his own story was the raw material which is to be utilised to produce such works which are entirely fiction; Graham Greene had thought it to be the "riskiest kind of fiction-writing"- there are no messages to be preached and no causes to be promoted:

> "Everything rested on the kind of characters that were created, and above all, the story itself. Such a writer, Greene pointed out, staked everything on his creativity. It is necessary to stress this point now, for in the world of today, far more than before, the prizes go to those who champion causes considered worthy. Creativity alone is not enough."[36]

The self-effacing Narayan, observe Susan and M. Ram[37], hates giving formal interviews; in the same way he detests the idea of unraveling any "meaning" in his works – he wants to remain a story-teller. And as long as Narayan tells the storys with sincerity and sympathy, which is his typical "touchstone method", Malgudi will continue to live on.

REFERENCES

1. Susanne K. Langer, *Feeling and Form, The Theory of Art,* Routledge and Kegan Paul Ltd, London, 1967, p. 213.
2. Morris Weitz, *Problems in Aesthethics*, Macmillan, London, 1970, p. 3.
3. Dewitt Parker, "The Nature of Art", *Problems in Aesthetics*, p. 76.
4. *Feeling and Form*, p. 291.
5. *Ibid.,* p. 292.
6. *Ibid.,* p. 296.
7. *Ibid.*
8. Rene Wellek and Austin Warren, *Theory of Literature*, Penguin Books, 1976, p. 78.

9. John Sturrock, *The Language of Autobiography*, Cambridge University Press, 1994, p. 20.

10. M.M. Bakhtin, P.N. Medvedev, *The Formal Method in Literary Scholarship,* The John Hopkins University Press, London, 1991, p. 154.

11. *Ibid.,* p.x.

12. William Walsh, *R.K. Narayan, A Critical Appreciation*, Allied Publishers, 1983, p. 51.

13. Glen Cavaliero, "Autobiography and Fiction", *Modern Selves*, Ed. Philip Dodd, Frank Cass, 1986, p. 157.

14. *Feeling and Form,* p. 292.

15. William Walsh, *R.K. Narayan*, p. 165.

16. *Feeling and Form*, p. 292.

17. Susan and N. Ram, "Narayan of Malgudi: Sixty-five years of story-telling", *Frontline*, Oct. 18, 1996.

18. William Walsh, *Indian Literature in English*, Longman, London, 1990, p. 74.

19. R.K. Narayan in first person, *Frontline*, Oct. 18, 1996.

20. Susan and N. Ram, *Frontline*, Oct. 18, 1996.

21. "R.K.Narayan: A fan's Adulation, *Anoop@linc.cis.upenn.edu.*

22. Susan and N. Ram, *Frontline*, Oct. 18, 1996.

23. A.O.J. Cockshut, *The Art of Autobiography in 19th & 20th Century England*, Yale University Press, New Haven and London, 1984, p. 3.

24. M.N. Srinivas, "A writer's world: A long-time friend reminisces", *Frontline*, Oct. 18, 1996.

25. R.K. narayan in first person, *Frontline*, Oct. 18, 1996.

26. Timothy F. Weiss, *On the Margins, The Art of Exile in V.S. Naipaul*, The University of Massachusetts Press, Amherst, 1992, p. 197.

27. *Ibid.,* p. 195.

28. *Ibid.,* p. 212.

29. K. Natwar Singh, "R.K.N: Evergreene at 90" *The Hindustan Times*, 6 October, 1996.

30. *The Art of Autobiography*, p. 69.

31. M.N. Srinivas, *Frontline*, Oct. 18, 1996.

32. *Ibid.*
33. Marjori Boulton, *The Anatomy of Prose*, Kalyani Publishers, New Delhi, 1993, p. 109.
34. *Anoop@linc.cis.upenn.edu.*
35. "Malgudi's very own Swami" An exclusive review of Susan and N. Ram's *R.K. Narayan – The Early Years: 1906 – 1945* by P.K. Balachanddran, *The Hindustan Times*, June 9, 1996.

CHAPTER 10

Nayantara Sahgal's Autobiographical Writings : A Quest for Inner Freedom

"Writing is a form of therapy", stated Graham Greene in *Ways of Escape* (1980), one of his autobiographical books. "Sometimes I wonder", he continued, "how all those who do not write, compose or paint can manage to escape the madness, the melancholia, the panic fear which is inherent in the human situation". The therapeutic value of writing has been recognised and emphasised throughout the ages by many writers who feel that "writing is liberation". At this point we may ask that if the act of writing is liberation then what is it from which the writer is trying to attain liberty or in other words freedom? The answer to this query is particularly relevant to the meaning of autobiography; this kind of writing is a reflection of the self and the life of the writer – the two are "completely intertwined and entangled, take on a certain form, assume a particular shape and image".[1] Psychoanalysts, says Georges Gusdorf[2], have made it known that the practice of confession of the past alters the present. Self-examination reconstructs and reforms the individual and his life. Autobiographical writings are representations of "the self's discovery that it is not simply an effect of history, but 'free'"[3]; this is particularly true in the case of the female self because in our tradition, women are far more restricted in their range of channels of self-expression than men.

Nayantara Sahgal, novelist and columnist of great repute, wrote two autobiographies *Prison and Chocolate*

Cake, From Fear Set Free (1962) and the recently published collection of her public addresses, *Point of View* (1997), delivered at literary conferences. Sahgal's fictional writings venture to break free of her "self" through a search for others' characters; in a few of them she tries to see some experiences of her life through her fictional creations and tries to understand herself. On the other hand her autobiographies reveal her efforts in attempting to confront her earlier "selves" which she had been perhaps trying to conceal. In an instance like this the autobiographical art acquires therapeautical dimensions. Sahgal endorses this quality of art when she says

> "Writing of any sort helps to put your own world in order, all the shapeless, bewildering fragments of it. It helps you to figure out what is happening in and around you ...There are things that will never be understood until they are written, and sometimes not even then. But writing helps the process."[4]

The act of writing brings about a psychological and emotional release for Sahgal and her autobiographical works have a common strain running through them: nostalgia for the past, which for her is always a happier place to dwell in; correlated with this theme is a quest for equilibrium and for "inward freedom".

Nayantara Sahgal was a part of the Nehru family, which was the hub of Indian politics and India's fight for freedom. Right from her childhood Nayantara Sahgal and her sisters were drawn into the freedom struggle. Her parents took part in the movement and went to jail several times. Gandhian ideals and teachings not only illumined the country but their lives too.

> "We were born and grew up at a time when India had come under the leadership of Gandhi and was maturing to nationhood under his guidance. My

> sisters and I were among the youngest of India's children to be touched by the spark with which Gandhi illumined our country. It touched our lives in innumerable small ways and penetrated our consciousness gradually, so that as we grew, it became a living part of us."[5]

Prison and Chocolate Cake, written during the autumn and winter of 1952-53, contains many domestic pictures of her family. The core of the book is personal experience through which she reaches for the liberation of her spirit. The book was not written for publication and the writer had not maintained records of any kind, these are necessary for "the stuff of which diaries and letters are made".

> "*Prison and Chocolate Cake* was intended for myself and my family, and for the circle of friends who had been part and parcel of the atmosphere it described".[6]

Does this statement confirm the initial argument that the book was written primarily for a remedial purpose? In such case the autobiography is not merely a recapitulation of the past, but a struggle of the self to draw the meaning from the life lived at a certain moment in history.

Early in life Nayantara Sahgal, with her sister, was sent to America; she would often wonder about the motive behind her parent's decision: "how did Mummie and Papu have the courage to send us to America in 1943?" The disconcerting question, which she frequently put to herself, had no answer even when she was married and had children. She could only make conjectures about her parents' resolution, which must have been a tough one, that perhaps the American sojourn was essential for a "training in courage and discipline." Close reading of *Prison and Chocolate Cake* enables us to discern various explanations to Sahgal's query – these are not discussed deliberately or consciously but are interwoven in the main body of the text and are a part of it. Sahgal's mother, Vijayalakshmi Pandit, was not very keen to send her daughters, Nayantara and Lekha, to America, which at that time was a *free* country. She was always inclined to be tearful whenever the proposition was brought up by her husband, Ranjit Pandit. She was apprehensive and felt a kind of trepidation at the idea of sending "such babies ..... so far away alone". On the other hand, Ranjit Pandit, showed great concern at letting his children remain in India where he could not give them the kind of freedom and security that they needed. He would frequently argue with his wife to convince her about America being a better place for their daughters:

> "Would you rather they stayed in India and became more and more embittered day by day by what is going on around them? That would be a complete negation of all that we have stood for and tried to teach them." 'No', Mummie agreed reluctantly, 'I should not like them to grow up bitter human beings, nursing grudges and hatreds'."[7]

Thus the "charmed hours of childhood" came to an end when Nayantara Sahgal with her sister set sail for America with a "coconut for good luck and a little box of carved wood containing a handful of Indian earth"[8] to fortify and console them in case a feeling of home sickness overwhelmed them and they longed for the homefront. Enroute to America, a fellow traveller, while talking to Nayantara Sahgal, suddenly put a question to her:

> "How come you decided to go abroad at a time like this"?
> "Because I'm not allowed to study at home", I replied. "You see at home students have to promise not to take part in political activities."
> "Political activities?" he asked, bewildered.
> I thought to myself: "For the past nine months all my family have been in Jail for wanting their country

> to be free, and nobody outside India knows anything about it." Out loud I patiently explained: "You see, at home we are not allowed to say what we think. If any one says he wants freedom for India, he gets locked up in prison."[9]

The journey to America was as much psychic as a physical voyage and it proved valuable and useful in more ways than one and was a widening experience. It favoured and promoted the growth of Sahgal's mind who had always been "encouraged to be venturesome, do the daring rather than the timid thing, taking risks rather than play safe, and I was keenly aware of the joy of being myself, like every other person a unique human being."[10]

Sahgal and her sister became India's "unofficial ambassadors" to America, where they had a wonderful time at college in a congenial and free atmosphere. The vacations were filled with fun and travelling to various parts of the country brought them into contact with a number of American celebrities who gave them a better understanding of that free land. Freedom was the main concern at home too, but it was mainly a political involvement and had proved to be quite traumatic to the young minds; freedom in America was an individual's business. The American voyage gave Sahgal

> "the first experience of a free country, for the first time we realised what it was like to live in one. In America, freedom – unlike in England, where a sophisticated and mature people, grown old in it, took it for granted – was still heady and intoxicating, like wine or a brand new, vibrant idea. People were ardent about it. 'This is a free country' was a joking rejoinder to remarks about whether one should make this or that choice, yet it was earnestly meant. Freedom was a cherished possession, belligerently defended. In India it had been haunting in its lack, a distant star

> on the horizon, something to work and ache for, often at stupendous personal cost. In America it was on one's lap, on one's tongue, where, I suddenly discovered, it belonged. It was one's very own."[11]

America's "freedom" was a "fatal encounter" for Sahgal and its spirit seeped through her very bones and she would relish its taste throughout her life:

> "The need for freedom, I knew once and for all, went far beyond political and economic definition. It no longer applied only to a country. From the depths of everything my parents had taught me and demonstrated through the way they lived and worked, it became a solid value. I knew that never in any circumstances, personal or national, whether in my capacity as student, or later as wife, mother or citizen, would I let it go. The freedom to think, to write, to *be,* what life was all about."[12]

For Sahgal the individual's freedom is an extremely important principle. She has recently revealed that as a child she was used to democracy: "we had it at home where no decision concerning us children was ever taken without a family council presided over by the youngest member."[13] Thus every form of coercion is an anathema to her whether in the realm of politics, marriage or religious practice. This according to her is the cornerstone of cultured behaviour. During her stay in America her sense of an individual's democratic rights was strengthened. Her portrayal of political dealings and human relationship everywhere imply the criterion of individual freedom. Individual and national freedom became an important part of Nayantara Sahgal's existence.

The world in which she was born and grown up was dominated by the presence and guidance of Mahatama Gandhi; it was at this time that India was trying to attain maturity as a nation. Gandhism not only united the country but became a living part of any Indian who came into contact with it. The main tenet of Gandhism being India's attainment of freedom, any sacrifice for the cause was not a deterrent to an individual, more so for "the children of Gandhi's India, born at a time when India was being reborn from an incarnation of darkness into one of light."[14] The nation became bewitched by Gandhi and people like Motilal Nehru gave up the luxurious way of life to join the cause of the country's freedom. The members of her family had been doggedly concerned with it and no loss incurred was great enough nor any hardship beyond tolerance for the cause. Nayantara Sahgal, with her sisters, had not been directly embroiled in the freedom movement but had observed it from extremely close quarters. Their parents too made sure that the girls had "untrammeled freedom of holidyas" whether it was at Almora or Khali.

Sahgal's father exercised an overwhelming influence on her young mind. Autobiographies, particularly by women, have extraordinarily etched out portraits of fathers; but with Nayantara Sahgal it was an unusually beautiful and loving relation. Both the parents were the "center" of their daughters' lives, but it was "the indulgent and proud father" who impressed Nayantara markedly. He was the pivot of her life and from him she learnt lessons in courage, freedom and self-respect; it was not a banal and conventional relationship. The two autobiographies *Prison and Chocolate Cake* and *From Fear Set Free* have significantly illustrated the instances where the father would encourage his daughters in their search of selfhood. Ranjit Pandit's influence and his lessons on the essence of freedom were specially meaningful to Sahgal:

> "Well, India is backward in many ways. That's why we must all work harder to make ourselves better people. The important thing is not to fight for freedom, but to fight to improve ourselves. Then freedom will come, and we will be worthy of it, as we were before."[15]

Her "gallant, laughter – loving father" died in prison in India while his daughters enjoyed the spirit of freedom in a foreign land. His death left not only a void in Sahgal's heart but filled it with rancour. It was not easy for her to get rid of bitterness, her father's most scorned enemy:

> "Bitterness filled me that he had to die, till I remembered that bitterness had been his most scorned enemy. He had sent us away so that we would grow up free from it, strong and proud, 'children of the light', as he had said. To bow before it now would be to deny all he had lived for and the purpose for which he had died."[16]

Nevertheless India without Papu would be "empty":

> ".......every familiar place echoing his gay voice, mirroring his smile, I wanted to run back through time into the security of his presence and his wisdom, canceling the years that had taken him from me, but I had to go forward. For me the lonely ordeal still remained."[17]

She strengthened herself to face the acute loneliness and desolation, fight the bitterness in her heart, and tried to establish a sense of equilibrium. She searched for freedom from the grief for all that she had lost while her country became free. It needed all her nerve and courage to get a firm hold on herself; Gandhi's advice to Vijaylakshmi Pandit to "find your courage within yourself" helped her in finding strength and fortitude. Nayantara had her mother's example before her and she decided she would return to India, to Delhi where her Mamu was the first Prime Minister of a free nation. Nehru's proximity made her feel as if she had "really come home." However, she did regret not being in India to watch and to follow the chain of events that had led to its freedom. Suddenly everything around her acquired an air of novelty, "but without the stranger's detachment" and whatever she saw and heard affected her deeply.

Gandhi's death was a trauma, which the nation faced with tears and shock; it signified the end of an era and of a way of life. Every effort was needed to ride over the tide of sorrow:

> "With an effort I roused myself from my imaginings .....were my values so fragile – had Bapu lived and died for nothing? – that I could so easily lose courage when he was no longer there? Millions of people would have been ordinary folk, living their humdrum lives unperturbed but for him. He had come to disturb them profoundly, to jolt them out of indifference, to awaken them to one another's suffering, and in so doing to make them reach for the stars .... The curtain had rung down over a great drama, but another one was about to begin. Gandhi was dead, but his India would live on in his children."[18]

The principal aim of autobiography, says Roy Pascal, must be a discovery of one's inner understanding, which should be revealed in the process of the narrative:

> "The life is represented in autobiography not as something established but as a process; it is not simply the narrative of the voyage, but also the voyage itself. There must be in it a sense of discovery, and where this is wanting, and the autobiography appears as an exposition of something understood from the outset, we feel it is a failure at any rate. .....self-knowledge is then a primary motive of autobiography."[19]

Many autobiographies do not necessarily facilitate our knowledge of the workings of the writer's mind. But in the case of Sahgal, the inner misgivings and apprehensions, the questionings to which she subjects herself, the doubts which assail her mind are all vividly depicted through her writings. The inner self of Sahgal finds its expression and embodiment in the portrayal of her life. This kind of depiction gives authenticity and merit to her books. *Prison and Chocolate Cake* and *From Fear Set Free* reveal the process of coming to terms with herself, with the world and her life. It was extremely important for Nayantara Sahgal to come to terms with the present, which she always saw in comparison with the past. The recollection of the past is done in a haphazard way, with a kind of chronological disorder and also a thematic disorganisation. There is no continuity because, as the author claims, *Prison and Chocolate Cake* was not intended for people outside the family and was not proposed for publication as a formal autobiographical work. Nayantara Sahgal's proficiency as a novelist aids her in adopting the technique of moving back and forth in time, and in culling out incidents and episodes from "memories store house."

Nayantara's decision of not making America her home was prompted by her affinity to her motherland and she realised that she could "never belong anywhere but in India" – India that had witnessed a "revolution of values" and where the people had brought about a change not through a legal battle but through the human heart. Gandhi's influence had dominated her household as it had the whole country. Gandhi breathed a life into every individual who came in contact with him. For Sahgal Gandhism symbolised not only "satyagraha" but a belief in one's self and a cleansing from fear and eventually from hate. She knew that it could lead to an inward freedom in an individual:

> "The outward freedom that we shall attain will only be in exact proportion to the inward freedom to which we may have grown at a given moment."[20]

Sahgal's source of inspiration was such teaching of Gandhi who was also a fountainhead of "spiritual reservoir" since her childhood. Thus she felt oddly out-of-place and strongly uncomfortable wherever she did not find the badge of Gandhism; the man she fell in love with and whom she eventually married "doubted the efficiency of Gandhi's teachings." Gautam, her husband, had witnessed the havoc wrought by partition upon millions of people – some of whom died and others were uprooted from the place where they had been born. Nayantara Sahgal was compelled to face certain queries surging in her mind about non-violence:

> "But how far, I thought, lying awake in the dark long after I had gone to bed, do we perform the good action knowing it to be the good? How often are we charitable or motivated by kindness knowing these to be the right? How closely does the actual ever resemble the ideal?"[21]

Nayantara Sahgal and Gautam were two individuals from two different world and an uncommon background, with the seeds of "potential conflict" lying dormant to erupt any moment; they decided to spend their lives together:

> "I worried about the differences between us, and soon learned that hesitation was not a part of Gautam's make-up ...... How could I enter his world or he mine? We could make a new one, said Gautam."[22]

Thus "caught between two opposing currents" Nayantara Sahgal entered her new world, where the "tug-of-war continued":

> "A part of me, deeply enmeshed in a political consciousness, strained every nerve in automatic response to what went on in India. This part was emotionally involved with India's future, and belonged to my uncle's home at the moment. The other part struggled to pull free and build a life as near normal as possible for myself."[23]

The marriage transported her from the familiar world of "Gandhi caps and Indian clothes" to the one "bequeathed by nearly two hundred years of British contact and rule." She became unsure of herself, of her capability of reconciling the two diverse worlds. The lure of the past made her want to escape from the present and any incident from her present life had to be paralleled and correlated to some event in the more familiar past. This becomes her method of narration particularly in her second autobiography, *From Fear Set Free*. Nostalgia for the past, whether it be a way of life, or relationships or of India's political ethos, is a significant trait of Sahgal in this book, which was written with the purpose of narrating her life after marriage. Autobiographies are not histories or life-accounts of only an individual; they become a contribution to the historical understanding of that particular period in which the writer lived. As such the autobiographical mode is used to expose not only the real determining instances in a person's life but it also becomes a kind of history-writing to explain the relationship between the past and the present. Her habit of story-telling, which once again reminds us that she is a novelist too, creeps in many times, as do the anecdotes, which are characteristically associated with autobiographical texts and help in enriching the organisation of experiences retrospectively. The urge for freedom becomes a persistent refrain in her writings.

From Fear Set Free does not blatantly condemn her marriage nor does it overtly express any feelings of suffocation or bondage, which Sahgal may have experienced during her married life. However, what she often alludes to is feeling of some kind of fear and being confined in a particular way of life. It is only when we correlate her other writings with the two life-narratives that the significance of her utterance of alienation within the four walls of her house becomes clear: "I still did not think of them as home." By traditional standards she should have been "happy" with the material comforts around her. But the lack of something as vital as oxygen suffocated her:

"My sickness went deep and every now and again it surfaced and made trouble, for its clamoring core was the inescapable truth that once you have lived in freedom, been truly yourself, you can never settle for less ......You cannot pretend other values, another outlook on life. You can't honestly serve what you don't believe in."[24]

Marriage had unsettled her "disastrously"; she had not anticipated an encounter with ego and ambition:

> "I was uneasy and restless adjusting to the demands of a personality and an environment whose goals and texture were different from anything I had known or been comfortable with. But if I had my hankerings, I suppressed them. I rigidly ignored the feeling that I was in a room two feet square with no opening but a tiny grating high up in one wall. I tried not to look up at it. Out there somewhere was sun light, and at night a forest of stars, but they were not for me. I was here in my two-feet-square room of my own choice. Nobody had forced me into it and I had no one else to blame."[25]

Paranoid at the idea of confinement Sahgal left her husband and found the courage to live separately in a flat found by E.N. Mangat Rai:

> "When it came to actually doing it, I couldn't. Living together without marriage held too many terrors. It might be all right in some place off the beaten track, but definitely not in the full avid glare and publicity of Delhi."[26]

The fear of the people, of the social and cultural values held her imprisoned and she balked at the idea of living together with Rai without marriage. Mangat Rai's devotion and his desire of "reaching for the stars" finally gave her the courage, which she lacked:

> "I packed my luggage and moved with the children to the house he had been allotted, and prepared to face the onslaught of Other People. We were not strangers to non-conformity but this, I thought, was going to be like hacking steps where no steps had ever been, in the cold rock face of a society unused to such situation. But though there was upheaval enough, involving ourselves, the storms of growing children and the adjustments to be made from past to present, Other People were not part of it. They unfolded along the way as a courteous and kindly breed, ready with interest, affection and help. Of one thing there was no sign – condemnation."[27]

The process of writing purges the human mind of all the fears and its cathartic effect makes the individual come to terms with herself. It also enables her to recognise and value her own self. This is characteristically true of Nayantara Sahgal who was judicious enough to perceive the utility of the written word:

> "I began, through the writing process, to unlearn all I had been taught, including that over powering mix, called history-culture-religion, and to discover who I was through the words I put on a page."[28]

An autobiographical work is more than a factual account of life's events and relationships; it is that "unique truth of life" as seen from inside. It is also a presentation of an "inner core" of the writer, of herself, which gives a new connotation and validity to her life. The self remains undefined and undetermined till the moment it is reviewed in retrospect through the technique of writing which establishes "the power of man in his realisation of an inner self that is as much compulsion as it is freedom ....True autobiography can be written only by men and women pledged to their innermost selves."[29]

Nayantara Sahgal's realisation of the truth about herself dawns on her as she writes her autobiographical works. Her "quest is not a search for transcendent wisdom, but for an inner harmony and contentment."[30] Montaigne's conviction "I have not made my book more than my book has made me," seems to ring true in Sahgal's case. Self-knowledge brings about equilibrium, an inner freedom and an emotional emancipation.

REFERENCES

1. James Olney, "Autobiography and the Cultural Moment: A Thematic, Historical, and Bibliographical Introduction" *Autobiography Essays Theoretical and Critical*, ed. James Olney, Princeton University Press, 1980, p. 22.
2. Georges Gusdorf, "Conditions and Limits of Autobiography" *Autobiography Essays Theoretical and Critical*, ed. James Olney, p. 38.
3. Philip Dodd, "Criticism and the Autobiographical Tradition", *Modern Selves Essays on Modern British and American Autobiography*, ed. Philip Dodd, Frank Cass, England, 1986, p. 9.
4. Nayantara Sahgal, *Point of View, A Personal Response to Life, Literature and Politics*, Prestige Books, New Delhi, 1997, p. 17.
5. Nayantara Sahgal, *Prison and Chocolate Cake*, Harper Collins Publishers, India, p. 18.
6. *Ibid.*, Introduction.
7. *Ibid.*, pp. 173-174.
8. *Ibid.*, p. 4.
9. *Ibid.*, p. 12.
10. Jasbir Jain, *Nayantara Sahgal*, Printwell, Jaipur, 1994, p.3.
11. *Point of View*, pp. 24-25.
12. *Ibid.*, p. 25.
13. Nayantara Sahgal, "India and America: A personal Memoir", *Span*, June/July/August 1997, p.4.
14. Nayantara Sahgal, *From Fear Set Free*, Hind Pocket Books, Delhi, 1962, p. 20.

15. *Prison and Chocolate*, p. 55.
16. *Ibid.*, p. 208.
17. *Ibid.*
18. *Ibid.*, p. 234.
19. Roy Pascal, *Design And Truth In Autobiography*, Harvard University Press, Cambridge, Massachusetts, 1960, p. 208.
20. *From Fear Set Free*, p. 6.
21. *Ibid.*, p. 27.
22. *Ibid.*, p. 21.
23. *Ibid.*, p. 31.
24. *Point of View*, p. 25.
25. *Ibid.*, p. 29.
26. *Ibid.*, p. 20.
27. *Ibid.*, p. 22.
28. *Ibid.*, p. 32.
29. *Design And Truth In Autobiography*, pp. 194-195.
30. A.O.J. Cockshut, *The Art of Autobiography In 19th and 20th Century England*, Yale University Press, New Haven and London, 1984, p. 156.

The God of Small Things : Memory and Art

"Memory", says Susanne K. Langer in ***Feeling and Form***, "is the great organiser of consciousness".[1] Real experience is composed of a medley of sounds, sights, feelings, anticipations and undeveloped reactions; memory is that special agency which sifts all the experiences to obtain and also to retain only the most distinctive and exclusive impressions of the past. It also simplifies and arranges our perceptions into "units of personal knowledge".

The recollection of the past experiences involves not only a process of remembering but also of its reconstruction through language; the doctrine of poesis or creativity demands the actual fact to be metamorphosed into something which is purely experiential with the aid of imagination. Thus in the whole creative process memory becomes a great artist and the writer who puts it to good use, technically as well as thematically, is clever enough to produce a great work of art. Out of the formless, chaotic, painful mass of emotions and experiences of life, the artist creates a pattern with a formal new beginning and meaning and subsequently with a definite aim.

> "Art formalises experience; form implies an end and an intention, and so a meaning ... Just as art has no substance without life, so life is meaningless without art, both poetic and autobiographic;..."[2]

Essentially life, which is represented in a literary work, is always a "unit of experience, a self-contained form"; in it each part is organically correlated to the other, "no matter how capricious or fragmentary the items are made to appear".[3] Consequently a good work of art reflects life and the writer's own feelings about it; this is how an artistic creation attains an intellectual essence. Any artist who makes use of the material from life must necessarily be in love with it to create a successful work of art. His own life's events may also be utilised and the work may comprise of his dreams, the real persons whom he may have known and many personal incidents – all that have a "timeless character". It is done to design and to develop an image of reality in the work of art. The artistic process involves not only a transformation of reality but its transmutation as well; autobiographers employ this method also to reconstruct their life's history through the narrative – the narrative that has the guise of memory.

Well-known writers like Montaigne in *Essays*, T.S.Eliot in *Four Quartets*, D.H.Lawrence in *Sons and Lovers*; R.K.Narayan in *The English Teacher*, *Swami and his Friends*, Kamala Das in her poems, Upamanayu Chatterjee in *English August*, and now Arundhati Roy in *The God of Small Things* have successfully converted their biography into brilliant works of art. The world created in a novel, or in any other literary genre, is a work of investigation that is very different from the actual world in which the hero or the heroine is entirely self-sufficient. Novelists are frequently impelled to base their fictions on their personal experiences:

> "The novel has apparent advantages that can be summed up as technical and may rapidly be enumerated. In the novel, events occurring outside the range of the author-hero may be evoked and imaginatively re-lived ...scenes and conversations may be constructed as a vivid actuality .....".[4]

There are additions, alterations and even inventions which are logical and suit the requirements of the character. This, in a sense, makes the world of fiction truer than life.

For actual life, with its "classic ineptitude", is "all inclusion and confusion" it "persistently blunders and deviates" while art draws "the right truth out of the so easy muddle of wrong truths is never more clearly in evidence than in the autobiographical novel."[5]

Arundhati Roy's fictional work, constructed out of the stuff of her life for a very specific purpose, may be termed an autobiographical novel. *The God of Small Things* has been designed and produced by Roy due to a feeling of urgency to make a reckoning with her past life; an endeavour to liberate herself from the matrix of the days gone by. Roy invents situations, adds data which could never have been actually available to her such as the erotic interlude between Ammu and Velutha and its subsequent repercussion. The incident, even in the novel, is wholly implausible because Roy neither develops the relationship nor gives any hint about it before the amorous episode takes place. Perhaps it has been used for highlighting the fundamental cause of caste and untouchability, of man and woman relationship, of the complexity and the frustrations ensuing from such relationships, of the violation of Love Laws. It is an action untrue of life, yet typical of the novel; a dramatic climax uncharacteristic of Ammu's own life and of a reaction against the Laws laid down by the society of Kerala. The incident sums up the book and at the same time rounds it off.

The God of Small Things, "a big book about the small things of life", is Roy's first book and as such it is heavily autobiographical, as all first works tend to be. Roy represents her life as a "sample" in its social setting and its ideological situation. The personalised story makes us assume that the writer must have felt her individuality to be unique, singular and specific; but she had to go "beyond the actuality also, inorder to uncover what was only potential."[6] It had all to be delineated more sharply than the actual life and hence the need for an artistic re-arrangement and invention. In this way the novel stands by itself though in the form of a "personal book". We can question Roy's impelling need to build the book out of personal experience and to transfer it to the characters in the situations which she invented to create a work of art. Her intentions in writing *The God of Small Things,* her method, her love and hatred for the background in which she grew up are specifically highlighted and elaborated in the numerous interviews she has given to various magazines and journals not only in India but in many other nations she visited after getting the Booker Prize. We have made an attempt in this paper to go beyond the novel, delve in the firsthand revealations and viewpoints of the author expressed in several publications, which were made available on the Internet. Arundhati Roy had been extremely forthcoming in these interviews and as such they help us in a better understanding of the novel. In one such tete-a-tete we find the answer to our query about the need for a persona to reveal her past in the book. She feels

> "Writing *The God of Small Things* was a fictional way of making sense of the world I lived in, and the novel was the technical key with which I did it. It touches things which I could not wish to address in my everyday life. It deals with the areas I do my best to avoid thinking about. It unleashes terrors which I have always tried to get away from. All I know is that there are things which form you before you form yourself. And these things will never go away, for they constitute the deepest part of me."[7]

Such fictional autobiographies are written to "authenticate the truthfulness of what they (the novelists) had to say ...we identify ourselves in the name we give others."[8] Thus Roy felt the need to put on the mask of Rahel, with whom the reader can empathise, to give impression to a traumatic childhood; through Rahel she revealed her native state and the Laws which governed the people who lived there. This transformation of personal life into art is not a "slavish transcription of actual life", but a presentation of biographical events in new combinations; the events are selected, altered and imbued with the brilliance of the various themes to suit the framework of the novel. Roy is a great artist and blends explicit realism with poetic myth and experience with imagination. The book is a chronicle of a life, which has been made meaningful and storiable. A life reconstructed out the memories of the past:

> "Roy's greatest gift is her power of memory, the kind of memory Charles Dickens and George Eliot had, which can bring alive for the reader what most of us have forgotten but can recall if jogged. What it felt like to be a child, 'a stranger and afraid in a world we never made'. Yet endowed with much or more ability to experience the supposedly adult emotions of anxiety, jealousy, grief, despair ... Love. Madness. Hope. Infinite Joy."[9]

There are memories of fear, of dirt, "the filth that laid siege to the Ayemenem house", in the "early amorphous years", of a life lived with long, unrelieved stretches of unhappiness:

> "Memory was that woman on the train. Insane in the way she sifted through dark things in a closet and emerged with the most unlikely ones – a fleeting look, a feeling. The smell of smoke. A windscreen wiper. A mother's marble eyes. Quite same in the way she left huge tracts of darkness veiled. Unremembered."(p.72)

It is about the "Heart of Darkness" at Aymanam (Ayemenem in the novel) where the Love Laws were made. "The laws that lay down who should be loved and how. And how much." The happenings Arundhati witnessed in this town, which is ten minutes drive from Kottayam in Kerala, "terrorised her". Treated creatively "Little events, ordinary things, smashed and reconstituted. Imbued with new meaning. Suddenly they become the bleached bones of a story."(p.33)

> "You know, I think, I know I can only bear to go back and flirt with the edges of it. I still have memories of just how deeply desperate I was when I was there. Even now, when I know I've escaped, I'm still scared of what it has done to me."[10]

However the landscape of the place held a special fascination for her; she loved it and yet she fears it. But she is compelled to write about it. The rustic idyll set in a quiet village in Kerala has aroused a worldwide interest. The vivid, exotic, pictorial and intimate description transports the reader to that part of southern India with which he may not be very familiar, but with which he gets acquainted as the book progresses. It is "a masterful creation from the hand of a gifted artist":

> "I think the kind of landscape that you grew up in, it lives in you. I don't think it's true of people who've grown up in cities so much, you may love a building but I don't think you can love it in the way that you love a tree or a river or the colour of the earth, it's a different kind of love ...If you spent your very early childhood catching fish and just learning to be quiet, the landscape just seeps into you. Even now I go back to Kerala and it makes me want to cry if something happens to that place."[11]

This "sense of place", says Ritu Menon of *Kali for Women*[12], which the novel evokes is "an important ingredient in Western literature (we remember Dickens and Hardy utilising it in English literature, R.K.Narayan in Indian Writing in English).

She wrote about the weather, the vegetation of Kerala with such evocative force, her flawless ear, her genius for the individuating detail is memorable; she evoked a "tropical splendour" with a dazzling command of language:

> "May in Ayemenem is hot, brooding month. The days are long and humid. The river shrinks and black crows gorge on·bright mangoes in still, dustgreen trees. Red bananas ripen. Jackfruits burst. Dissolute bluebottles hum vacuously in the fruity air. Then they stun themselves against clear windowpanes and die, fatly baffled in the sun.
>
> But by early June the south-west monsoon breaks and there are three months of wind and water with short spells of sharp, glittering sunshine that thrilled children snatch to play with. The countryside turns an immodest green. Boundaries blur as tapioca fences take root and bloom. Brick walls turn mossgreen. Pepper vines snake up electric poles. Wild creepers burst through laterite banks and spill across the flooded roads. Boats ply in the bazaars. And small fish appear in the puddles that fill the PWD potholes on the highways."(p.1)

The sluggish river Meenachal (Meenachil in reality) overflows out of the pages of the novel. This Kerala setting of 1969, "not so much sultry as dripping with decay, disappointment, family pettiness and social calcification"[13], is out-and-out autobiographical.

> "I grew up in Kerala and a lot of the atmosphere of *The God of Small Things* is based on my experiences of what it was like there."[14]

The quintessence of Roy's life provides interesting material for biography *The God of Small Things* presents material the novelist's journey into her past, to her childhood days; the book embodies the life of the twins in the verdant backwaters of Kerala. Like Rahel, Arundhati was the child of an unhappy marriage of a Christian woman, who broke all conventional norms by marrying a Bengali Hindu, and then separating from him and going back to Kerala to live in sufferance with Arundhati and her brother Lalit. Rahel, in the novel, with her "wild hair", with a tiny diamond gleaming in one nostril, with "absurdly beautiful collarbones"(p.18) is the slim-hipped author herself. But she has never known a twin brother:

> "I'm not a twin, and I've never known twins. The book really delves, very deep I think, into human nature. The story tells of the brutality we're capable of, but also that aching, intimate love. And for me the twins are what that is about ...the ability to actually dream each other's dreams and to share each other's happiness and pain."[15]

The novel portrays the unhappiness and pain with no positive relationships – marriages take place but end in divorce; the loved ones are separated; alcoholism and beatings pervade the families; the twins have to suffer the pain of separation; deaths occur commonly even in the very young. Should we conclude that the unhappiness seeping through the pages of the novel represents Roy's personal view? Does she think that happiness is unsubstantial and chimerical? Does she feel that true love is condemned and cursed?

> "Actually I wouldn't see the book that way ..the way in which the story is told, or the structure of the book, tells you a different story. The structure of the book ambushes the story – by that I mean the novel ends more or less in the middle of the story and it ends with Ammu and Velutha making love and it ends on the word tomorrow. Though you know that what tomorrow brings is terrible it is saying that the fact that this happened at all is wonderful ..I don't think I offer you one thing. If there's tragedy there's also comedy going on somewhere on the side. If there's sadness there's also happiness, there's also joy."[16]

She feels that the world around us has nothing much to offer; it is not possible for people to live happily ever after and so "There's no candy at the end of the story."

The novel, which is about human nature, spans three decades and accentuates the class division seen in the Kottayam society with layering detail upon detail. Mary Roy and her children did not live in the centre of the traditional community of Kerala. They were unprotected from any uncertainty and insecurity; a feeling of reliability and dependability of a conventional family life, which is the demand of any normal individual, was denied to them. However, the only advantage of an unshielded, defenseless and precarious life seems to be that though the people who live on the borders of these communities may have nothing to do with each other but at sometime of their life they do come across one another. This point has been emphasised in the novel and we realise that Arundhati Roy identifies with her fictional creations:

> "I grew up in very similar circumstances to the children in the book. My mother was divorced, I lived on the edge of the community in a very vulnerable fashion. I was an unprotected child in some ways ... Then when I was sixteen I left home and lived on my own, sort of ... you know it wasn't awful, it was just sort of precarious living in a squatter's colony in Delhi. Looking at life from the outside and not being part of this world where you grow up and then are married and sent off. You know it's actually terrifying for those ensconced in traditional societies and in many ways I escaped that. Having an arranged life and being sent off to some stranger's house. But on other hand escaping that meant watching it from the outside and not knowing exactly what would happen to you."[17]

Roy thinks that the class division, which forms another theme of the novel, especially in Ammu's forbidden, tragic relationship with a Paravan, is still a divisive force in India; it is particularly reflected in Indian politics and in the marriages. India, she thinks, exists in several centuries simultaneously. So on the one hand where there are intellectuals like Roy herself, with a particularly Bohemian life style, there are others who are much behind in times. It is no doubt a kind of strange situation with a chasm dividing people at different levels of the society. Roy is not very hopeful of the narrowing of this breach between the two opposite groups. Perhaps this dismay has led to a feeling of anger and defiance in the novel; anger at the subordinate and marginalised position of women in the society, particularly in the society in which she grew up where, she says, the only real conflict was between women and men:

> "What I meant by biology having been subdued is that when I go back to Kerala, I see these incredible beautiful human beings, who are just so attractive. And yet I know of girls who despite being so lovely can't get married because they don't have enough money to pay a dowry. There's no question of their marrying lower-caste men ...They are lower caste and therefore almost not men! It's like different species, like cats and dogs. I've spoken to people who've read my book and liked it, but are completely unable to accept the relationship between Ammu and Velutha. 'It can't happen', they say."[18]

Ammu, a woman of grit and courage, was denied higher education by Pappachi who "insisted that a college education was an unnecessary expense for a girl."(p.38) She waited, like all the girls in Ayemenem, for marriage proposals, which did not come, as there was no money to pay for dowry:

> "Unnoticed, or at least unremarked upon by her parents. Ammu grew desperate. All day she dreamed of escaping from Ayemenem and the clutches of her ill-tempered father and bitter, long-suffering mother."(p.38)

She finally fled to Calcutta to end up in marriage to an alcoholic Bengali. Roy's novel reveals not only the inward problems and struggles, but also many more issues central to the character of Ammu. Rahel, like Arundhati, was born out of a marriage doomed from the start and was the child of a broken home. The "emotionally – precarious childhood" gave Roy a kind of vulnerability which makes her "absolutely terrified"[19] of ever having children. It is due to a mentally scarred childhood that she finds it difficult to speak of her father whom she does not know and has met only a couple of times.

Mary Roy's status of a single mother was the cause of much antipathy and aversion in Kottayam's insular, traditional community. Being a daughter, she, like Ammu, had no claim to the property and no "Locusts Stand I".(p.57) Mary Roy created history of sorts by fighting the provisions of the Christian Succession Act in the Supreme Court, which gave a favourable ruling to the Christian women, who were then allowed an equal share, with their brothers, in the father's property. When interviewed by *India Today* (October 27, 1997) Mary Roy revealed her insecure position in the conservative Kerala society:

> "There was much trauma for me in the '60s as Kottayam did not accept me as I was a woman separated from my husband. We are not divorced, though I tried to hide the pain from my children. It is only when I read her book that I realised that even at five she was conscious that we were unwelcome in the native home and that I expected her to be able to stand on her own feet, so that she would never be in such a weak position as I was."

But she does not agree with the critics that 'Ammu' in the novel, who was ostracised by her family and society, has been modeled on her. Her daughter, says Mary Roy, has only used her bio-data as the bare bones for 'Ammu's' character.

Arundhati now shared a beautiful relationship with her mother. She left home at eighteen and did not return for some six years or so, was a willful girl who hated anyone telling her what to do. Only her mother, who supported her, had that privilege and authority and in the course of time, this relationship matured into a strong bond as is evident from the dedication of the book. The mother runs the Corpus Christi School where the social elite of Kottayam send their children to learn the Western way of education. Arundhati had the advantage of spending her formative years in this school. Later she had her architectural training in the Delhi School of Architecture, where she met and married classmate Gerard Da Cunha. The marriage, which could not be made official in the Registrar's office due to the long queue there, broke after four years. Roy's nonconformist and offbeat life style is reflected in Rahel's character, .who marries Larry McCaslin, goes to America with him and later split up with him. Rahel "never returned to Ayemenem. Not when Mammachi died. Not when Chacko emigrated to Canada."(p.18) Ajaz Ahmad's commentary on Arundhati's way of life brings her attitude into sharp focus:

> "The leaving of the family home and the sowing of the wild oats endows her with the autonomous self that would have been denied to her, as it was denied to her mother, in the stifling world of the provincial caste-bound gentility of the family."[20]

These are not the only autobiographical reflections in *The God of Small Things*. Mary Roy's estranged brother, George Isaac, is featured in the book as Uncle Chacko, the only male in the house. As the England-returned Uncle he is at the maelstrom of the emotional tension within the family.

He convincingly states that Mary Roy "is 'Ammu'".[21] But he does not want to disclose the identity of Velutha. The "Ayemenem House" of the novel cannot be found in the Aymanam village; however it is not entirely fictional:

> "An architect by training, Arundhati has borrowed brick and timber from two old buildings in the, Puliyampallil House and Shanti House to construct her "Ayemenem House"'.[22]

Puliyapallil is an elegant, early 20th century building "with its steep gabled roof pulled over its ears like a low hat".(p.1) Mary Roy agrees that it does resemble the "Ayemenem House". It now belongs to one of Arundhati's Aunts. The Shanti House, which in its interiors resembles any European House, was designed in early sixties by Isaac's divorced wife, Cacilia Philipson, who is more or less 'Margaret' in the novel. But there is no 'Baby Kochamma' to be identified in the real life.

"Paradise Pickles" factory in *The God of Small Things* (pp.30, 46) is the "Palat Pickles" and it was started by Isaac and is located near his ancestral house, Palathinkal. It bears the same slogan as the one in the novel, "Emperor in the realm of taste". The Aymanam temple figures in the novel as a prominent venue for the annual Kathakali festival (pp.228-237). This beautiful, compelling and energetic dance from Kerala has now been taken, through the pages of the novel, beyond the state and beyond the country, into the whole wide world as India's rich cultural heritage.

Donald Eichert in *The Week* (October 26, 1997) comes to the conclusion that Aymanam with 7000 houses and a number of dish antennae may not be the same old-fashioned village of the sixties. Social prejudices have dissolved to a greater extent. But even today an affair between a low caste man and an upper caste woman is unthinkable and can cause its people to react not too congenially.

Communism gained a stronghold in Kerala and the party proved to be quite successful. Arundhati observed its influence not only on the state but on its people too. Kerala, she found, was

> "the only place in the world where religions coincide, there's Christianity, Hinduism, Marxism and Islam and they all live together and rub each other down. When I grew up it was the Marxism that was very strong, it was like the revolution was coming next week. I was aware of the different cultures when I was growing up and I am still aware of them now. When you see all the competing beliefs against the same background you realise how they all wear each other down. To me, I couldn't think of a better location for a book about human beings."[23]

However, supporters of Marxism are not too happy at the way its leaders have been depicted in the book. Roy's "ideological opposition to communism" in the book, says Aijaz Ahmad, does not come as a surprise; it is a common attitude of mind among the "cosmopolitan intelligentsia" not only in India but elsewhere in the world too. However, what is surprising is that even though she is a Keralite, Roy lacks the "rudimentary knowledge" about communist politics. Her lampooning of E.M.S.Namboodripad in the novel stems not from a lack of intelligence but from "settled ideological hostility". Moreover, Namboodripad's ancestral home does not exist anywhere near Kottayam; Arundhati has converted this home into a hotel in the novel while the communist workers become the hotel boys. This was done, remarked the Chief Minister of Kerala, E.K.Nayanar, to portray the commercialisation of communism. However, it is difficult to agree with Nayanar's gibe that the "anti-communist venom" in *The God of Small Things* and the caricaturing of the communist leaders helped Roy in getting the prestigious Booker. The observation is uncalled for and has not been fairly spoken.

It has not been the aim of this paper to correlate all the events and persons in the novel with the facts of Arundhati Roy's life and her home in Kerala. Nevertheless the interviews given by the author, her mother and her uncle help in identifying evidences of biographical details in *The God of Small Things*. It is not for the first time that a writer has mingled fact with fabrication in her work of art; R.K.Narayan's statement in his autobiography *My Days* that "fiction outlasts facts"[24] bears testimony to this method. We can presume that Roy thought the same and mingled incidents and people from her life with the figments of her imagination. It is a well-known artistic manoeuver to immortalise one's life-experience by giving it the form of a story; the process embellishes the novel with a kind of richness and the endeavaer may have been done "to reduce a chaos of experience to some sort of order and a hungry curiosity."[25]

Roy's first attempt at novel-writing, is a work of fiction with its own technique of stream of consciousness of a small girl, using a daring formula, unfolded through a language which is highly indigenised and which, being a part of Roy's personality, is very important to her:

> "My language is mine, it's the way I think and the way I write. You know I don't scrabble around and try and I don't sweat the language. I don't rewrite. It was just a lot of arranging."[26]

It was this 'arranging' or 'designing' the book, of slipping back and forth between several time frames, of zooming on certain events of her life and leaving out many others which makes her novel read like a "ferociously reinvented memoir, and Roy says that in some ways *Small Things* is a story that has 'always been with her'."[27]

Any individual's life, however dull or insipid it may be, can become significant and worthwhile when it is transformed into a story. Roy's early life may have been traumatic and painful when she and her mother were plagued and distressed quite frequently by their unhappy living condition; but when the same story is transferred to fictional characters in fictional situations, it becomes a gripping tale with various thematic connotations. The novelist reconstructs the facts of her life to write a memorable book, which has become a milestone in the history of Indian Writing in English. A critic writing in *India Today* (March 15, 1997) said about the book that "It is all so real, it had to be fiction" and Arundhati Roy, perhaps wanting to immortalise her life, borrowed her autobiographical resources for the purpose of its reconstruction into art. The raw materials from her past are exploited and reorganised; the practice gives credence to the hypothesis that "Fact, in order to survive, must become fiction."[28] The two are complementary to each other and the truth of reality has to be "fragmented by the prism of fiction" to become an engrossing and profound work of art with a universal appeal.

REFERENCES

1. "Virtual Memory", *Feelings and Form*, A theory of Art Developed From *Philosophy In A New Key*, By Susanne K. Langer, Routledge & Kegan Paul Limited, 1967, p. 262.
2. *Metaphors of Self, the meaning of autobiography*, By James Olney, Princeton University Press, 1972, pp. 270, 271.
3. Susanne K. Langer, *Feeling and Form*, p. 262.
4. "The Autobiographical Novel", *Design And Truth In Autobiography*, Roy Pascal, Harvard University Press, Cambridge, Massachusetts, 1960, p. 164.
5. *Ibid.,* p.168.
6. *Ibid.,* p.171.
7. *Frontline*, August 8,1997, Interviewed by Praveen Swami.
8. Glen Cavaliero, "Autobiography and Fiction", in *Modern Selves, Essays on Modern British & American Autobiography,* ed. By Philip Dodd, Frank Cass Company Limited, London, 1986, p. 157.

9. Ruth Vanita, *Book Review: No Small Achievement*, Issue no.103/ 1997.
10. *Frontline*, August 8, 1997.
11. Interview with Arundhati Roy, "Capturing Landscapes Which Become a Part of You", and "How Small Things Grow Into Something Far Greater", reported at website http://www.harpercollin.co.uk/intv1/017/roy2.htm.
12. *The Hindu*, October 17, 1997.
13. Anthony Spaeth, "No Small Thing", *Time*, April 14, 1997.
14. Interview with Arundhati Roy, "Capturing Landscapes Which Become a Part of You" and "How Small Things Grow into Something Far Greater", reported at website http://harpercollin.co.uk/intv1/017/roy2.htm.
15. Emily Gutheinz, Wordsworth Books: Interview with Arundhati Roy, 15.6.97.
16. *Ibid.*
17. *Ibid.*
18. *Frontline*, August 8,1997.
19. Shobha Tsering Bhalla, "Live being stroked and slapped", The Strats Times Interactive, Feb. 28, 1998.
20. *Frontline*, August 8, 1997.
21. Venu Menon, Rediff On The NeT, 1997, *Who's Ammu?*
22. Donald Eichert, "To The Booker Born", *The Week*, October 26, 1997.
23. Website http://harpercollin.co.uk/intv1/017/roy2.htm.
24. *My Days, An Autobiography*, Orient Paperbacks, 1991, p. 122.
25. Graham Greene, *A Sort of Life*, Penguin Books, 1971, p. 9.
26. "A conversation with Arundhati Roy", Interview with Amazon.com.
27. *Time*, April 14,1997.
28. Robert Scholes, *Elements of Fiction*, Oxford University Press, 1968, p. 3.

CHAPTER 12

Writing A Woman's Life : The Scope of Happiness

Anonymity is naturally believed to be the proper condition of a woman and she has to justify her encroachment on the autobiographical genre of writing, which is supposedly a male monopoly. "The more male self dominated autobiography the better the genre".[1] For a woman the creative act in this case becomes an instance of defying the predetermined life-patterns and the necessity of fitting into the socially defined slots. Queries like "why have you written your autobiography?" are frequently hurled at her as she is appropriated to be a female rather than a human being. The Indian constitution guarantees a woman not only the freedom of speech but also of expression. Denying her the right to life writing is a way of opposing her the write to power. Inorder to retain their status of authority, it becomes imperative for men to disallow any kind of position of eminence to the woman who desires to be at the helm of affairs. Autobiographical writing is one such means to focus attention on one's self and on one's life which the male dominance seeks to wipe out.

A woman's writing has generally been considered to be "valueless art" and "dismissed as 'confession'".[2] But the reality is far from it – we read a woman's autobiography for other reasons than we read her novels, where the self may be fictionalised. These life narratives by historical figures delineate and reveal how they found their own voice to express their feelings in writings; thus these autobiographies become a "priviledged site of historical agency for women". Some of these life narratives have emphatically demonstrated how the assumption of power comes naturally to any woman of substance who can successfully avoid being marginalised to move into the centre of life's activities.

The Scope of Happiness (1979) by Vijaya Lakshmi Pandit is a fine piece of autobiographical writing besides being a valuable document as it validates the rightful position of women in the Indian society. It is work which seeks to focus not only upon some of the conservatisms followed by the Nehru family but also on the human rights, which signified "the need to work for freedom from oppressions that continue to crush humanity in so many parts of the world".[3] The Gandhian ideals, which were tenaciously followed and adopted by the family, helped in transforming a young, timid girl from Allahabad into a confident and extraordinary individual who played an active and positive role in developing an image of India on the world scene.

Patricia Spacks's[4] observations of women's autobiographies are not relevant to Mrs. Pandit's work. Spacks had said that it is very rare to find "the theme of accomplishment" dominating these narratives though the genre demands "self-assertion and self-display". This remark is not valid in the case of this charming Indian woman's "well-written and informative autobiography" which "gives an insight into a remarkable" individual:

> "Hers is a story of selfless dedication not only to her mother country, India, but to the cause of freedom, peace, and understanding throughout the world. She has truly proved herself to be a good citizen of the world".[5]

Vijaya Lakshmi Pandit's involvement in the affairs of the country gave her the opportunity of "self-discovery of her identity", which is not "grounded through relation to the chosen other". Carolyn G Heilbrun, a feminist critic, while reviewing women's autobiographies had commented:

> "There are no recognisable career stages in such a life, as there would be for a man. Nor have women a tone of voice in which to speak with authority".[6]

However Mrs. Pandit's autobiography breaks down all the established theoretical norms, including the "narrative flatness", discerned by the western feminist critics in the writings by women. It is legitimately argued that such writings by women cannot serve as role models. This is not the case with Mrs. Pandit who seizes her own life's story and tells it directly to enlighten the readers; *The Scope of Happiness* can therefore be slotted in the "gender-neutral-realm". More over the work does not have a sub-title like many of the autobiographies written by the Indian women to specify their sex.

Though belonging to a privileged family, at a time of "startling contradictions and contrasts", Mrs. Pandit's life style was completely transformed in 1921, when her family decided to join Gandhi's National Movement; the move revolutionised the lives of the Nehrus.

> "From then on she devoted her life to the cause of freedom in India. This involved her in great hardships, including terms in prison and the loss of her beloved husband, Ranjit, who died as a direct result of the conditions he suffered in prison. And yet this diminutive woman with a large heart never became embittered, and her love and affection for the British and her friendship with the British monarchy are beyond question".[7]

This is the story of a woman who found a voice of her own and also used it; a woman who could have been the Vice-President of India, not because her brother was the Prime Minister of the country but because of her "vast political and diplomatic knowledge, and her unique ability to make friends with all levels of people of all nations".[8] This life-narrative validates the rightful position of a woman in the Indian society.

Born as Sarup Kumari in a family which was traditional as well as unorthodox, she received education from an English governess, who changed her pet name "Nanhi" to "Nan" and "Nan" she remained to those who knew her closely. She became Vijaya Lakshmi after marriage to Ranjit Pandit; the name signified "victory". The Nehru family taught its women to be devoted and have steadfast loyalty; her mother's concern did not go beyond her family – her life was simple, dedicated and faithful to husband and the family, which was also the typical attitude of any Indian woman. This was combined with an inner strength, which proved to be a sustaining force in the uncongenial atmosphere of a country under the colonial rule. It was a family, which was dismayed at the birth of a girl child, Indira, who later went on to become the Prime Minister of India. Vijaya Lakshmi's aunt, though a beautiful and intelligent woman, who "could have expressed herself in many ways", was "condemned to a life of work for others". She was a widow. Ranjit Pandit's family had seen his great grandmother become a *sati* on the death of her husband.

Motilal Nehru was a champion of women's rights and thus there was a constant stream of women visitors like Annie Besant and Sarojini Naidu in the household. Mrs. Pandit received no formal education in any university and was always sore about it till she met Gandhiji: "my values were ultimately set straight by Gandhiji, but it took a national revolution to start a revolution in my mind".[9]

She received training in life under Bapu at Sabarmati Ashram, who, she realised "radiated a quiet serenity". Many women like Rajkumari Amrit Kaur from the House of Kapurthala, were inspired by the Gandhian ideals and served the country under him. The influence of Gandhi on the Nehrus was tremendous and they abandoned their luxurious way of life to live in simplicity and austerity. Both Mrs. Pandit and her husband joined the political movement under Gandhiji in which all the Nehru women as well as those from the different parts of the country who were anxiously willing to work. Gandhiji's concept of an egalitarian society ascertained equal rights and equal opportunities for both men and women. They were bound together to fight for the common cause and hence there was no question of women being marginalised.

> "Kamala was actively organising women's civil disobedience, and the manner in which sheltered women had responded to Gandhiji's call to participate in the national struggle was dramatic. From this time on, more and more women came forward to take this responsibility and they did a splendid job".[10]

Gandhiji's teachings emphasised the removal of any discrimination from the Indian society. His views on women are valid even today:

> "Woman is not helpless. She must never regard herself as weaker than man. She should not ....beg for any man's mercy, nor depend on him".[11]

Encouraged by such teachings Mrs. Pandit devoted her life to the cause of freedom. The Gandhian philosophy, she says, had "come to have a special meaning in many parts of the world where human dignity and rights continue to be violated".[12] The Indian woman, an embodiment of faith and courage, had allowed stoicism to become a part of her personality; these attributes coupled with the Gandhian principles helped many women, including Mrs. Pandit, in surviving the ordeal of imprisonment. Going to jail for the cause of freedom of the nation has been mentioned in the autobiography several times; what is significant about such incidents is that there used to be no weeping or wailing on the part of Mrs. Pandit's children. She also used to settle quickly to a prison life as her mind was "adjusted to doing so". The result was a personality well-moulded and perfectly formed to suit the various offices Mrs. Pandit was to occupy in her life. Her election as the chairperson of the Education Committee of the Municipal Board was the first step in an extremely active and fulfilling political career. She campaigned for the Congress party and was its first woman minister. Mrs. Pandit was chosen by Gandhiji to go to the U.S.A to acquaint the Americans with the conditions of India under the colonial rule. On Gandhiji's recommendation she was also asked to lead a delegation to the First General Assembly of the United Nations, which was then referred to as the "conscience of humanity". There Mrs. Pandit came in contact with Mrs. Roosevelt who dealt with the problems of human rights. Mrs. Pandit, a greatly accomplished woman with well marked administrative capabilities was made the first ambassador of a free India to Moscow. She played a key role in propagating India's policy in the two big nations of the world. The most prestigious assignment given to her, as she says, was the post of the President of the General Assembly – she was the first woman to hold that office and her election was acclaimed by the world. At a press conference she was asked to describe the sari she was wearing; her sharp retort was significant of her training in gender neutrality:

> "'Did you ask my predecessor to describe his suit?' I was very put out that in this age of women's emancipation, and after all the years I had been in public life, such inane queries should be put to me simply because I was a woman. No man would have been asked these meaningless questions by the world press".[13]

Another important diplomatic post was that of Indian High Commissioner in London which did immense amount of good to cement Anglo-Indian relations. She also came to know the Mountbattens extremely well. One of the many advantages of the positions she held in her career was her contact with unusual and interesting people. With some she maintained official relationships but some informal friendships sustained her throughout her life.

The Scope of Happiness is significant not only because of the portrait of a high-profile woman but also due to certain legal prejudices against the women of the time. It is important to note that even a pre-eminent woman like Mrs. Pandit was denied any accession to her husband's money after his death. In the absence of any will the Hindu Inheritance Law for women disallowed her the right to their joint account and she had to forfeit any claim whatsoever to her husband's money:

> "As the widow of a man who died intestate and was a member of a joint Hindu family, because I had no 'offspring' meaning a son, I was not entitled to any part of the joint immovable property. It seemed that this also applied to money".[14]

Mrs. Pandit signed a document to give up her personal claims and that of her unborn grandsons, if any. But such abrasions were always put in the background as Mrs. Pandit invariably had more important things to do and which helped her in keeping her mind off herself. Ofcourse the influence of Gandhiji was always a source of strength, which reinforced and restored her confidence in herself. For him physical weakness was not to be worried over but the weakness of the mind was fatal and so he wrote to her:

> "You are the daughter, sister, wife of great men. I will not condole with you. Come to me as soon as you can".[15]

Mrs. Pandit's autobiography reveals certain patriarchal relationships very distinctly. It is no exaggeration to say that the life story shows how the father, Motilal Nehru, had been used as a pivot on which the new awareness turns. She was very intimate with him and there was no terror evident in her analysis of her relationship with him. Her brother had a very special position in her life and she would frequently accept her Bhai's views without questioning. Carolyn G. Heilbrun[16] is of the view that "marriage is the most persistent of myths imprisoning women" evident in their autobiographies. Not so with Mrs. Pandit; in her case marriage was a system of mutual support. She was fortunate to have got Ranjit Pandit as her husband, who was of lively and sympathetic nature and encouraged her in almost everything. Their marriage was both conventional and mandatory.

The autobiography concludes on a note of satisfaction and contentment at a life well lived, with Mrs. Pandit at peace with herself:

> "As I look at the mountains I give thanks for the abundance of God's blessings, above all for His having given me the strength to keep faith with my ideals ....I have lived most of my life in the sunlight and enjoyed it. Now that the twilight has come, I welcome it, for I know that the darkness that follows will be the beginning of another day".[17]

If the woman's autobiography in India has taken a great leap it has done so only due to the "new and revolutionary" form of writing as that of Mrs. Pandit; she is a "self-realised" woman not only in the nation's history but also in that of the world. By and large the autobiographical writings by women have been found to have distinctive qualities which cannot be seen in those by men writers. Most of the life-narratives by women focus primarily on the various emotional relationships whereas it has been observed that men are generally concerned with their life-achievements with "recognisable career stages". The critics have observed that women do not have “a tone of voice in which to speak with authority”.[18] Mrs. Pandit's story of her life is remarkable for various reasons but most importantly for being a work which not only highlights the loving relationships in her life with her parents, her husband, her daughters but also for being a success story of her accomplishments as one of the leaders of the country. **The Scope of Happines** is more generalised than particularised and it is a case “”where concepts of subject, self, and author collapse into the act of producing a text”.[19] There is no self-consciousness or any kind of obsession with her identity as woman. Such stories can determine new ways of writing the lives of women as women themselves.

REFERENCES

1. Cynthia Huff, “Delivery: The Cultural Re-presentation of Childbirth”, in *Autobiography and Questions of GenderB,* ed. Shrley Neuman, Frank Cass, Great Britain, 1991, p. 108.
2. Carolin G Heilbrun, *Writing a Woman's Life*, The Womans Press, 1988, p. 21.
3. Vijaya Lakshmi Pandit, *The Scope of Happiness*, Vikas Publishing House Pvt. Ltd., 1979, p. 23.
4. Carolyn G Heilbrun, “Women's Autobiographical Writings: New Forms”, in *Modern Selves Essays on Modern British and American Autobiography*, ed. Philip Dodd, Frank Cass, 1986, p. 16.
5. *The Scope of Happiness*, p. XI.
6. Carolyn G Heilbrun, “Woman's Autobiographical Writings: New Forms”, *Modern Selves*, p. 17.
7. *The Scope of Happiness*, p. X.
8. *Ibid.*
9. *Ibid.,* p. 60.
10. *Ibid.,* p. 97.
11. *Ibid.,* p. 295.
12. *Ibid.,* p. 247.
13. *Ibid.,* p. 276.

14. *Ibid.,* p. 178.
15. *Ibid.,* p. 177.
16. Carolyn G Heilbrun, "Woman's Autobiographical Writings: New Forms", *Modern Selves*, p. 77.
17. *The Scope of Happiness*, p. 325.
18. Carolyn G Heilbrun, "Woman's Autobiographical Writings: New Forms", *Modern Selves*, p. 17.
19. Shirley Neuman, "Autobiography and Questions of Gender", p. 1.

CHAPTER 13

Kamala Das's My Story : "A Voyage of Inner Discovery"

Ever since Augustine wrote his *Confessions* between the years 397-400 A.D., a work which recorded his moral development and a spiritual journey, "journeying and return" have remained the most primary and noteworthy motifs of the autobiographical form of writing. *Confessions* proved to be a testimony of a great and powerful mind undergoing religious conversion. Critics of autobiography have made it almost mandatory that the life-narratives answer the question, though not consciously or deliberately, "How did I become what I am?" Nietzsche's autobiography *Ecce Homo* has an almost similar query as its subtitle "How one becomes what one is". It is the story through narrative, says John Sturrock, of Nietzsche's "philosophical becoming", and thus the autobiography becomes "the certificate of a unique human passage through time"[1]. It involves a search for the writer's identity where the narrative is suitable for a "literary reconstruction" of life, done, no doubt, with great discrimination. The journey into the past may

> "choose to focus on specific episodes in the greater narrative of journeying: the idyllic childhood and the dawn of self-consciousness, or the time following, of severance and departure, and the loss of roots, home, or motherland."[2]

Though the autobiographer is himself the thesis of his book, he views himself as if he were another person writing about himself. This happens because the journeying into the past is a tedious process where he has to be very careful and accurate in depicting and reshaping the incidents of his life which shaped his personality or which touched him in a very special way. On this journey of self-discovery,

> "remembering does not just happen. Instead, it is a skill that must be learned, a socially motivated activity with a specific developmental history in early childhood."[3]

The issue to be argued is that why does the writer undertakes this journey into the past, which like all journeys may not be without pitfalls, hurdles and stumbling blocks. The individual, who is the producer of his life-history thinks himself to be unique and exceptional, who for reasons known to him, may like to leave some record and evidence of his existence on this earth. Critics like Georges Gusdorf have made the following observation,

> "The man who takes delight in thus drawing his own image believes himself worthy of a special interest. Each of us tends to think of himself as the center of a living space: I count, my existence is significant to the world, and my death will leave the world incomplete."[4]

We know that it is not only the ordinary man who has been tempted to utilise the autobiographic form to depict his life-history, but kings and monarchs have also sought recourse to such life-narratives as a testimony of their life and for recording the events of the time spent on this earth.

> " ...using all the narrative devices and restrictions like accuracy, impartiality and inclusiveness; it is not merely a recapitulation of the past but also an attempt by the autobiographer to reconstruct himself in his own likeness."[5]

It also becomes essential for the writer to withdraw himself from the society, though temporarily, inorder to perform the act of reconstructing the past.[6] Hence the relevance of the question "How did I become what I am?" and its subsequent reply in the narrative. In the process the writer discovers the past "I" to be different from the present "I", where the past events have played a crucial role in making him "what he presently is". Therefore, though the writer is himself the thesis of his book, he views his persona as that of a stranger.

The autobiographical form of writing helps to bring into focus "the search for self-definition" through the "lifelines". The journey into the past uses the skill of remembering, and proves to be cathartic and is a "catalyst for healing". *My Story* by Kamala Das is one such autobiographical journey which was not only cathartic for the poetess, but also helped her in coming to terms with herself and providing abundant happiness in the process:

> "I have written several books in my lifetime, but none of them provided the pleasure the writing of *My Story* has given me. I have nothing more to say."[7]

The writing was started to distract her mind, to help her recover from a grave illness and also to take care of the hospital bills. She no longer wanted to evade her private life and

> "found the courage to move forward into as yet unnarrated and unexplored ways of living."[8]

The time had come when Kamala Das found a voice of her own, but it was only when she realised that she was face to face with Death.

> " ...I wanted to empty myself of all the secrets so that I could depart when the time came, with a scrubbed-out conscience."[9]

The carrying back process took a journey in the past to reveal her urges, yearnings and her inner self. She knows that

> "One's real world is not what is outside him. It is the immeasurable world inside him that is real. Only the one who has decided to travel inwards, will realise that his route has no end."[10]

It is a peeling of layer upon layer of her conscience; the writings have psychological overtones and provide a privileged insight into the autobiographer's unnarrated past. The mysteries of the self are revealed, as are the creation; for her the act is a deliverance from the ghosts of the past, which otherwise would have continued to haunt her. The "scrubbed-out conscience" is attained only after reaching her destination.

> " All the ancient hungers that had once tormented my lithe body were fulfilled. Not even the best-looking man in the world would any longer arouse in me an appetite for love."

"If my desires were lotuses in a pond, closing their petals at dusk and opening out at dawn at one time, they were now totally dead, rotted and dissolved, and for them there was no more to be a re-sprouting. The pond had cleared itself of all growth. It was placid."[11]

My Story opens with Kamala's childhood in Calcutta, when the "British ruled India". The writings in the autobiographical tradition, should begin "with a memory of mother or nurse, or a visual impression of nursery or garden, or sometimes facts about parentage and ancestry."[12]

She was a brown child who along with her brother suffered humiliation in a European school in Calcutta and sang the National Anthem during British. They were tortured and inflicted injuries by the children of those who ruled India.

"Blackie, your blood is red" would be the exclamation from the bully of the class when Kamala's brother bled. Suffering tortures secretly became necessary to "hold together the tatters" of their self-respect from the days of childhood:

> "When the visitors came the brown children were always discreetly hidden away, swept under the carpet, told to wait in the corridor behind the lavatories where the school ayahs kept them company."[13]

Her birth was the result of an "arid union" and the parents were "horribly mismatched". The mother was "vague and indifferent, spent her time lying on her belly on a large four-post bed, composing poems in Malayalm."[14] Kamala Das spent the happiest days of her childhood and life in her hometown in Malabar in the Nalapat house. The inherited richness of her family was in a sharp contrast to the condition in which she was born. The journeys to and fro from Calcutta and Nalapat were well defined and underlined the impact of the two cities on her. Calcutta made her feel unwanted and inferior whereas Nalapat provided the security and confidence not only in childhood but also after her ill-fated marriage. These voyages from the metropolitan to the serene Nalapat are described frequently in *My Story* and help in focussing the swift, sudden changes and development which took place in Das's personality on reaching the two destinations. The journey motif might have been deliberately employed by her to accentuate the changes taking place in her personality. All these journeys involved a search for her identity, with contradictions, happiness and sorrow forming a large part of the narrative.

My Story has no dates, which is not unusual, says Shirley Newman; for a woman's autobiography has "discontinuity and fragmentation ...as opposed to chronological, linear and coherent narratives by men."[15] The book moves back and forth in time as one episode views the Vannery children's Dramatic Society at Nalapat, and the other takes us inside a boarding school where her father put her, as he was convinced that only the Mother Superior and the other Roman Catholic nuns would be able to reform the ways of his "rustic" daughter. Not conversant with a proper dress code, the daughter did not wear a chemise under her mill-khaddar frock; she suffered the ridicule and jeers of the Anglo-Indian girls who tauntingly sang "she had nothing under when she came". Her brown skin became the symbol of her inferiority and her grandmother's raw turmeric remedies did not help much in lightening its colour. She was the odd one amongst fair-skinned students.

Later in Calcutta, Kamala Das's father employed an art-tutor for her, who was a young Bengali and she often admired his pink earlobes. This was her first encounter with a man who could attract her; she took to wearing sari for her tuition classes. The sudden change in her appearance was not to be missed by her parents and the classes were discontinued. She felt distracted and heart-broken and decided to visit the man at his place of work. However, her depression and sorrow increased when the rich Bengali took her to him home and he did not offered even a kiss to her and left her with a number of unanswered questions.

> "Why did he not kiss me? Why didn't he make love to me?"[16]

Bildungsroman has been established as a female form of writing and *My Story* marks the various stages in Kamala Das's character development: the time of the awakening of a carnal desire, her consciousness of being born in a particular religion and being a Hindu, some of her friends being Muslims. But the most significant aspect of her personality and its unraveling is described in her loveless marriage to a cousin who found her "cold and frigid".

Before Kamala Das arrived on the scene, women, generally princesses, political leaders, social workers had been writing their life-narratives. But these autobiographies were not provocative and delineated the women and their lives lived in the shadow of their husbands; their roles were well defined on the basis of their relationships with others, especially with the men in their lives. A couple of women had revolted against the pre-determined life-patterns; but by and large a woman's autobiography was a definition of her subjectivity as seen against the backdrop of something more powerful. With Kamala Das emerges a new kind of woman's writing, which is not only bold, daring and tantalising but is self-assertive. It retaliates against the worn out social values and traditions which forever hinder and retard the development of a woman's personality, emotionally as well as intellectually.

The account of her physical relationship with her husband and his obsession with her body must have shocked many conservative readers. Since a woman is taught to be docile and reserved about the details of her sexual relationships, she cannot indulge in revealing such accounts in her writings. But with Kamala Das no such inhibitions could shackle the outpourings of deeper feelings on her journey of "female psychological development."[17]

> "The rape was unsuccessful but he comforted me when I expressed my fear that I was perhaps not equipped for sexual progress. Perhaps I am not normal, perhaps I am only a eunuch, I said ...Again and again throughout that unhappy night he hurt me and all the while the Kathakali drums throbbed dully against our window and the singers sang of Damayanti's plight in the jungle."[18]

The frank and confessional language, which helped in transcending her 'marginal self', prompted her critics, to brand her as an exhibitionist. She had viewed marriage through tinted glasses of romance,

> "I thought then that love was flowers in the hair, it was the yellow moon lighting up a familiar face and soft words whispered in the ear ..At the end of the month, experiencing rejection, jealousy and bitterness I grew old suddenly, my face changed from a child's to a woman's and my limbs were sore and fatigue."[19]

Her husband's brutality left her gasping her for love. To the other members of the household, her marriage was a show of richness and wealth and the "bride was unimportant and her happiness a minor issue."[20]

The essence of *My Story* is its authenticity about the autobiographer's feminine sensibility. In it she introduced herself as a daughter, a mother, a wife, a poet; but what was more important was that she was conscious of her woman's identity which was an amalgam of all these personalities. Identity to Kamala Das did not mean fitting in a predefined slot,

> "Dress in saris, be girl
> Be wife, they said. Be embroiderer, be cook
> Be a mareller with servants. Fin in, oh,
> Belong, cried the categorizers."
>
> (*An Introduction*)

Kamala Das learnt to defy these pre-established canons of feminine identity; for her it was important to be a woman and a lover with a body and a soul. The autobiography becomes a vehicle for voicing an "inner privacy", and a protest against the senseless restrictions which force a sensitive and woman to lead an insipid life. *My Story,* like her poems (which are also self-revealatory), interests us due to its naivete and sincerity.

Her marriage made her realise that she was to be "the victim of a young man's carnal hunger" and out of this forced union would born some children.

"I would be a middle-class housewife, and walk along the vegetable shop carrying a string bag and wearing faded chappals on my feet."[21]

Kamala Das's father had made a wrong decision in choosing her mate; but being a male autocrat he would not have realised that he had chosen a wrong man. Although she hated her husband for physical assault, Kamala disliked the idea of leaving him. To have her first-child she went to her grand mother's place. The husband had grown weary of her temperament and thus decided to send her to Nalapat.

"Tearing myself away from the man who did not ever learn to love me, I went back to Malabar with an uncle who had been sent to take me home."[22]

After the birth of her son Kamala Das felt that she had been given a toy to play with; the husband, not excited at all after becoming a father, hated the child's cries at night.

Cynthia Huff in her essay "Delivery: The Cultural Re-presentation of Childbirth" observes that a woman's life

"delineates a significant life event rather than the form of a life lived, describes an experience which *only* women can have, and, furthermore, characterizes a cultural phenomenon which metaphorically embodies physical as well as textual creation."[23]

For these reasons, feels Cynthia Huff, it becomes necessary to examine the personal accounts of childbirth, if found in any autobiography:

"The metaphors that affect our responses to childbirth attenuate our analysis of birth itself, thus subverting its autobiographical import and in effect silencing birth as a cultural expression of a woman's life."[24]

These personal narratives in women's autobiographies are expressions of her birth experience; they could either be of a woman giving birth to a child or helping in the process of delivery. What Kamala Das's *My Story* signifies is "the delivery of her experience of parturition textually", probably for the first time in the history Indian autobiographies by women writers. These are described by Kamala Das as "one of life's major milestones".

Her first experience of carrying a baby in her womb was when she felt a "quickening" in her womb and know that her child "had become a live being."[25] Later the process of labour is briefly narrated:

> "When the labour began, I put old records on the gramophone and chatted courageously with my cousins who had come to watch me to have the baby. All of them sat outside my door, leaning against the verandah wall. The most excited of all was my younger brother who kept asking me every minute or so if the baby was coming out.

I was not prepared for the great pain that finally brought the baby sliding along my left thigh, and I could not smother my scream."[26]

Childbirth in India is more of familial, social and cultural significance rather than a private event and in Kamala Das's family, deliveries usually took place inside the homes, where the whole family, with aunts, uncles, grandfather, grandmother and cousins, would excitedly await the cry of the newborn. These were the culturally recognised events and Kamala Das's *My Story* has composed textual accounts of three such physical creations. The subsequent two pregnancies made her temperamental with her cravings for alcoholic beverages. Her creativity would be at its zenith and she would sit up all night to write poetry.

Delivery at home was risky and involved health hazards; women, if they were lucky to have escaped death in the process, often became victims of puerperal fever and other diseases. Kamala Das suffered such illnesses and was lucky to have been nursed by her grandmother and mother-in-law at Nalapat.

Defining the self in Das's case becomes an intricate process and her autobiographical text, the "biographies of birth give us accounts which highlight the intricate relationships between the physical, cultural, and textual construction of delivery."[27] Motherhood brought in a "metamorphosis" in her; she shed all her "carnal desire" and became religious. After the birth of her third child she decided to settle in Malabar, where her relatives were not too happy to see her without her husband and thought that her twenty-four year old marriage was at rocks. But she could not have cared less. She dressed traditionally in "the white blouses and heavy gold jewellry." She cultivated her lands and fields with hands and became the mistress of Nalapat House. She wrote extremely well. However, another bout of illness, this time a heart attack, took her once more to Bombay. Her life had come full circle:

> "Illness and my writing helped me to turn into an island. People had to go out of their way to visit me ... I wanted only love and kindness."[28]

Her hungers were "fulfilled", her desires were purged and she questioned the validity of her life,

"What did I finally gain from life? Only the vague hope that there were a few readers who loved reading my books although they have not wished to inform me of it. It is for each of them that I continue to write, although the abusive letters keep pouring in. I tweak the noses of the puritans but I am that corny creature, the sad clown, who knows that the performance is over ..."[29]

Death, she realised, would not be able to end the world; the world and the life in it shall go on, her sons shall produce "brilliant children",

"My descendants shall populate this earth. It is enough for me. It is more than enough. ..."[30]

The journey narrative should naturally culminate in homecoming, which could signify one of such moods – either of celebration or of disillusionment depending upon whether the autobiographer has come to terms with herself or not.[31] Kamala Das's autobiographical journey prompted by the "lure of the self" prove to be rewarding. She felt liberated after recounting her past.

REFERENCES

1. John Sturrock, *The Language of Autobiography*, Cambridge University Press, 1994, p. 3.
2. Elleke Boehmer, *Colonial and Postcolonial Literature*, OUP, Oxford, 1995, p. 200.
3. Ulric Neisser and Robyn Fivush, *The Remembering Self, Construction and accuracy in the self-narrative*, Cambridge University Press, 1994, p. VII.
4. Georges Gusdorf, "*Conditions and Limits of Autobiography*", translated by James Olney in *Autobiography Essays Theoretical and Critical*, ed. James Olney, Princeton University Press, 1980, p. 29.
5. Meena Sodhi, "*Autobiography: A recreation of the self*", *Points of View*, Vol.III, Number 1, Summer 1996, p. 96.
6. *The Language of Autobiography*, p. 290.
7. Kamala Das, *My Story*, Sterling Publisher Private Limited., 1991, p. V.
8. Carolyn Heilbrun, "*Woman's Autobiographical Writings: New Forms*", in *Modern Selves, Essays on Modern British & American Autobiography*", ed. Philip Dodd, p. 21.
9. *My Story*, p. V.
10. Ibid., p. 109.
11. Ibid., p. 209.
12. A.O.J. Cockshut, *The Art of Autobiography in 19th & 20th Century England*, Yale University Press, 1984, p. 55.
13. *My Story*, p. 3.

14. *Ibid.*, p. 2.
15. Shirley Neuman, ed, *Autobiography & Questions of Gender*, Frank Cass, 1991, p. 2.
16. *My Story*, p. 72.
17. *Autobiography and Questions of Gender*, p. 2.
18. *My Story*, p. 90.
19. *Ibid.*
20. *Ibid.*, p.87.
21. *Ibid.*, p.85.
22. *Ibid.*, p.92.
23. *Autobiography and Questions of Gender*, p.108.
24. *Ibid.*,
25. *My Story*, p. 92.
26. *Ibid.*, p. 93.
27. *Autobiography and Question of Gender*, pp. 119-120.
28. *My Story*, p. 208.
29. *Ibid.*, pp. 209-210.
30. *Ibid.*, p. 219.
31. Elleke Boehmer, *Colonial & Postcolonial Literature*, p. 201.

Kamala Das's Reinventing Self

The outcry rose over the conversion of one of our exceptionally talented Poets and also "one of the first fine modern writers to assert her femininity as a human in Indian literature", compels the readers of Kamala Das to re-read her poems and also the story of her life in a new perspective. Perhaps we can discover some clues in her past writings, which may help us in focusing on her present frame of mind. There are no definite clues except that the dominant note only too apparent in all her writings continues to be the urge for freedom, the need to establish her identity and liberation as an individual and as "one of the most electric women in India".

If we consult newspaper reports and magazine articles, we find that the response to her problematic action has been largely emotional. But as, we shall do better if we try to analyse some of the reasons behind her conversion, which can be interpreted from many remarks made by the Poet, who still believes in always recreating herself. She has become the target of many attacks and insinuations and her detractors coolly ignore the fact that it was essentially and totally her personal decision. They keenly emphasise the flexibility of Hindu religion, which, they insist, grants any individual the right to read either the Koran or the Bible. Some of the Vishwa Hindu Parishad leaders planned to "seek judicial redressal" and condemned certain remarks of the Poet on Hinduism[1]. The allegations and indictment do not stop at this point and Das is censured for showing her obligation to the International film-maker, Ismail Merchant, who is reportedly making a film on her *My Story*.

Perhaps Kamala Das exults in creating a storm of sorts and being in the centre of it. But this time she had become involved in a controversy, which could have far-reaching repercussions. In an interview given to *The Times of India* (19 December 1999) she claimed that she was attracted to the orthodox lifestyle of the Muslim women and hence her decision to embrace Islam. Though she had resolved to convert some twenty-seven years back, she restrained from doing so as her children were not settled in life. She found Hinduism "too lenient" and it permitted her plenty of freedom. Wasn't it this freedom, which had spared her for writing not only numerous bold autobiographical poems but also an exceptionally flamboyant and revealing account of her life in *My Story?*

A retired Professor and a CPI (M) activist Nabeesa Ummal has observed, "I challenge her to write a book like *My Story* now. She will face the same fatwa and fate as Bangladeshi writer Taslima Nasreen"[2]. However Kamala Das's remarks emphasise her dare-devil attitude. In keeping with her exhibitionist, bold and reckless attitude, she attended a seminar on "Indian Muslim agenda for the 21st century" organised by the Khair-Ummat Trust on January 24-2000 and proclaimed:

> "I will not run away like Salman Rushdie and Taslima Nasreen did from their motherland. I am born an Indian and will die as one"[3].

Kamala's conversion shocked the Keralites who were made to retort "It hurts the pride of the lay man and the literate alike; we nurtured a rebel of sorts in our midst for so long, and look how she rejects us for the aliens". Perhaps they failed to realise that everyone needs to reinvent oneself and it was very likely that Kamala Das wanted to do it more frequently. Now she seemed to have found her "misplaced father in Allah"[4]. May be the Hindu tolerance is unable to approve the conversion of a woman's libber, who had till now been endured her outspoken, saucy, strip-tease style of writing. But she had not been the target of abuse only, some people have applauded her for her "bold" decision. Being bold and uninhibited comes naturally to Kamala Das and she had for long time wrote on subjects related to sex, which were always considered a taboo not only for women but for male writers too. With the publication of *My Story* in 1976 there emerged a new kind of woman's writing, which was not only daring and tantalising but also presumptuous and self-assertive. Here was a writer who defied all conventional models to retaliate against the worn out social values and traditions, which forever hinder and retard the development of a woman's personality, emotionally as well as intellectually.

The autobiography aimed at redefining the male-female relationship and was not only a challenging account of the writer's experiences of her life but of her body as well. In Kamala Das we have a woman conscious of her femininity and determined to vindicate it against the male supremacy. The autobiography emphasised the personality of Kamala Das as it had been made by the dictates of the society. Thus a "good" girl was made to rebel against the established socio-cultural barriers of feminine modesty which at times shocked the conservative readers. The frank and confessional language, which helped in transcending her "marginal self", prompted her critics to brand her as an exhibitionist.

Now her admirers are nostalgic for the "musty smell in the attic of Nalapat home" with which they had become as familiar as did the readers of R.K. Narayan with Malgudi. Bibi Suraiya has overturned all that. Her statements regarding the Hindu Gods and Hindus at large are not in the right taste. Hindu deities, she says, punish and *Allah*, she feels forgives all the sins: "Hindus have only hurt me, scandalised me. This is a new birth for me"[5]. Speaking to

The Hindu she was at pains to emphasise that she could not feel that she belonged to any religion till she converted to Islam:

> "How long can I remain an unclaimed parcel with the address stamped on me. There should be someone to claim me. I want love from all"[6].

Her conversion with "*Allah's* mercy" made her feel well and healthy once again. She has not lived an easy life and has always been searching for solace, safety and contentment. Let us review what Kamala Das has to say about the state of her mind after taking over the "*burqa*":

> "From the first birthday of memory till today, this life was a red hot desert. Now I walk after shedding my heavy load, toward the mirage in the desert with date palms, clear pools. The home of *Allah*, the empire of Love of *Allah* .... I have always been searching for God. I found him in Islam and I took shelter under it. I did not expect such a furore over it. I never thought so many cases would be filed against me simply because of the change in religion. Conversion is a simple procedure. It is a search for God"[7].

Her penchant for truth made her react in anger at her critics; they were speculating the reason for her newfound happiness, more so after her surprising announcement that she planned to get married again! But the name of the prospective suitor had been kept a closely guarded secret. She always desired to be completely possessed by a man:

> "Even if it had been a poor, labourer who said to me 'I want nothing else but you', I would have followed him ..... Even my Krishna poems, I think, were attempts to realise that"[8].

She shuns the concept of old people visiting only temples and passing their time in prayers.

Autobiographical writing for women has always been a way of exploring their sense of identity and the process helps them in redefining their own lives too. Kamala Das continues to redefine herself even without writing a sequel to her autobiography. *My Story* is the work of a poet, famous for her honesty. The life narrative depicts some very intensely personal experiences including "her growth into womanhood, her unsuccessful quest for love in and outside marriage and life in her matriarchal rural south India after inheriting her ancestral home. While at home, the rich families try to kill her with magic because they fear that her writing will reveal their immortality in it"[9]. She alleges the Keralites for "treating her shabbily and spurning her with contempt"[10].

The writings of Kamala Das were by and large have been ego-centred, as was *My Story*. The essence of the autobiography was its authenticity about the autobiographer's feminine sensibility. In it she introduced herself as a daughter, a mother, a wife, a poet; but what was more important in the book was her being conscious of her woman's identity which was an amalgam of all these personalities. Identity to Kamala Das did not mean fitting in a predefined slot:

> "Dress in saris, be girl
> Be wife, they said. Be an embroiderer, be a cook,
> Be a quareller with servants, Fit in, oh,
> Belong, cried the categorizers"
>
> (An Introduction)

Kamala Das learnt to defy these pre-established canons of feminine identity; for her it was important to be a woman and a lover with a body and a soul. The autobiography became for her a vehicle for voicing an "inner privacy", and a protest against the senseless restrictions which force a sensitive woman to lead an insipid life.

A significant and important aspect of *My Story* was the description of such experiences, which only a woman could have. These are the personal accounts of childbirth which, Cynthia Huff, in her essay "Delivery: The Cultural Representation Childbirth" observes is the characteristic of a cultural phenomenon; it also embodies metaphorically physical as well as external creation. Kamala Das's autobiography had three such textual accounts of physical creations, narrated probably for the first time in the history of Indian women's writings in English.The writing was started to distract her mind, to help her recover from a grave illness and also to take care of hospital bills. The time had come when Kamala Das found a voice of her own, but it was only when she realised that she was face to face with death.

> "I wanted to empty myself of all the secrets so that I could depart when the time came, with a scrubbed-out conscience"[11]

Autobiographical writing can prove to be cathartic as it can help the writer in coming to terms with herself. In the case of Kamala Das, *My Story* gave her "the courage to move forward into as yet unnarrated and unexplored ways of living"[12]. And in the process it also gave her abundant happiness:

> "I have written several books in my lifetime, but none of them provided the pleasure the writing of *My Story* has given me. I have nothing more to say."[13]

We read a woman's autobiography for other reasons than we read her novels, diaries, and letters or edited papers. We read these feminine writings to hear from, learn from some specific historical figures about how they found their own voice not only in these autobiographical writings but as a product of historical forces. This is what makes an autobiography a privileged form of historical agency for a woman, an act of finding a voice of her own and expressing it freely. However, now Kamala Das was wary of emancipation and unconstraint and for her the "burqa" had become a symbol of "protection" and at the age of sixty-five she need it more than ever! From demanding complete freedom on independence in sexual matters, she had gone back to total denial of freedom by her conversion to an orthodox Muslim way of life. The freedom, which she enjoyed as a Hindu, will not be allowed to her now. "Who needs freedom?" retorts Suraiya. Speaking to a national daily she rejected her earlier demand for freedom:

> "I don't want freedom. I had enough of it thrust on me. Freedom had become a burden for me ......I want a master to protect me. I wanted protection and not freedom. I want to be subservient to *Allah*"[14]

The Kamala Das of earlier days, the femme fatale of Indian Women's writings, had been undergoing a metamorphosis of sorts even earlier to her conversion:

> "Before I was the rebellious type I used to move around a lot, involve myself in various activities; most of the time taking risks and living dangerously. Now I have changed. I have become a virtuous, clean woman. A puritan in all senses who prays daily, wears white clothes and is conservative in thinking".[15]

However, she has been transformed into a woman who says she loves the orthodox lifestyle of Muslim women:

> "I want guidelines to regulate and discipline my life. I want a master to protect me .... My husband died seven years ago and I am now a lonely widow who is 67 years old. When he was there he provided me with protection. I had not to bother about getting tickets, passport, visas and such other things. I just had to follow him".[16]

It is apparent that the swallow of earlier days had really been tamed and now it missed the master and was lonely. But can the conversion also be viewed as an evolution of a woman who had come full circle? Her comments in her other writings seemed to suggest that she might have longed for a more circumscribed existence for some years now. Nevertheless what needs to be questioned is the sincerity of her decision not only now but in her earlier life too. How genuine were her expressions in *My Story* and how sincere are they now? They may be "bold" and "unconventional", but somewhere in the mind of the reader there lurks the doubt to regard all her statements and actions, flamboyant gestures as publicity gimmicks. Nevertheless we cannot but agree with Dom Moraes's recent remark that "much may be forgiven those who write well".

REFERENCES

1. www.timesofindia.com
2. *India Today*, Dec. 27, 1999.
3. *Deccan Herald,* Tuesday, January 25, 2000, "Religion must never spread hatred: Suraiya".
4. www.timesofindia.com
5. Mohinddin Anwar, "More stories on Kamala Das's conversion".mohinddin@netzero.net
6. "Kamala Das embraces Islam", Online Edition on India server.com, Sunday, December 12, 1999.
7. Kamala Das wants to die like a 'true Muslim', from *India Abroad*, January 21, 2000.
8. "High priestess of love", Charmy Hari Krishnan, daily.htm events, Dec.26, 1999.
9. "Kamala Das: Creating a voice by seizing and reinterpreting religions tradition", Shoshana M. Landow 91 (Anthropology 302, Princeton University, 1989).
10. "Kamala Das' decision". Online edition on indiaserver.com, Thursday, December 16, 1999.
11. Kamala Das, *My Story*, Sterling Publishers Pvt. Ltd., 1991, Preface.
12. Carolyn G. Heilbrun, "Women's Autobiographical Writings: New Forms", in *Modern Selves, Essays on Modern British & American Autobiography*, ed. Philip C. Dodd, p. 21.
13. *My Story*, Preface.
14. http:www.timesofindia.com/191299/19conim3.htm
15. *Ibid.*
16. *Ibid.*

CHAPTER 15

From *Krishna* to *Allah* : The Experiencing Self in Kamala Das

Autobiographical writings by women tend to express an original and personal vision and verbalise vast areas of female experience, generally overlooked by men. Women's understanding of the world and its affairs have determined a unique pattern of living, produced in literature with a very distinct perspective that has readily conceptualised itself as an alternative literature. Thus seen from socio-historical perspective women's autobiographical writings are documents, which are verifiable, showcasing the emergence of this dispossessed group into the realm of the essentially public. These scripts are a reflection of the self, a self striving to reassemble itself and in the process make the female the chronicle.

As a personal portrait, the autobiography reflects the voyage of the individual through life, eventually making a self-discovery as well as a self-reconciliation, thus answering the question "How did I become what I am". Oscar Wilde had stated, "All artistic creation is absolutely subjective". Having said that it has to be pointed out that the borderline between autobiography and other miscellaneous forms of personal writings is hard to define – they share the same concern and the same reflective impulses and often the autobiography tends to slide noiselessly into the domain of a memoir or a poem. James Olney in *The Ontology of Autobiography* has argued:

> I maintain that just as it is possible to have a work that is "autobiographical" without its being "an autobiography" so also – nor am I being wantonly paradoxical – it is possible to have a work without its being "autobiographical"[1].

He further elaborates that a poem is "an autobiography (in contrast to an "autobiographical" poem) is not a matter of content but of form; it is through the formal device of "recapitulation and recall" that the *bios* or life of a poet is revealed[2].

In order to analyse and interpret the essence of Kamala Das's revealation of the self, it is imperative to consider not only her autobiography, *My Story,* but also her autobiographical poems from different collections, including the ones on *Krishna* and finally some of her creations from *"Ya Allah"* to trace the portrait of her inimitable self, as she thought it to be. In this "confessional" mode she discovered a form for her uninhibited autobiographical impulses.

Readers are constantly trying to unravel the mystery behind the 'purdah' of the most exceptional feminine poet of the last century. Apart from being sensational, her creativity is poignant and penetrating, where a woman is looking for authentic love and a sense of security from very early days. Born out of an "arid union"[3], she was always lonely (9) and felt unwanted. Sadly, her marriage also did not provide the much needed solace and love and her mind became

> ......an old Playhouse with all its lights put out,[4]

Her "soul balked at this diet of ash" (4). Having "failed in love" loneliness enveloped her and

> .... The heart
> An empty cistern, waiting
> Through long hours, fills itself
> With coiling snakes of silence.[5]

In *Composition*, a poem which expressively shows the manifestation of the self, she narrates "the ordinary events of an ordinary life[6]. Ordinarily she definitely wanted tenderness so she was forever looking for "tenderness" in her relationships and when she did not find it, she deliberately whipped up

> ....A froth of desire
> a passion to suit the occasion,
> I must let my mind striptease
> I must extrude autobiography.[7]

The Indian woman in Kamala Das does not move from her position of a cultural "other" or a "subaltern" status; rather she uses this position to her own advantage:

> I must linger on,
> trapped in immortality
> my only freedom being
> the freedom to discompose,[8]

Writing about her own life and her own self helped her to carve out a cultural space for herself and conceptualise her presence in a male-dominated society:

> I am a freak. It's only
> To save my face, I flaunt, at
> Times, a grand, flamboyant lust.[9]

A lonely childhood and an unhappy marriage, nurtured feelings of isolation and depression. Pain became the central force of her existence and she wanted to be "completely involved" and "walk into the sea and lie there." She desperately tried to break the shackles of authority imposed by her husband and to reaffirm her own identity:

> .... I am sinner
> I am saint. I am the beloved and the betrayed.
> I have no joys which are not yours, no
> Aches which are not yours, I too call myself "I"[10]

My Story expresses her pain in a tone which is profound and compelling:

> Like arms looking for a begging bowl was my love which only sought for a receptacle. At the hour of worship even a stone becomes an idol. I was perhaps seeking a familiar face that blossomed like a blue lotus in water of my dreams. It was to get closer to that bodyless one that I approached other forms and lost my way. I may have gone astray, but not once did I forget my destination..[11]

The search for something more than "physical hungers" led her to *Krishna*, the ideal lover, who has been immortalised by the sixteenth century poet, Mira Bai. The *Krishna* motif in any creative writing exhibits the paradigm of "supremacy of spirit over matter, soul over body, timeless over the temporal"[12]. Such consciousness, as reflected in Kamala Das's writings, suggests the growth of her mind and a sense of maturity. We find the *Krishna* leitmotif not only in her poems, but also in her autobiography. Her initial encounter with Him was when she found the *Krishna* Poems written by her great grandmother's younger sister Ammalu. Many times during her tumultuous and unhappy marriage, the bhajans of Meera gave her the much-needed succour and she yearned for "a new life".

> I was looking for an ideal lover. I was looking for the one who went to Mathura and forgot to return to his *Radha*. Perhaps I was seeking the cruelty that lies in the depths of a man's heart. Otherwise why did I not get peace in the arms of my husband?[13]

She found a kindred soul in *Radha* and her poem *The Maggots* expresses the anguish of women, which *Radha* feels in her husband's arms:

> At sunset, on the river bank, *Krishna*
> Loved her for the last time and left...
> That night in her husband's arms, *Radha* felt
> So dead that he asked, What is wrong,
> Do you mind my kisses, love? And she said,
> No not at all, but thought, What is
> It to the corpse if the maggots nip?[14]

Search for love entangled her in a number of relationships and in every man she would seek *Krishna*; not finding him there she would break off the ties.

Free from the last of human bondage, I turned to *Krishna*..Then he came...In the old playhouse of my mind, in its echoing hollowness His voice was sweet. He had come to claim me, ultimately. Thereafter He dwelt in my dreams. Often I sat crosslegged before a lamp reciting mantras in His praise.[15]

Her efforts to conquer the physicality, to make the spirit dominate the body and write about the mythic lover had a therapeutic effect on her:

> We are burdened with perishable bodies which strike up bonds which are also unreal, and perishable. The only relationship that is permanent is the one which we form with God. My mate is He. He shall come to me in myriad shapes. In many shall I surrender to His desire...I shall pass through all the pathways of this world, condemning none, understanding all and then become part of Him. Then for me there shall be no return journey..[16]

Ready to succumb to her to her ideal lover, her mystical longings find a reflection in *Ghanshyam:*

> You have like a koel built a nest in the arbour of my heart.
> My life until now a sleeping jungle is at last stir with music.

> You lead me along a route I have never known before
> But at each turn when I hear you
> Like a spectral flame you vanish.[17]

Sarojini Naidu in her *Radha-Krishna* poems had made the relationship a metaphor for the affiliation between the *Atman* and *Paramatman*. In Kamala Das the relationship is that of ideal lovers and does not rise to the 'divine level'. Women writers of the "Bhakti " movement in Medieval India had displayed an intensity and a "mystic experience of personal devotion"[18]. Each writer had her own idiom and broke free from the institutionalised decorum of the society and their families; they also developed a freedom of expression. Mira, the sixteenth century poet, is still considered the most representative figure of such devotional writings: a rebel at heart, she did not succumb to the family norms.

Even within the mainstream popular tradition, the intensity of Mira's devotion and her courage in resisting every pressure to deviate from her chosen way of life can be a source of strength to women who regard her as an intimate and personal support in their suffering and pain.[19]

Kamala Das's poetical writings are much in tune with these " bhakti" poets and her reactionary zeal towards the predefined societal norms corresponds to the revolt by the women of the movement. As she approached middle age *Krishna* became her friend and a patriarch. She, as A.N. Dwivedi remarks,

> ... is merely searching for a relationship which gives both genuine love and impenetrable security. That's why she sometimes gives a mythical framework to her search for true love, and identifies it with *Radha-Krishna* syndrome or with Mira Bai, relinquishing the ties of marriage in pursuit of Lord *Krishna*, the true divine lover[20].

Kamala Das continuously redefines and attempts to recreate herself as a woman and a Poet. Self for her became the nucleus of creativity from which her poetry was born; in *Composition* she had said, "The tragedy of life, is not death but growth." Her growth as a Poet took an upward leap when she decided to experience a new way of life. In December 1999 her ever-domineering restlessness took her away from *Krishna* to *Allah*: Kamala Das became Kamala *Suraiya*. The Malayalees were appalled as they had been on a previous occasion when her autobiography was published or when she had painted nudes. But she was unmoved by all the admonition and censure, rather she exulted like a child who had made a new discovery:

> Look at me. Am I not ebullient with happiness, with joy and zest for a life with *Allah*... This is the last time I am shocking you all.[21]

The idol of Lord *Krishna* and other gods were shifted to the guestroom and like devout follower of Islam, Kamala *Suraiya* started praying five times a day. Many rumour mills started working overtime and the assumption was that she had a Muslim lover whom she planned to marry. The other conjecture was that Ismail Merchant, the renowned film director, had chosen her for his new venture. The lady was unfazed and retorted, "I am what I am." However in a more condescending mood she conceded to two incentives for having embraced Islam:

> One is 'purdah'...the most wonderful dress for women in the world. And I always loved to wear the 'purdah'. It gives protection to women. I have been lonely all through my life. At nights I used to sleep by embracing a pillow. But I am no longer a loner. Islam is my company. Therefore I converted.[22]

Seeking refuge in *Allah* appeared attractive and Islam seemed a protective force; earlier she had sought the patriarch in *Krishna*. Thus after the death of her husband embracing this religion appeared the only alternative and she found unnarrated and unexplored ways of living, with well-defined guidelines:

> I don't want freedom. I had enough of it thrust on me. Freedom had become a burden for me ... I want a master to protect me... I want to be subservient to *Allah*.[23]

This confession may make one question the authenticity and sincerity of *My Story*. Was it, as some critics claim, fiction? In an interview given to a national daily, her response confirmed the apprehension about the legitimacy of the book and aroused much curiosity:

> So what if I added a few imaginary characters? Literature uses this as an alloy. And anyway, where was the time to have love affairs? I was working all day, writing all night. I never even walked on the streets alone. There was always my husband or my sons with me...And how much the book sold![24]

Writing about once life is a work of art. No doubt the writer needs materials from life but the process of selection and putting them together is a work of art. Thus "the truth or falsity of autobiography is .... subordinated to the creativity, the design, the 'inner' truth of the narrative"[25]. The autobiographer is only creating and not remembering her past life, thus making this genre identical to other forms of "imaginative" literature.

Kamala Das's experience of conversion and her intense identification first with *Krishna* and then with *Allah*, led her to a religious self-examination; the innovative dimensions of her religious thought, especially her modifications, co-relate with her new image of the self. She dares to narrate a religious experiment and writing her new "Ya Allah" poems was an exercise of autobiographical reflection in which she discovered and clarified her sense of personal identity in a communicable form. Rapt in her own world and oblivious of the furor she had created, she wrote poems in praise of *Allah*:

> *Ya Allah*!
> Unbound
> Religious shell, you are!
> Epitome of unbridled freedom, you are!!
> Your light
> And your shade;
> For happiness I seek .....
> I worship thee.[26]

The Islamic Publishing House first published her collection of "Ya Allah" poems in 2002 in Malayalam in Kerala. They were translated into English by Dubai based Kalim Ahmed in 2008. All these poems depict *Allah* as boundless and express the intensity of her emotions towards him.

> My lord!!
> I am your sunflower,
> Basking in the sun
> That you are,
> Both in my hours of sleep,
> And in my conscience,
> I have felt you.[27]

As Kamala *Suraiya* she found the serenity and peace, which she had been looking for everywhere during her entire life. Anonymous letters criticising her conversion were sent to her, which hurt her enormously. She was asked whether she would be able to exorcise the *Radha* in her. And what about *Krishna* who had been her constant mate since childhood? Perhaps she regretted embracing a new religion, but then one's religion is a very private and personal way of life. Her selfhood was transformed, her God's identity changed. The "Ya Allah" poems reveal an intense spiritual personality and show her in state where she is totally

"Speechless and powerless" in front of the Supreme Power. In these poems she relives her life, only now *Allah* is with her:

> You are not alone, *Suraiya*!
> *Allah's* deep love is like the soft moonlight.
> You have worn it as a shield:[28]

Fervent and suffused with "bhakti" for her God she eulogises her faith in him:

> *Ya Allah,*
> I was a girl,
> Playing in the courtyard of my home,
> Celebrating the feel of the youth sun'.
> ....
> It was you
> Who put me through
> The appalling tests.
> ....
> A fraud Woman and a liar,
> They called me
> My lord,
> Was it for
> You sprung up inside me,
> Like a banyan sprout?
> And you bathed me in
> Your soft starlit moonlight always?[29]

Kamala Suraiyya's 'bios' as a poet and spiritual explorer of her inner self is revealed in these autobiographical writings and as such they are justified in their worth, reflecting her religious belief.

Women writers, who unfold their inner self either through their biographical poems / fiction, tend to be more candid about their personal experiences, cordially inviting the reader to inhibit their own privatised space. While Kamala Das in *My Story* reveals a highly sensitised mind, her life graph as a poet established her as one of the leading poets of the Indian subcontinent. Her poems uncover the dark continent of her mind and body and effectively break down the cultural barriers of feminine modesty. In them she celebrated her unique self and established the eternal relationship with *Krishna* and *Allah*; wrote about love, sex, family, deprivation and fulfillment. These poems are manifestly autobiographical; written in "first person" they relate with life. It may appear at first sight that there is a metamorphosis of the self in Kamala Das. But when we read the poems deeply we find a consistency in the development of the self, in the sense that the original yearnings and critical experiences are based on the same urges in all her writings, including her autobiography, thus producing a larger and more inclusive view of the self.

REFERENCES

1. Olney, James, ed. *Autobiography. Essays: Theoretical and Critical.* New Jersy: Princeton University Press. 1980, p. 250.
2. *Ibid.,* p. 252.
3. Das, Kamala. *My Story*. New Delhi: Sterling Publishers Pvt Ltd. 1991, p. 5.
4. *The Old Playhouse and Other Poems*. Orient Longman Ltd. 1991, p. 1.
5. *Ibid.,* p. 11.
6. *Ibid.* p. 7.
7. *Ibid.,* p. 5.
8. *Ibid.,* p. 10.
9. *Ibid.,* p. 11.
10. *Ibid.,* p. 27.
11. *My Story*, p. 118.
12. Dodiya, Jaydipsinh. *Critical Essays on Indian Writing in English.* New Delhi: Sarup & sons. 2006, p. 1.
13. *My Story*, p. 171.
14. *The Descendants.* Calcutta: Writers Workshop, 1967.

15. *My Story*, p. 185.
16. *Ibid.,* p. 185-186.
17. *The Descendants.*
18. Tharu,Susie,Lalita.K. *Women Writing in India. 600BC To The Present. Vol.I.* New Delhi: Oxford University Press, 1993, p. 561.
19. *Ibid.,* p. 19.
20. Dwivedi, A.N. *Kamala Das and Her Poetry.* New Delhi: Atlantic Publishers and Distributers, 2006, p. 3.
21. www.rediff.com/news/1999/dec/14kamala.htm.
22. *Ibid.*
23. www.timesofindia.com/191299/19conim3.htm.
24. *The Hindustan Times*, New Delhi: 12 Jan., 2003.
25. *Autobiography. Essays: Theoretical and Critical*, p. 25.
26. www.JAIHOON.COM.
27. *Ibid.,* "I am safe".
28. *Ibid.,* "A forlorn Woman".
29. *Ibid.,* "Experiment".

CHAPTER 16

Rassundari Devi's Autobiography : The Extra Dimension

Writings by women in India have been copious and the two volumes on women's writing edited by Susie Tharu and K. Lalita bear testimony to this fact. Women writers have not been recalcitrant when it comes to writing about their own lives in many of the regional languages and in English as well. But the later part of the nineteenth century was perhaps the time which can be viewed by the critics as the beginning of a new era for women writers venturing into the arena of autobiographical writings[1]. It was a period when women became aware of a new sense of worth as "individuals" and took up the creative process of recording their lives. These nineteenth century autobiographies focus on themes like a woman's adoration for her progressive husband, her venture into education and the new vistas it opened for her. However, at times we do get a glimpse of a sense of frustration she might feel in living the monotony of day-to-day existence which was not free from hardship.

> "... the pain of being constantly watched and corrected; the feeling that they were not good enough; the exhausting demands of the new housework; the uncertainty and anxiety involved in raising children in the new mode, outside the reassuring circle of the traditional family; the longing for the support of a world they had lost, and so on"[2].

Rassundari Devi's *Amar Jiban (My Life)* is not only the first life narrative by a Bengali woman[3] but may perhaps be the first autobiography by any Indian woman. Rassundari Devi, born in a remote village of Potajia in Bengal in 1809 lived most of her life in Ramdia, decided to write the story of her life at the age of eighty-eight years; part of this story was subsequently published in 1868[4]. Putting the slight confusion of the year of first publication or Rassundari Devi's exact age at the time of writing behind us, we have to acknowledge that without any formal training in education she is successful in recreating "her life and her times in an astonishingly simple, lucid and purposeful manner"[5]. Writing about the book Sri Dinesh Chandra Sen observes that the estimate of her life cannot be treated only as personal because it is "a factual document of the life of an old Hindu woman". He further says

> "The book *Amar Jiban* is thus not merely the account of Rassundari but a story of all Hindu women of her time. We do not have a second book of this kind in our Bengali literature where the situation of women is so exactly and frankly drawn. Come to think of it if this book had not been written, an entire chapter of Bengali literature would have remained incomplete"[6].

Amar Jiban thus presents not only a picture of the Hindu society but is a reflection of the socio-cultural scenario in the India of nineteenth century. At the same time it is a first-hand account of the development of a woman from a "daughter to a new bride, from a bride to the mistress of the house and eventually to a mother". However this autobiographical description, as observed in the book, has to be understood as "socially and historically constructed and multiply positioned in complex worlds and discourses"[7].

There are no career stages in Rassundari Devi's life story, which we would normally find in other female life writers.

Her book unwittingly takes us into a world very similar to the one we find in the fiction of Jane Austen[8] who dealt with interesting situations of life, which can notably take place even at home. Otherwise there appears to be no reason why the narration of day to day events like preparing huge amount of food, caring for a blind mother-in-law, "the sea of housework through day and night", and lastly but most importantly worshipping the family deity, Madan Gopal, compels the reader not to put the book down. We have to agree with Jasbir Jain that Rassundari Devi had no choice in the roles she had to fulfill and at the same time struggle to seek self-expression in "staid, straight forward simple narration, where the ego is subdued and timid"[9]. In Rassundari Devi we find a woman who has no desire to imitate any male activity and therefore she is unambiguously a woman; hers is the story of a woman worth telling. We read her "as the avatar of a simpler world, with simpler values broadly accepted"[10].

Nevertheless, the story of her life does not lay much emphasis on her role as a wife and it is very indistinct and undefined; she barely mentions her husband in the first part of the book and is quite aware of it:

> "I have written an account of my life but it does not include anything about my husband. That has made the book incomplete. However I may not be the fittest person to describe all his virtues. All I can say is that he was a good man, the like of whom is not easy to come". (p.89)

What follows is an extremely brief account of his kind nature, his competency in solving law suits, his great authority which made him a terror. All in all he appears to have been a powerful and intelligent personality with whom she had nothing much to do as he did not play a big role in her life. Yet his presence in her life had placed a "gold crown" on her head that tumbled with his death, and she plunged into the state of widowhood, which she found not only unfortunate but also embarrassing to talk about:

> "but I do not mind. I am content to be in whatever condition God wishes to keep me". (p.74)

This is the kind of spiritual optimism found in the autobiography of Rassundari Devi, which is remarkable as she utilises the resources of the soul to establish peace with God. Feminist critics may call her an independent and spirited woman; or was she too self-centered? Being a mother of eleven children, she gives a brief and casual chronological account of the birth of her each child (p.46). She hardly discusses her daughters-in-law or her relationship with her daughters. The only bond which appears to be close to her is that with her mother, whose teachings guided her throughout her life. Rassundari's marriage at the age of twelve years made her cry for days together and she questioned her mother:

> "Mother why did you give me away to strangers?" (p.38)

Being separated from her mother caused her a lot of pain:

> "I regret to say that I have not taken good care of my own mother, who was so affectionate. A mother is a very precious thing – it is my misfortune that I did not understand it. She suffered so much for my sake. ..She used to cry for me and wanted to have me over. But I am a virtual prisoner here". (p.49)

Her childhood, which formed the first three compositions, was a happy time for her and we have many instances where she mentioned her mother. This period was spent in the company of the people she loved. However when it came to elaborating her role as a mother, she was mysteriously silent and dismissed any details by saying, "Now I am everybody's mother"(p.88). Perhaps unintentionally, through this statement, she had conveyed a kind of power, the power of having "the senior most position in the family":

> "It seemed to me that I was not me but somebody else. All my weakness was gone, I was strong and brave. My assets grew – children, servants, subjects. As I watched my prosperity I felt I am a real householder now – what a strange thing to happen. Most of the people address me as Karta Thakurani". (p.57)

Nonetheless Rassundari Devi, like all other women of her time, was denied the power of education. A woman had to fit into the sociologically predefined, predetermined roles of a daughter, a sister, a sister-in-law, a daughter-in-law, a wife and finally a mother. The role of an educated female was not for her. As a child of eight years she did sit in the Bengali school in her home and heard the boys read the alphabets aloud. At sixteen the desire to read became strong in her:

> "But unfortunately girls were not supposed to read in those days. 'What is the world coming to?' they used to say. 'To think that women will be doing the work of men! Never heard of it before'". (p.44)

She felt terrified at voicing her urge for reading and did not know what to do. Moreover with the amount of housework, cooking and caring for the children that she did, left hardly any time for education. Miserable as she was, her only thought was to pray to God:

> "Please, God, help me learn, so that I can read religious books. ...Please God, teach me how to read. If you don't, who else will? That was my constant prayer". (p.44, 53)

And God did come to her rescue and help; she started reading *Chaitanya Bhagvata*, which her husband left for eldest son to read. She stealthily detached one sheet from the book and hid it. With a lot of determination and a great deal of pain and difficulty she learnt to read and eventually the encouragement from her seventh son, Kishori Lai, taught her to write letters to him.

> "The process of my education was not easy at all. It was really a painstaking one. It makes me wonder when I think of those days. It seems as if God was my teacher, otherwise learning to read and write was impossible in the situation I was in. I consider it my great good fortune that I am able to write some letters". (p.71)

This brings us to assess the condition of women in the nineteenth century in India, which was, as Rassundari Devi says "like the life of a bird in the cage." Even though she shows her gratitude to her Maker many times in the book, we cannot overlook such outpourings from her which occur quite often. She triumphed over all the hindrances she encountered with the only help being her faith in God who, she feels, made her achieve the impossible. Women of her times were completely "under the control of men" and if a woman dared to become famous she was a threat to a "decent man", who would soon lose his caste. At times an anguished cry would emanate from her heart:

> "Why was I ever born a woman? Shame on my life! ... I am helpless. I am a caged bird". (p.50)

She was a woman, a married one at that, and a daughter-in-law of the family – that put more restrictions on her. It was believed that if a Hindu wife touched a book or a pen, she faced the risk of losing her husband. Susie Tharu and K. Lalita have cryptically observed that

> "as Rassundari Devi scratches her letters, like a prisoner in solitary confinement, onto the blackened kitchen wall, she also subverts the reform movement's educational project into a totally different, personal one. Her desire for literacy ... has a composition quite different from that postulated by the new individualism. There is absolutely no place in her hunger to read for domesticity or motherhood, or indeed for any of the other much-flaunted ends of female education"[11].

Despite being denied any kind of formal education (she was convinced that the "school of life" gave her enough education) there is no sense of pessimism in her autobiography and she could easily come to terms with her life and herself; though the undercurrent of impatience and discontent may be discerned in the narrative. Her essence of spirituality enabled her to face the drudgery of domesticity:

> "My father – the king of all kings. Why should I feel so miserable since I am the daughter of such a king? Is it possible for a king's daughter to be miserable"? (p.56)

Rassundari Devi's attempt was to interpret her own personal existence as an "experienceable sign" of god's creation. Though at times the narrative breaks into an agonised cry of a woman, she soon overcame it in a powerful way; as a critic says "she followed the system but she is neither unaware of her plight nor is she completely reconciled to it"[12].

The portrait, which emerges from Amar Jiban, is of a woman who, despite the uncongenial atmosphere, carved a niche for herself, did not violate any of the norms prevalent in the society and was successful in achieving her goal and fulfilling the mission of her life. And how does she do it? Much as the critics would like to refute a very important aspect of the book, this remarkable woman obtained her peace of mind due to a very strong religious and spiritual impulse; the instinct was implanted in her psyche from very early times by a person who played a significant role in her childhood - her mother, who had on many occasions, advised her to pray to "Dayamadhav" or "Parameshwar":

> "Why are you afraid. There is nothing to fear. ...We have Dayamadhav, so don't worry. Whenever you feel scared call Dayamadhav all your fears will disappear. ...He is almighty God, he is everywhere, that is why he can hear us all. ...He is no ordinary person. He is God". (p. 25, 30)

The teachings of the mother left an indelible imprint on the young girl's mind:

> "Since that day the *mantra* given by my mother – the name of Parameshwar had entered my heart". (p.30)

She would call on God only because her mother had asked her to do so; it gave her the courage which she otherwise lacked due to her fearful nature.

Writing about the spirituality in *Amar Jiban*, Susie Tharu and K.Lalita have said:

> "Literary historians often emphasise Rassundari Devi's pious conclusions to promote her autobiography as that of a god-fearing Bengali housewife. In the process they blur over other, less "exemplary" aspects of her unusual self, which form the body of her work: the strength of her bond with her mother, the shadowy presence of her husband (who seems a totally unimportant figure in her life), and the brief mention she makes even of her children"[13].

We have seen that the confessions of this "god-fearing Bengali housewife" involve many facets of her life but nevertheless the spiritual or the religious theme which runs throughout the book, and dominates the second part, does form an important fulcrum of her life-narrative. She has "written in the old genre of female autobiography, which tends to find beauty even in pain and to transform rage into spiritual acceptance"[14].

Autobiographical writings in the West came into prominence with Augustine's *Confessions*, which is exclusively a spiritual book. This autobiography has formed the groundwork for many western critics to formulate a theory of life-writings, particularly the religious ones. Such books, says Roy Pascal, have particular characteristics:

> "Relatively few experiences are chosen, few personal relationships are dwelt on, and these are closely linked as stages in ... spiritual progress"[15].

However the most important element of such life-narratives is the intensity of religious experience which is accompanied by a loss of individuality. Roy Pascal's assessment is that such autobiographies are not to be criticised and the religious experiences should not be taken as hallucinations, because subjectively they are as compelling and convincing as other experiences. Autobiographical writers who venture to portray their soul's dialogue with God have a tough mission than the one who describe only the external events which shaped their lives. The intensity of faith makes communication of religious experiences a formidable task for two reasons: firstly because they are extremely subjective and therefore not easy to be challenged or disputed. We should not be tempted to provoke the plausibility of religious experiences because they are not the only ones in writer's life; and secondly because we have to analyse the autobiographer's individuality in totality which is an amalgam of many incidents, the religious being just one of many.

> "We are not meant to read the philosophical passages of the autobiography as a mere personal confession of faith, but as a conclusion of truth; and if we boggle at the philosophy, we tend to view the actual personality with some distrust"[16].

At this point we have to take into consideration the observations of Alladi Uma who views *Amar Jiban* a medium for expression of Rassundari Devi's desires, both religious and non-spiritual, as well as for her creative impulse. Thus her autobiography comprises of two parts: the first one dealing with her activities in the household, that too with the grace of God and the second with her devotion and suppliance to the Almighty. Significantly the book starts with an invocation to Goddess Saraswati, followed by different sections, titled as compositions instead of chapters and once again mixes "the religious with the material for we tend to think both the religious composition of a saint, poet and the composing of the life of an individual. One way she does this is to use the poetic mode for God and prose for her life"[17].

As a young child she had "no idea of what was meant by the word God" (p.30). But there was an instinctive feeling in her that told her He would always help her when she needed Him: "Please be with me, God", became her constant plea. Her mother's advice "Speak the name of God if you are afraid" (p. 36) was sown deep in her heart:

> "O you Lord of the world, all pervading, on whom rests the world
> God of the world you are everywhere.
> Leaving the protection of my mother I appeal to you in dire distress and fright." (p.35)

Rassundari Devi dismissed her troubles as the "will of god", it was her defence against any kind of indulgence in self-pity. Her deep faith in God influenced her entire personality; her physical growth was accompanied by her mental progress towards a deep involvement in the Supreme Being:

> "Merciful God, dear father, I know how kind you are. Because I was afraid, I used to appeal to you day and night. I was not aware of the virtues associated with your name. My mother had told me to remember God in case I was afraid. That was the reason I used to call you desperately". (p. 38)

But she could never reveal her "relationship" with God to anyone: hers was "a silent communication" with Dayamadhav in her mother's house and Madangopal in her husband's place. He was the Merciful Father of whom she was never afraid, He was her teacher and with God in her heart she "plunged into the work" in her house which she found was not so difficult after all.

Her poems at the beginning of each composition are suffused with deep philosophy of life and we find it strangely credible to believe that a woman of nineteenth century who never went to a school, nor to a sage or a saint to learn the gospel of life, is able to portray such depth of feeling. It only proves that religion and faith in God was a way of life with her:

> "You came here alone and that is how you will depart
> The one who has sent you here will call you back at his side
> Why are you then enamoured of an illusion which has got you into a trap.
>
> ....
>
> If you take refuge in him you will be rid of the fear of death
> Since you intend to cross over the sea of life
> Do not make a mistake
> Merciful God, friend of the poor
> Is all you have in your voyage". (p.43)

He, as the "saviour of the fallen" and "kind friend of the poor" resided in her heart; He gave her the courage to expose her misdeeds and follow His laws; it was an "act of God" when she went without food for two days and He still allowed her to have an excellent health. Despite her blind faith in God she knew that "the ways of God are beyond comprehension" and "no work can be accomplished without the will of God" (p.67). With her mind "always full of happiness and love, due to the mercy of God" she accomplished every task which confronted her.

The second part of the autobiography becomes more spiritual with longer poems in praise of God; but here the prose also is a medium for the outpourings of her heart in articulating praises of God. Her deep faith in God was continuously being reaffirmed and she cites an incident to exemplify the power and will of the Creator. She lost her nose-ring while taking a bath in a tank adjoining her house when she was twenty-two years old; all efforts to find it were futile. Later the tank dried up and the accumulated mud was taken to build a wall and the tank reconstructed. Many years later part of the wall collapsed and on the broken wall was found her lost nose-ring after sixty years.

> "It was indeed one of God's miracles. It made my heart beat faster. ...Nothing is beyond God's power. This ring fell in the water 60 years ago. ...Oh Ocean of mercy ...you intended to hand over the nose-ring to this wretched person". (p.100)

She was not thrilled to have her gold back but because the recovery of nose-ring symbolised the benevolence shown by the "kind master". From then the nose-ring was pinned on the headdress of Madangopal. This part of the autobiography is full of deep outpourings in praise of God and her complete faith in Him. She views the world as a theatre and God as the "Proprietor Sir", the world's creator and destroyer.

"You are the owner of this huge theatre. Everything happens according to your wish, You have brought me to this theatre. For the last eighty-eight years. I have been given a seat from which I have not moved". (p.101)

Amar Jiban narrates two episodes, which we can only describe as spiritual happenings; otherwise in no way can they be taken as real. Rassundari Devi's faith in God perhaps made her experience "visions" which she describes in her traditional way, but which not only serve the purpose of the narrative but also amplify the significance of Rassundari Devi's story, "especially in moments of epiphany charging it with dramatic intensity"[18]. Did she have psychic powers? We do not know. On a couple of occasions she did have "visions" or strong intuitions of some impending doom. Her revealations had a foreboding of things to come, in which she said her twenty-three year old son Pyarilal was on his death bed in Behrampur college, where he studied. She even saw his cremation on the banks of the Ganga, she was standing nearby and weeping bitterly. When she woke up she found her bed sheets wet with tears. Her dream proved to be true and it came to be known that Pyarilal had died on the same day, at the same time. Another vision she describes related to her eldest son, Bipinbehari, who while going to the police station on a horseback fell and broke his pelvis. Rassundari Devi "saw" the whole incident while being busy with the household chores. Later hearing the accident being narrated she wept not for her son but "because of the wonderful act of God. ...How could I see these events so clearly from my own house? Can anything be stranger?" (p.84).

The strange powers of the mind are described in that part of the book which is called "The Idea of Death". Here she describes her own death which she saw when she was suffering from high fever. She could see herself being laid on the floor and her children weeping for her. But she survived and when she regained consciousness she was taken inside the house. All these incidents were not narrated to anyone for fear of being called a liar. But we, as readers of autobiography, willingly suspend our disbelief and believe everything she shares with us without any misgivings. Perhaps it is the characteristic essentiality of this genre which compels and demands the writers to convey the truth to hold its readers in its grip. We tend to believe that may be Rassundari Devi had a wonderful mind with supernatural powers.

Rassundari Devi's *Amar Jiban* (My Life) is thus the story of personal conversion and illumination about the will of God; here by 'conversion' we do not mean a change of belief or attitude, but a transformation and development of personality which is typical of any autobiography. The narrative shows moments of doubt and despair but the writer always returns to the serenity of achieved understanding; and the ultimate impression which the book leaves on the mind of the reader is a sense of peace attained not only by the writer but also experienced by the readers, whom she urges to read her autobiography:

> "This book is written by my own hand. I am not literate in the real sense. Do not neglect it, my dear readers, do not look down upon it. I need not elaborate. You are aware of everything so please do the needful so that my labour is rewarded". (p.122)

No reader after picking up this "factual document" written by an old Hindu woman can put down the book till he read the whole life narrative. The ultimate frame for both her conversion tale and her picaresque progress in the story of the book's composition; in creating her text she was recreating her exemplary life.

> "Rassundari Devi's autobiography is so astonishing because she grew up, reared her children, and struggled in secret to learn how to read in a village,

a long distance away from the metropolis of Calcutta where debating societies were arguing about women's education, and long before the new schools for women had been set up in the city"[19].

Why did she write the autobiography? Susie Tharu and K. Lalita are of the view that perhaps it was due to a desire to escape, or may be the love of words, or the nostalgia for her paternal home which prompts her to indulge in creating the story of her life.

"But it is also a powerful sense of self-worth as well as the need to extend the spiritual dimensions of her life that drives her"[20].

Rassundari Devi feels that she wasted her valuable life "in the hell-hole of material things, a wretched slave of illusion. Alas, my human birth has been useless. This rare human birth was not spent in singing the praise of *Radha-Krishna*. ...I squandered my time" (p.106). But we, the readers of *Amar Jiban* do not agree with her. She was the woman who "followed the system but was neither unaware of her plight nor completely reconciled to it"[21]. We should read *Amar Jiban* not only because it presents a picture of the times, not only because it shows the helplessness of a woman being denied the rights of education, but predominantly because it is a narrative written with an honest heart, a clear mind and a devoted faith.

REFERENCES

1. *Women Writing in India*, ed. Susie Tharu & K. Lalita, Vol. 1, OUP, 1993.
2. *Ibid.*, p. 160.
3. Jasbir Jain, Review of *Amar Jiban* in Indian Book Chronicle, Sept. 2000.
4. The complete book in its present form was published in 1906. There have been many more publications, which hint at the discrepancy in the dates of publication. Or as Alladi Uma

explains while reviewing the book for *Journal of Indian Writing in English*, "an eighty-eight year old has made a slight miscalculation regarding her age".

5. *Ibid.*
6. "About this Book", Dinesh Chandra Sen in *Amar Jiban* (My Life) translated in English by Enakshi Chatterjee, Writers Workshop, 1999, p. 11. The subsequent quotations from the autobiography are from this book.
7. Betty Bergland, "Post modernism and the Autobiographical subjects: Reconstructing the 'Other'", in *Autobiography & post Modernism*, ed. By Kathleen Ashley, Leigh Gilmore, Gerald Peters, The University of Massachusetts Press, 1994, p.131.
8. Carolyn Heilbrun, *Writing a woman's life*, The Woman's Press, New York, 1988, p. 13.
9. Jasbir Jain, "A woman's Life in a 19th century Bengali Household", *India Book Chronicle*, September 2000, p. 6.
10. *Writing a Woman's Life*, p. 14.
11. *Women Writing in India*, p. 164.
12. Alladi Uma, *The Journal of Indian Writing in English.*, Vol. 28, No.2, July 2000, pp. 53-55.
13. *Women Writing in India*, p. 161.
14. *Writing a Woman's Life*, p. 12.
15. Roy Pascal, *Design And Truth in Autobiography*, Harvard University Press, 1960, p. 96.
16. *Ibid.*, p. 102.
17. *The Journal of Indian Writing in English*, p. 55.
18. Mary G. Mason, "Autobiography of Women Writers", in *Autobiographical Essays Theoretical and Critical*, edited by James Olney, Princeton University Press, 1980, p. 214.
19. *Women writing in India*, p. 164.
20. *Ibid.*
21. *The Journal of Indian Writing in English*, p. 54.

CHAPTER 17

Voice from the Margin : A Life Less Ordinary

Much before the dawn of twenty first century women's literature came to be accepted as very different from the male-centred philosophy of writing and frame of reference, including subjectivity. The issue of identifying and formulating the distinctiveness of feminine narrative in autobiography has involved a great deal of controversy. Female fiction writers had faced a similar handicap of using a prose "which is essentially a male instrument fashioned for male purposes"[1].

Critics like Domna Stanton, Susan Friedman, Mary Mason, Showalter have confronted the androcentric intention of the genre and cogently argued for an alternative poetics and form of autobiography that would address issues of gender and subjectivity.

Indian women have also ventured into this mode of writing, which had been represented under an unconscious presumption of undisputed subjectivity, invariably male as early as 1868. This was an era in history when women were not only deprived of education and financial independence but had also to contend and resist the dogma which disapproved and suppressed any kind of expression or speech.

Rassundari Debi's *Amar Jiban*(1868), said to be one of the first life writings by a woman in India, subverted the predetermined, preset order of the "other". In recent years there has been a deliberate reconstitution and recognition of the feminine point of view in autobiographical discourse. A purposeful and definitive feminist reconstruction of women's life narratives has promoted and facilitated the establishment of the personal narrative as an effective means of self-revealation. The genre has thus the potency and ability to become an impressive and persuasive agent of social change.

A Life Less Ordinary (2006) by Baby Haldar is the life writing by a woman, who survived and withstood mental and physical trauma, became a housemaid and finally found courage to represent her brutalisation and dehumanisation, her despair and secret hopes through autobiographical expression. The autobiography has multiple dimensions but the two most prominent and important perspectives are immediately seen by the readers are the writer's plight as a woman and the other as a maid. Baby Haldar wrote about her life much before the approved norm of middle-age criteria and the book is more than a "confession". It is not a recreation on some finally perceived ideals; she sort and recapitulates the moments at which she realised she had the courage to move forward into unnarrated and unexplored ways of living. The book is an emotionless account of the life of Baby Haldar, a young woman of thirty-four: a much abused individual, working as a domestic help in a house in Delhi. This is an autobiography which almost numbs the senses of the reader, who is baffled by the extent of violence, which, when it becomes an everyday predicament and scenario can make people stop reacting the way, that many others do.

The development of new elites within independent societies, often buttressed by neo-colonial institutions; the development of internal divisions based on racial, linguistic or religious discriminations; the continuing unequal treatment of indigenous peoples in settler/invader societies – all these testify to the fact that post-colonialism is a continuing process of resistance and reconstruction[2].

The raw honesty of the narrative is a cruel slap in the face of the society, which treats its women, especially the ones coming from the downtrodden segment, with such contempt and derision. "One is not born, but rather becomes a woman", Simone de Beauvoir's remark proves the point in the case of Baby Haldar, where the "civilization as a whole" has produced "this creature intermediate between male and eunuch, which is described as feminine." (*The Second Sex* 295) No wonder then that K. Sachidanandan calls it "one of the best subaltern autobiographies," as it not only projects the sufferings and drudgery of a woman, "the other", in her own house but also in the society in which she lives as a single parent in later part of the book. The autobiography thus becomes a crucial site of cultural struggle and discrimination with far-reaching results. Helen Cixous had remarked that this kind of writing is a unique product celebrating the female physiology.

Women must write through their bodies, they must invent impregnable language that will wreck partitions, classes, and rhetorics, regulations and codes, they must submerge, cut through, get beyond the ultimate reserve-discourse, including the one that laughs at the very idea of pronouncing the word 'silence'... Such is the strength of women that, sweeping away syntax, breaking that famous thread ...which acts for men as a surrogate umbilical cord[3].

Baby Haldar's painful narrative begins very methodically and analytically:

> Where should I start? Should I begin with how when I was seven years old my mother suddenly left us by thrusting a coin each in our hands, or tell you about how my nephew told my Baba that he saw his father strangling his mother, my Didi, to death, or how my Baba used to suddenly vanish from our life and resurface or should I tell you about my husband to whom I was married off when I was twelve and why I left him and came to Delhi with my three children[4].

The mother's absence at a tender age is a frequent refrain in the early part of the book as are the pangs of hunger. Baby Haldar very often wished that it was her father who had gone out of her life rather than her mother, "It is a painful fact that a nurturing father, who replaces rather than complements a mother, must be loved at the mother's expense, whatever the reasons for the mother's absence"[5]. Baby was no longer "the apple of his eye, but more like a thorn in his flesh". However, there were rare moments of tenderness between the two, which were terminated by the stepmother's abnormal, vicious and bitter reaction, suspecting an unnatural bond between a twelve-year old and her father; she felt terrified of analysing her relationship with her father. The image of fatherhood becomes a representative of Patriarchy, as are other male members. Carolyn G. Heilbrun's analytical remark that in dealing with father, women are not "dealing with abstractions of a vaguely defined 'patriarchy' but talking about actual men and thus a complex picture begins to emerge of 'manhood' and 'fatherhood'" proves the point[6].

Although Baby Haldar did not have a very intimate relationship with her father, she could never bear to see him sad: "whenever he was unhappy, whenever he shed tears, I would also weep". The autobiographical narrative frequently shifts from first person to third as if the writer is distancing herself from the traumatic experiences which were so painful.

Poor Baby! What else could one say of her? Imagine a childhood so brief, so ephemeral, that you could sit down and the whole thing could unravel in front of you in barely half an hour! And yet her childhood fascinates Baby. Perhaps everyone is fascinated by the things they've been deprived of, the things they long for. Baby remembers her childhood, she savours every moment of it, she licks it just as a cow would her newborn calf, tasting every part[7].

It may be an act of acknowledging the real presence and recognition of another consciousness and the disclosure of self gets linked to the identification of some "other."

This recognition of another consciousness – this grounding of identity through relation to the chosen other, seems to enable women to write openly about themselves[8].

However a change in the narrative can be perceived as the life story progresses and she lingers over the events of her life. In the Foreword to the autobiography, Sheela Reddy observes that it is as if the painful memories, which had never been disclosed earlier, perhaps not even to herself, had always needed the healing touch of her words. Thus the autobiographical mode becomes a salubrious enterprise and the narrative enacts the triumph over the conditions of her life.

Marriage for Baby Haldar should have been a joyous occasion, but it meant opening of fresh avenues of pain and suffering:

Now when she thinks back, Baby wonders how she spent that day of sorrow in such merriment. Little did Baby know that this was the beginning of her days of grief and pain, little did she know what the future held for her. On the seventeenth day, a Wednesday in the month of Agrahayan, Baby was married[9].

Simone De Beauvoir in *The Second Sex* reviews the concept of marriage, which she says, normally "subordinates wife to husband" and "the problem of their mutual relations is posed most sharply to the female. The paradox of marriage lies in the fact that it has at once an erotic and a social function"[10]. As a young wife, the woman feels it to be her duty to herself and to the society to love her husband and to be happy.

Married to a man who traumatised her very often, Baby became pregnant at the age of thirteen, did all the housework and suffered morning sickness. The excessive pain for long hours at the time of delivery is not only unbearable to Baby but to her readers as well who can sympathise with her sufferings. The third person narrative saves her by giving objectivity to the whole process.

After the doctor had left, they took Baby off the table, and tried to stand her up but she fainted and fell to the floor. The ayah ran to call the doctor ..... Then they picked Baby up and put her on a stretcher and took her to bed ..... They tried to put her on drip, but they could not find a vein in her hand[11].

The birth of a son did not pacify her husband, who treated her as if she "was an animal". In frequent bouts of disgust she mused: "If I had no happiness and peace in his house, was it necessary that I should stay on there in that living hell?"[12]

Violence against women says Simone de Beauvoir, is a common phenomenon as women generally are "unfamiliar with violence, they have not been through the tussles of childhood and youth as have men; and now the girl is laid hold of, swept away in a bodily struggle in which the man is the stronger"[13]. And when violence becomes an everyday situation, as it did in Haldar's case, it can make people stop responding to it in the way that many others do. However Baby Haldar did react in a decisive way to give the best to her children and was determined to educate them. Her fight for dignity made her courageous enough to walk out on her marriage and take a train to Delhi: a city where many miserable women seek house jobs in anticipation of a better life, in the houses of capital's rising middle class.

Her bold move is commendable as she ventured into an unknown city with her children, leaving the husband forever: a move, which did not meet the approval of the father. In Delhi she let her eldest son work as an under-age domestic servant in the homes of abusive employers. This is the story of poverty and economic migration and it does not end here; Baby's decision to work as a housemaid brought in a new phase of distress and misfortune, as her search for a job became futile in the absence of a husband by her side. Determinedly she did find work at a number of households of "memsahibs" who made her work day and night for a very meager salary.

Finally fate was benevolent and she found a model employer in Prabodh Kumar, the grand son of Premchand at Gurgaon, who treated her with dignity and humaneness. He encouraged her to read and write and the first book she read was Taslima Nasreen's *Amar Meyabela* (My Girlhood).

It was if she was reading about her own life. Here was a writer, her rage at 9, and the humiliation of being born a woman in a poor society[14].

With no dearth of sympathy and encouragement from her employer, she wrote *Aalo Aandhari* (2004), soon to be followed by the Hindi translation in 2006. The book is a simple description of a grim existence, the life's story is told in plain language without a trace of self-pity. In writing her book she was creating a proper image of herself, and through the creation of her text she was recreating her exemplary life and came to be called "the new Ashapurna Devi". Writing was a therapeutic enterprise for her.

When I wrote, I felt like I was talking to someone, and after writing I would feel lighter, as if I had taken some sort of revenge against my father, who never took care of me as a father should, and against my husband. I never thought that other people might be interested in reading my story[15].

The narrative both relates and enacts triumphant emergence over conditions that had drained her energies, threatened her physical and mental health. She had committed her secrets to writing and in the process had purged herself of all the sorrow. It is her way of setting the record straight.

Giving her pen and notebook Prabodh Kumar gifted her the divine power to discover her own self, layer by layer.

It is as if, given a pen and paper asked to write about her life, Baby is assiduously extracting with a surgeon's precision and professional lack of sentiment, all the hurts and traumas that made up her childhood[16]

Too many issues emerge from this one book: Prabodh Kumar, Baby Haldar's employer, occupies one end of the wide range of employers. He encouraged her not only to write the tragic experiences of her life, but supported her in getting it published. There are others who ill-treat and abuse female employees. And between the two are the majority of us, who though not too unkind, are disinterested or are patronising, viewing domestic workers as a necessary evil, something without which we cannot do. One of the most noticed power struggles frequently seen and observed in Indian society at large is the one between the employer and the domestic worker, which generally leads to bitterness with apparently little hope of reconciliation. But a change can be brought about if domestic work is regularised and for once the law sets the parameters of what is acceptable. Many employers then would perhaps feel compelled to do the right thing. Every working person is an employee and should have the right to lead a dignified life. It isn't so with the domestic workers, who are treated as though they have no distinct life of their own.

Child Labour Act (1986) which bans the employment of children under 14, the Unrecognised Sector Worker Bill (2004) are Bills which need to get implemented to help the powerless domestic workers in India. We know that the history of servitude can be traced back to centuries, but after 61 years of Independence it is now time to grant them legal status of 'worker' and the benefits of minimum wages and a pension.

What is commendable and praiseworthy about this autobiography is that although her sorrow seems never to end, there is no anger expressed at either the individuals or the society. As Amit Bhargava says in the *International Tribune*.

Ms Haldar never articulates her rage directly and rarely blames her father or her husband for the cruelty she experienced, but the facts stand powerfully for themselves.

This is a simple description of a grim existence and has no need of embellishment with literary tricks.

A Life Less Ordinary can be read as a unique Bildungsroman, the development of a female Life, a process of "triumphant self-discovery". The events in the autobiography are a true representation, which lead towards the construction of gender identity. The writer not only discovers a unique individuality and selfhood but also a mission in life. Like Catherine in *Wuthering Heights,* her marriage had locked her into a social system, which subsequently denied and subjugated herself. The writing process helped in the recovery of the 'subaltern voice" and is a formidable task. Gayatri Chakravorty Spivak voiced her concern for maintaining "a special position" for "the subaltern who were trying to survive and establish its identity in its difference"[17]. Baby Haldar lived as the "other", as a woman and as a poverty stricken one at that, being exploited and facing cultural erasure. These are the "complexities in the central fabric" which need to be addressed directly if we have to see the "elusive nature of identity that emerges from the margins"[18], to re-establish a voice of it's own.

REFERENCES

1. Barry Peter, *Beginning Theory.* Manchester University Press, 2007, p. 126.
2. Ashcroft Bill, et al. *The Post Colonial Studies Reader*. Routledge, 2004, p. 2.
3. *Beginning Theory,* p. 128.
4. *The Hindu*, May 15, 2006.
5. Dodd Philip, Ed. *Modern Selves*: *Essays on Modern British and American Autobiography*. Frank Cass, London, 1986, p. 24.
6. *Ibid.,* p. 65.
7. Haldar Baby. *A Life Less Ordinary.* Zubaan, Penguin Books, New Delhi, 2006, p. 28.
8. Olney James, Ed. *Autobiography: Essays Theoretical and Critical*. Princeton University Press, 1980. p. 210.

9. *A Life Less Ordinary,* p. 34.
10. *The Second Sex*. Beauvoir Simone de, *The Second Sex*. Picador, London, 1988, p. 480.
11. *A Life Less Ordinary,* p. 56.
12. *Ibid.,* p. 12.
13. *The Second Sex*, p. 403.
14. *A Life Less Ordinary,* p. vii.
15. *The New York Times, August 2, 2006.*
16. Sheela Reddy, *Outlook*, www.zubaanbooks.com/rc2006.pdf.
17. *The Post Colonial Studies Reader*. Routledge, 2004, p. 8.
18. Tharu Susie, Lalita, K. *Women Writing In India*: 600 BC to The Present, Vol.I. OUP, New Delhi, 1991, p. xix.

Bibliography

SECONDARY SOURCES

1. Anderson, Linda. *Autobiography, The New Critical Idiom*. London, Routledge, 2007.
2. Ashcroft, Bill, et al. *The post Colonial Studies Reader*. Routledge, 2004.
3. Bakhtin, M.M. and Medvedev, P.N. *The Formal Method in Literary Scholarship*. London: The John Hopkins University Press, 1991.
4. Bary, Peter. *Beginning Theory*. Manchester University Press, 2007.
5. Beauvouvoir, Simone de. *The Second Sex*. Picador, London, 1988.
6. Boehmer, Elleke. *Colonial and Post Colonial Literature.* Oxford: Oxford University Press, 1995.
7. Booth, Wayne C. *The Rhetoric of Fiction.* The University of Chicago Press, 1970.
8. Boulton, Marjorie. *The Anatomy of Prose*. New Delhi: Kalyani Publishers, 1993.
9. Cassel's Encyclopedia of Literature, Vol. I, London, 1953.
10. Coburn, Kathleen. *The Notebooks of Samuel Taylor Coleridge.* London: Routledge and Kegan Paul, 1957.
11. Cockshut, A.O.J. *The Art of Autobiography in 19th and 20th Century England.* New Haven: Yale University Press, 1984.
12. DeMan, Paul. *'Autobiography as De-Facement'* Modern Language Notes 94, 5 (Dec.1979).
13. Dodd, Philip. (ed.) *Modern Selves: Essays on Modern British and American Autobiography*. London: Frank Cass, 1986.
14. Dodiya, Jaydipsinh. *Critical Essays on Indian Writing in English*, New Delhi: Sarup & Sons, 2006.

15. Dwivesi, A.N. *Kamala Das and Her Poetry*. New Delhi: Atlantic Publishers and Distributors, 2006.
16. Eakin, John Paul. American Autobiography:*Retrospect and Prospect*. The University of Wisconsin Press, 1991.
17. Eliot, T.S. *The Sacred Wood.* Methuen & Co. Ltd., 1967.
18. Ford, Boris. (ed.) *The New Pelican Guide to English Literature*, 1983.
19. Frye, Northop. *Anatomy of Criticism.* Princeton University Press, 1957.
20. Greene, Graham. *A Soat of Life*. Harmondsworth, Penguin Books, 1971.
21. Habib, M.A.R. *A History of Literary Cricism*. Blackwell Publishing, 2008.
22. Heilburn, Carolyn. *Writing a Woman's Life.* London: The Woman's Press, 1989.
23. Hiriyanna, M. *Outlines of Indian Philosophy*. London: George Allen and Unwin, 1951.
24. Iyengar, K.R. Srinivasa. *Indian Writing in English.* New Delhi: Sterling Publishers, 1993.
25. Jacobs, Hans. *Western Psycho-therapy and Hindu Sadhana.* London: George and Unwin, 1961.
26. Jelinek, Estelle. (ed.) *Women's Autobiography: Essays in Criticism.* Bloomington: Indiana University Press, 1980.
27. Kristeva, Julie. *Estragers a nous-memes.* Paris: Fayard, 1988.
28. Langer, Susanne K. *Feeling and Form: The Theory of Art.* London: Routledge & Kegan Paul, 1967.
29. Lodge, David. (ed.) *Modern Criticism and Theory.* London and New York: Longman, 1989.
30. Marcus, Laura. *Autobiographical Discourses: Theory, Criticism, Practice.* Manchester and New York: Manchester University Press, 1994.
31. Mukherjee, Meenakshi. (ed.) *Considerations.* Bombay: Allied Publishers, 1977.
32. Nabar, Vrinda. *The Endless Female Hungers: A study of Kamala Das.* New Delhi: Sterling Publishers, 1994.
33. Naik, M.K. *A History of Indian English Literature.* New Delhi: Sahitya Akademi, 1995.
34. Narasimhaiah, C.D.N. *Essays in Commonwealth Literature: Heirloom of Multiple Heritage.* Delhi: Pencraft International,1995.

35. Neisser, Ulric and Fivush, Robyn. *The Remembering Self.* Cambridge University Press, 1994.

36. Neuman, Shirley. (ed.) *Autobiography and Questions of Gender.* London: Frank Cass, 1991.

37. O'Flaherty, Wendy Deniger. (trans.) *The Rig Veda.* New Delhi: Penguin, 1994.

38. Olney, James. *Metaphors of Self: The Meaning of Autobiography.* Princeton University Press, 1972.

39. __________ (ed.) *Autobiography: Essays Theoretical and Critical.* Princeton University Press, 1980.

40. __________ (ed.) *Studies in Autobiography.* New York and Oxford: Oxford University Press, 1988.

41. Palmer, Pauline. *Contemporary Women's Fiction.* Harvester Wheatsheaf, 1989.

42. Parthasarthy, R. *Ten Twentieth Century Indian Poets.* Delhi: Oxford University Press, 1983.

43. Pascal, Roy. *Design and Truth in Autobiography.* London: Routledge and Kegan Paul, 1960.

44. Radhakrishnan, S and Raju, P.T. (ed.) *The Concept of Man.* New Delhi: Indus, Harper Collins, 1995.

45. Rahman, Anisur. *Expressive Form in the Poetry of Kamala Das.* New Delhi: Abhinav Publishers, 1981.

46. Ram, N. and Susan. *R.K. Narayan – The Early Years: 1906-1945,* Penguin India, 1996.

47. Rao, Raja. *Kanthapura.* Delhi: Oxford University Press, 1989.

48. Rice, Philip and Waugh, Patricia. (ed.) *Modern Literary Theory: A Reader.* Edward Arnold, 1992.

49. Rushdie, Salman. *Imaginary Homelands. Essays and Criticism* 1981-91. Granta Books, London, 1992.

50. Sayre, Robert F. *The Examined Self.* The University of Wisconsin Press, 1988.

51. Scholes, Robert. *Elements of Fiction.* London, Oxford University Press, 1968.

52. Shaw, Bernard. *Candida.* Orient Longmans, 1957.

53. Sheringham, Michael. *French Autobiography: Devices and Desires.* Oxford: Clarendon Press, 1993.

54. Showalter, Elaine. (ed.) *Women's Liberation and Literature.* New York: Harcourt Brace Javanovich, 1971.

55. ______________________ *A Literature of Their Own.* Princeton University Press, 1977.

56. Sinari, R.N. (ed.) *Concept of Man in Philosophy.* New Delhi: B.R. Publishing Corporation, 1991.

57. Sinha, R.C.P. *The Indian Autobiographies in English.* New Delhi: S. Chand, 1978.

58. Sodhi, Meena. *Indian English Writing: The Autobiographical Mode.* New Delhi: Creative Books,1999.

59. Spacks, Patricia. *Imagining a Self: Autobiography and Novel in Eighteenth-Century England.* Cambridge, Mass.: Harvard University Press, 1976.

60. Stone, Albert E. (ed.) *The American Autobiography.* Englewood Cliffs, NJ: Prentice-Hall, 1981.

61. Sturrock, John. *The Language of Autobiography: Studies in the First Person Singular.* Cambridge University Press, 1994.

62. ______________ (ed.) *The Oxford Guide to Contemporary Writing.* OUP, 1996.

63. Tagore, R.N. *Sadhna*. Macmillan, 1988.

64. Tharu, Susie, Lalita. K. *Women Writing in India, 600 B.C. to the Present.* Vols. I & II. New Delhi,:Oxford University Press, 1993.

65. Walsh, William. *R.K. Narayan: A Critical Appreciation.* Allied Publishers, 1983.

66. ______________ *Indian Literature in English.* London: Longman, 1990.

67. Weiss, Timothy F. *On the Margins: The Art of Exile in V.S. Naipaul.* Amherst: The University of Massachusetts Press, 1992.

68. Weitz, Morris. *Problems in Aesthetics.* London: Macmillan, 1970.

69. Wellek, Rene and Warren, Austin. *Theory of Literature.* Penguin Books, 1976.

70. Wurson, J.O. & Ree, Jonathan. (ed.) *The Concise Encyclopedia of Western Philosophy and Philosophers.* London: Unwin Hyman, 1989.

71. Yaravintelinath, Balram Gupta, Venugopal, Amritjit Singh. (ed.) *New Perspectives in Indian Literature in English.* New Delhi: Sterling Publishers, 1995.

ARTICLES

1. Alladi, Uma. The Journal of Indian Writing in English, Vol.28. No.2. July 2000.

2. Deccan Herlad, January 25, 2000.
3. Frontline, 8 August 1997.
4. India Today, Nov.30, 1993.
5. India Today, December 27, 1999.
6. Indian Literature. Sahitya Akademi Bi-Monthly Journal, No.149, May-June, 1992.
7. Jain, Jasbir. "A Woman's Life in a 19th century Bengali Household", *Indian Book Chronicle*, September 2000.
8. Narasimhaiah, C.D.N. (ed.) *The Literary Criterion*, Vol.XXXI, No.182, 1996.
9. Pathak, R.S. (ed.) *Quest for Identity in Indian English Writing*. Vol.II, New Delhi: Bahri Publications, 1992.
10. Rajan, P.K. (ed.) LITTCRIT. Vol.18, No.1 & 2, June-December,1992.
11. Rajnath. (ed.) *The Journal of Literary Criticism*. Vol.5, No.2, Dec. 1989.
12. Nayantara Sahgal. *"India and America: A Personal Memoir"*, Span, June/July/August, 1997.
13. Saturday Times. June 25, 1995.
14. Saxena, D.C. (ed.) *Occasional papers*. Vol.IV, No.1, 1995-96.
15. Sharma, K.K. (ed.) *Points of View*. Vol.III, No.1, Summer 1996.
16. Spaeth, Anthony. "No Small Thing", *Times*, 14 April 1997.
17. Tharyan, P. *The Hindustan Times*, Feb.20, 1993.
18. The Hindustan Times. New Delhi: 12 January 2003.
19. The Hindu. 17 October, 1997.
20. Vanita, Ruth. "No Small Achievement", *Book Review*, 1997.
21. The Handyreader. India Today, April 26, 2010.

PRIMARY SOURCES

1. Anand, Mulk Raj. *Apology for Heroism*. New Delhi: Arnold-Heinemann,1986.
2. Augustine, A. *The Confessions of St. Augustine*. trans. E.B. Pusey, Grolier Classics, Classic Appreciation Society, 1956.
3. Bachchan, Harivansh Rai. *The Afternoon of Time*. trans. Dr. Rupert Snell. New Delhi: Penguin.
4. Bond, Ruskin. *Scenes From a Writer's Life: A Memoir*. New Delhi: Penguin, 1997.

5. Chattopadhya, Kamladevi. *Inner Recesses Outer Spaces.* New Delhi: Navrang, 1986.
6. Chaudhuri, Nirad C. *Thy Hand, Great Anarch!* Wokingham: Addison-Wesley, 1988.
7. ________________ *The Autobiography of an Unknown Indian.* Jaico Publishing House, 1991.
8. Das, Kamala. *My Story.* New Delhi: Sterling Publishers, 1976, Reprint 1991.
9. Das, Kamala. *The Old Playhouse and other Poems.* Oriental Longman Ltd. 1991.
10. Das, Kamala. *The Descendants.* Calcutta: Writers Workshop, 1967.
11. Das, Shoilabala. *A Look Before and After.* Cuttack: Orissa Mission Press, 1956.
12. Deshmukh, Durgabai. *Chintaman and I.* New Delhi: Allied Publishers,1980.
13. Devee, Sunity. *The Autobiography of an Indian Princess.* London: John Murray,1972.
14. Devi, Gayatri. *The Princess Remembers.* New York: Weildenfield & Nicolson, 1976.
15. Devi, Rassundari. *Amar Jiban*, translated in English by Enakshi Chatterjee, Writers Workshop, 1999.
16. Dingerkery, Kamala. *On the Wings of Time.* Bombay: Bharatiya Vidya Sabha, 1968.
17. Gandhi, M.K. *The Story of My Experiments with Truth.* trans. Mahadev Desai. Ahmedabad: Navajivan Publishing House, 1992.
18. Giri, V.V. *My Life and Time.* Delhi: Macmillan, 1976.
19. Gujral, Satish. *A Brush With Life: An Autobiography.* New Delhi: Viking, Penguin,1997.
20. Haldar, Baby. *A Life Less Ordinary.* Zubaan, Penguin Books, New Delhi, 2006.
21. Haskar, Urmila. *The Future That Was.* New Delhi: Allied Publishers, 1972.
22. Hutheesing, Krishna. *With No Regrets: An Autobiography.* Bombay: Padma Publication, 1943.
23. Jain, Jasbir. N*ayantara Sahgal.* Jaipur, Printwell, 1994.
24. Kaul, T.N. *My Years Through Raj to Swaraj.* Vikas, 1995.

25. Kriyananda, Swami. *The Path: Autobiography of a Western Yogi.* Delhi: Goyal Saab, 1988.
26. Lal, P. *Lessons*. A Writers Workshop Publication, 1991.
27. Maharani, Brinda. *The Story of an Indian Princess*. New York: Henry Holt, 1953.
28. Mazumdar, Shudha. *A Pattern of Life.* New Delhi: Manohar, 1977.
29. Mehta, Ved. *Up At Oxford*. John Murray, 1993.
30. Moraes, Dom. *My Son's Father.* Penguin, 1990.
31. __________. *Never at Home.* Viking, Penguin, 1992.
32. Mukherjee, Sujit. *Autobiography of an Unknown Cricketer.* Delhi: Ravi Dayal Publishers, 1996.
33. Naipaul, V.S. *An Area of Darkness.* Penguin, 1968.
34. __________. *India: A Wounded Civilization.* Penguin, 1979.
35. __________. *Finding the Centre.* Penguin, 1984.
36. __________. *India: A Multi-Mutinies Now.* Minerva, 1991.
37. Nanda, Savitri Devi. *The City of Two Gateways: The Autobiography of an Indian Girl.* London: George Allen and Unwin, 1950.
38. Narasimhaiah, C.D.N. *'N' for Nobody: The Autobiography of an English Teacher*. Delhi: B.R. Publishing Corporation, 1991.
39. Narayan, R.K. *My Days.* Orient Paperbacks, 1991.
40. __________. *The English Teacher*. Mysore: Indian Thought Publications, 1992.
41. __________. *Swami and Friends.* Mysore: Indian Thought Publications, 1994.
42. Nehru, Jawaharlal. *An Autobiography.* Jawaharlal Memorial Fund. Oxford University Press, 1980.
43. Norman, K.R. (trans.) *The Elder's Verses – Theragatha.* London: Pali Text Society, 1969.
44. __________. (trans.) *The Elder's Verses – Therigatha.* Vol.II. London: Pali Text Society, 1971.
45. Pandit, Vijaya Lakshmi. *The Scope of Happiness.* New Delhi: Vikas Publishing House, 1979.
46. Paul, Swaraj. *Beyond Bounderies: A Memoir.* New Delhi: Viking, 1998.
47. Pseud, Ishvani. *Girl in Bombay*. London: The Pilot Press Ltd., 1947.

48. Rathnamal, Sita. *Beyond the Jungle.* London: William Blackwood, 1968.
49. Rau, Dhanwanti Rama. *An Inheritance.* New Delhi: Allied Publishers, 1977.
50. Roy, Arundhati.
51. Sahgal, Nayantara. *Prison and Chocolate Cake.* London: Victor Gollanez, 1954.
52. ________________. *From Fear Set Free.* Delhi: Orient, 1962.
53. ________________. *Point of View, A Personal Response to Life, Literature and Politics,* New Delhi: Prestige Books, 1997.
54. Scindia, Vijayraje. *Princess, The Autobiography.* New Delhi: The Books International, 1985.
55. Singh, Karan. *Autobiography* (1931-1967). Delhi: Oxford University Press, 1989.
56. Singh, Khushwant. *Truth, Love and a Little Malice.* New Delhi: Ravi Dayal, 1995.
57. Sorabji, Cornelia. *India Calling.* London: Nisbet, 1935.
58. Venkataraman, R. *My Presidential Years.* New Delhi: Indus, 1994.

WEB SITES

1. www.JAIHOON.COM
2. www.timesofindia.com/191299/19conism3.html
3. www.rediffcom/news/1999/dec/14kamala.html
4. www.zubaanbooks.com/Sheela Reddy,outlook
5. www.harpercollin.co.uk/intvl/017/roy2.html
6. www.indiatoday.com

Index

❑❑❑